Holiday Programs
for
Boys and Girls

by

AILEEN FISHER

New, Revised Edition

Publishers   **PLAYS, INC.**   *Boston*

Library of Congress Cataloging in Publication Data

Fisher, Aileen Lucia, 1906-
 Holiday programs for boys and girls.

 1. Schools—Exercises and recreations.
I. Title.
LB3015.F58   1980   371.8'9   80-18642
 ISBN 0-8238-0244-2

HOLIDAY PROGRAMS
for
BOYS AND GIRLS

Acknowledgments

Thanks are due to the following publications for permission to reprint some of the plays and verses: *Child Life*, *Children's Activities*, *Plays: The Drama Magazine for Young People*, *Story Parade*, and *Young America Magazines*.

Table of Contents

CONTENTS

CONTENTS

WASHINGTON'S BIRTHDAY

ST. PATRICK'S DAY

EASTER

EARTH DAY

ARBOR DAY

MOTHER'S DAY

CONTENTS

MEMORIAL DAY

GRADUATION

THE SEASONS
(Group Readings)

COLUMBUS DAY

The Weaver's Son

Characters

CHRISTOPHER COLUMBUS, *14*
SUSANNA, *his mother*
DOMENICO, *his father*
BIANCHINETTA, *his sister, 7*
BARTHOLOMEW, *12*

TIME: *A spring day in 1465.*
SETTING: *The combination workroom-living room of the Colum-bus family in Genoa.*
AT RISE: BIANCHINETTA *is seated on a low stool near a basket of tangled wool yarn. She is trying to get order out of the tangles, winding the different colors on balls. In a few moments her mother,* SUSANNA, *comes in, wiping her hands on her apron.*

SUSANNA: There, I have done with the dyeing of the blue yarn. Always so much stirring and stirring! And to keep the big vats boiling, that is not easy. (*Looks at yarn basket*) Good, Bianchinetta. You are getting all the snarls out of the old yarn.
BIANCHINETTA: I have the black almost untangled.
SUSANNA: I am glad that my daughter, at least, is dependable in this house.

BIANCHINETTA: Bartholomew is busy, Mama. At the heap of new wool Papa bought.

SUSANNA: Bartholomew is carding it?

BIANCHINETTA: Yes, Mama. When I looked in the wool room he was combing so hard he did not see me.

SUSANNA: Or perhaps he was looking so hard out the window? (*Shakes her head*) No, I am afraid my sons are not weavers at heart. And Christopher is not back *yet*. Two hours he has been gone. Two hours! And on such a busy morning.

BIANCHINETTA: He had the woven cloth to deliver for Papa, you know.

SUSANNA: And how long does that take? Not two hours, I am sure. He promised to come home directly.

BIANCHINETTA: I saw him start out running.

SUSANNA: Then he should be back the sooner.

BIANCHINETTA: Mama, do you know why Christopher runs when he has errands to do? I know. It is to save time . . . so he can stop at the docks and watch the ships.

SUSANNA: Yes, or stand around at the map makers! As if there were nothing for him to do at home. (*Shakes head*) He is no weaver's son, with his head full of the sea. Yet we must live . . . and to live means to work. Especially when your father . . . Where is your father, by the way?

BIANCHINETTA: He said he had to meet a member of the guild at the wine dealer. On business.

SUSANNA: So? At the wine dealer? I do not see much business in that, except for the wine dealer.

BIANCHINETTA: Papa said he would not be long.

SUSANNA: Yet he has been gone all the time I was dyeing the yarn. Business, indeed! I must send Bartholomew to fetch him. Oh, Bianchinetta, a woman's lot is not an easy one. Work, work, work. And keep track of the menfolk besides. It is not easy, I tell you. (*Calls*) Bartholomew! (*Looks at work basket*) There, near the bottom, is more of the black. (*Calls*) Bartholomew! (BARTHOLOMEW, *a slight, dark-haired lad, enters.*)

BARTHOLOMEW: Yes, Mama.

SUSANNA: Is Christopher helping with the carding?

BARTHOLOMEW: He is not back yet from delivering the cloth.

SUSANNA: How do you explain that it takes him so long?

BARTHOLOMEW (*Shrugging*): It would take a long time to get way to the other side of the docks.

SUSANNA: Yes, when one keeps stubbing his toe from looking so hard at the ships. Go find him, Bartholomew, and bring him to me when you return. He was to have come home directly. That was a promise.

BARTHOLOMEW: Yes, Mama.

SUSANNA: And as you pass the wine dealer's shop, tell your father he is wanted at home immediately. It is important. Do you hear?

BARTHOLOMEW: Yes, Mama. Immediately. Important.

SUSANNA: Now, run. This is a busy morning. And my back aches from work already. (BARTHOLOMEW *runs out.* SU-SANNA *and* BIANCHINETTA *work at the yarn.*)

BIANCHINETTA: Mama . . .

SUSANNA: Yes, daughter.

BIANCHINETTA: Is there to be a feast day soon?

SUSANNA: Not soon. Why do you ask?

BIANCHINETTA: Because of the cheeses.

SUSANNA: What cheeses?

BIANCHINETTA: The cheeses in the dark closet under the stair-way.

SUSANNA: What are you talking of, Bianchinetta?

BIANCHINETTA: I was looking for my old doll this morning, and I saw them. Three big wonderful cheeses.

SUSANNA: Are you sure?

BIANCHINETTA: Yes, yes, Mama. Is it a surprise?

SUSANNA (*Sighing*): Yes . . . a surprise to me. Your father,

Bianchinetta, is full of surprises. Now he probably wishes to deal in cheeses instead of woolen cloth! Last month it was wine. He could see a fortune in dealing in wine, he said! To your father the far pasture is always the greenest.

BIANCHINETTA: Doesn't Papa like to be a weaver?

SUSANNA: I am afraid he likes most what he does not have to do. So now it is cheeses! Well. Is it any wonder his sons do not keep their minds on their work, seeing the example of their father? You and I cannot tend to everything, daughter . . . (DOMENICO *is heard singing offstage as he approaches.*)

BIANCHINETTA: I think that is Papa now.

SUSANNA: There is no doubt of it. Run out into the court-yard, Bianchinetta, while I speak to him. (BIANCHINETTA *exits.* DOMENICO *sings.* SUSANNA *works nervously at the yarn.*)

DOMENICO (*Still offstage*):
A jug of wine and a loaf of bread
And a lovely yellow cheese
And a jolly song in a fellow's head,
Oh, what is better than these?
Oh, what is better than these?
(DOMENICO *comes in.*)
My dear wife, here I am immediately. And what is so important?

SUSANNA: What is important is Christopher, Domenico.

DOMENICO: Christopher? Is anything the matter with Christopher?

SUSANNA: Yes. And I am afraid it is your fault.

DOMENICO: My fault? What has happened? Have I not been a good father? Have I not apprenticed my sons to a good trade?

SUSANNA: A good father! Is it a good father, Domenico, to make promise after promise that you do not keep? To set such an example to your sons? Time and again you tell me you will not go to the wine dealer's in the midst of a busy morning. Yet you go.

DOMENICO (*Weakly*): I have business with members of the guild of master clothiers, Susanna.

SUSANNA: At the shop of the wine dealer! Why must it always be at the wine dealer's? You come home without a coin in your pocket. (DOMENICO *feels in his pockets. They are empty.*) Time and again you promise to stick to the workshop as becomes a good weaver. But do you keep your mind on your weaving? No. Your head is full of cheeses!

DOMENICO (*Taken aback*): Cheeses?

SUSANNA: Yes, cheeses. What do you plan to do now, Domenico? Become a cheesemonger? And where did you get the money to buy three cheeses?

DOMENICO: Dear wife, I borrowed it. I have friends. I will pay it back. (*Catches himself*) What three cheeses, may I ask?

SUSANNA: The cheeses in the dark closet under the stairs. Oh, Domenico, do you not see what you are doing? How can we hope to raise our sons to be upright and dependable when their father . . .

DOMENICO: When their father is so undependable? (*He becomes very repentant.*) Dear little wife, flower of my heart, rose of my soul, I know what you say is true. I dream big dreams, and they keep me from tending to my business. Every morning, believe me, I wake up full of fire. "Today," I say, "I will work my fingers to the bone. Today I will weave the finest wool cloth in Genoa. Today I will show my dear Susanna what a man she married . . ."

SUSANNA (*Resignedly*): You show me, all right.

DOMENICO: Every morning this fire of ambition burns in my breast.

SUSANNA: And then the fire burns to ashes. (*She wipes her*

eyes) That itself is bad, but it is not the worst. Your sons suffer from your example! And I had such hopes for them, Domenico. A lad must learn discipline, or he will fail as a man. A lad must keep his promise. He must drive straight ahead and let nothing stand in his way. How long, Domenico, should it have taken Christopher to deliver the cloth this morning?

DOMENICO: Oh, an hour, perhaps. Maybe more.

SUSANNA: He has now been gone more than two hours, and he promised to return directly.

DOMENICO: That is bad. Indeed, dear wife, that is bad. But Christopher is a good lad. It does not happen often, you know.

SUSANNA: Too often. This is not the first time. For his own good, Domenico, you must punish him.

DOMENICO: Do you think so?

SUSANNA: I am sure of it. (*Looks at him pointedly*) It is so easy to get into bad habits.

DOMENICO (*Sighing*): Delightfully easy. (*Catches himself*) What punishment would you suggest, wife?

SUSANNA: Give him more to do; more responsibility, perhaps. Make him work harder, and longer. Then he will have less time for distractions. Promise me, Domenico. For his own good, promise me you will punish him. Then I will try to forget about the cheeses.

DOMENICO: Rest assured, little flower, I promise. Longer hours, you say? More to do? Responsibility? Yes, I will find a way. (BIANCHINETTA *runs in.*)

BIANCHINETTA: They are coming—Bartholomew and Christopher. And running, too.

DOMENICO (*Affectionately*): And you, little rose in the bud, have you not a kiss for Papa after all this time? (BIANCHI-NETTA *kisses him fondly and returns to unravelling the wool.*

BARTHOLOMEW *and* CHRISTOPHER *hurry in.* CHRISTOPHER *is a sturdy, fair-complexioned lad, with reddish hair.*)

SUSANNA: So, Christopher. You are home at last. And what has happened to your promise in the meantime?

CHRISTOPHER: But I *did* come home directly, Mama. Only the wind was against me.

SUSANNA: The wind? And are you a bird, to be concerned with the wind?

BARTHOLOMEW (*Grinning*): You should see his wings, Mama. (*Makes shape of a square-rigged sail with gestures*) How they fly in the wind!

DOMENICO: Come, what is all this talk in riddles? You send a great confusion through my poor head.

SUSANNA (*Giving him a look*): I am afraid it is not only riddles that make a confusion in your head, husband. (*To* CHRISTOPHER) Well, what do you mean, Christopher, that you came home directly, only the wind was against you?

CHRISTOPHER: I am sorry, Mama. But, you see, when the wind on the bay is against you, *directly* may mean having to sail in a zigzag fashion. Still it is as directly as possible.

SUSANNA: Sail? On the bay? What are you talking about, Christopher? (CHRISTOPHER *is hesitant.* BARTHOLOMEW *speaks up.*)

BARTHOLOMEW: Well . . . you see . . . whenever there is a moment, Vittorio lets Christopher sail his little boat.

CHRISTOPHER: A beautiful little boat with square sails. And Vittorio says I have the feel of sailing in my hands . . . and in my heart.

SUSANNA: Oh, la. A weaver's son. Sailing a boat!

DOMENICO: And who is this Vittorio, may I ask?

BARTHOLOMEW: A fisherman. We have met him often at the docks, Papa. He is a wonderful man.

SUSANNA (*Turning to* DOMENICO): So. You see what I mean, Domenico. Something must be done, and immediately.

BIANCHINETTA: Oh, Christopher. That is why you are always running. So you can sail like a bird.

CHRISTOPHER: But for a sudden wind that came up, Mama, I could have come home much more directly. I am sorry. (*Brightens*) But Vittorio says I handled the sail like one born to it.

SUSANNA: What is the world coming to! (*Looks from* DOMENICO *to* CHRISTOPHER) A weaver with his head full of cheeses. And a weaver's son with his nostrils full of the sea. Oh, Bianchinetta, it seems the weight of this household is indeed on the shoulders of the womenfolk.

DOMENICO (*Soothingly*): We could not manage without our womenfolk, for a truth. On the rosebush of our home you are indeed the roses . . . and we, (*Looking at* CHRISTOPHER) the thorns. But how you bloom, Susanna and Bianchinetta!

SUSANNA: Always honey on your tongue, Domenico. You are like a bee who never misses his way to a flower. So be it. Now back to your carding, Bartholomew. And you, Christopher . . . your father has some words to say to you. Come, Bianchinetta. (*As she leaves, she turns back to* DOMENICO) You remember your promise?

DOMENICO: Indeed, I remember. How could I forget? (SUSANNA *and* BIANCHINETTA *exit.* BARTHOLOMEW *lingers.*)

BARTHOLOMEW: Do not punish too hard, Papa. Can he help it if his heart is not with his hands in carding the wool? I know how he feels. I would rather draw maps than comb the oily wool . . .

DOMENICO (*Throwing up his hands*): What a weaver I must be, to have two such sons! Go along, Bartholomew. Christopher will not suffer too much, I promise you. (*Smiles*) Oh, la, today I am full of promises. (BARTHOLOMEW *exits.*) Well, Christopher, what have you to say?

CHRISTOPHER: I have said I was sorry. But (*He hesitates*) . . .

I must tell you the truth, Papa. Only part of me is sorry. It is the sea I love, not the workroom. The smell of salt, not of wool.

DOMENICO (*Sympathetically*): I know. As I love the smell of wine . . . and cheeses. (*Catches himself*) But I should not be agreeing with you. (*Sternly*) A lad must learn discipline, Christopher, or he will fail as a man. A lad must keep his promise. A lad must be dependable. Am I not right?

CHRISTOPHER: Yes, you are right.

DOMENICO: You have in this household a noble example to follow. I do not mean your father, Christopher. Unfortunately, your father is not an example to follow. But your mother! You see how she works, how she plans, how she drives ahead. Yet in her heart, I suppose, she does not like the oily smell of the wool or the bitter tang of the dye any more than you and I.

CHRISTOPHER: I had not thought of it, Papa.

DOMENICO: Then think of it from now on. (*There is silence as* DOMENICO *paces back and forth. Suddenly he gets an idea. His face beams.*) Your mother and I agreed you must be punished for not sticking to business. And I have thought of the way!

CHRISTOPHER: Yes, Papa?

DOMENICO: You are . . . how old? I keep forgetting.

CHRISTOPHER: I will be fifteen in September.

DOMENICO: Not a boy any more. How the time passes! But fifteen in the fall . . . that is good. Your mother and I have agreed that a lad of your age would take his work more seriously if he had more to do.

CHRISTOPHER: But there is so little time now for what pleases me most. Could you not give me a beating instead, and be done with it?

DOMENICO: Now wait. Not so fast. Your back is very tender —I am not in the habit of beating you.

CHRISTOPHER: But the day is mostly work already.

DOMENICO (*Mysteriously*): There is work . . . and work. This Vittorio, now. He says you are a good sailor?

CHRISTOPHER: He says I am born to it.

DOMENICO: And you can already handle a small boat?

CHRISTOPHER: Yes. Vittorio will tell you.

DOMENICO: Then here is how I keep my promise to your mother for extra work, longer hours! Listen, son. I am a weaver, yes. But my head is not only full of wool. Every morning I wake up with a fire in my breast. Today I will show Susanna what a man she married! I will gather in the liras! I will become a rich man! Now, at last, I see a way to do it.

CHRISTOPHER: By making me work doubly hard. Is that it, Papa?

DOMENICO: Come, come. I have said there is work and work. (*Confidentially*) This is a dream I have been fondling for a long time: I have been thinking if I were a wine dealer as well as a weaver, if I were a cheesemonger as well as a weaver, I could be a success. And now I see the way of weaving the many patterns with one shuttle, as it were.

CHRISTOPHER: How do you mean?

DOMENICO: I will buy a little boat. I have friends who will lend me the money, until I can repay. Your father has friends, Christopher. All right. I will buy a little boat with a square-rigged sail. You, Christopher, shall sail it. Oh, there will be long enough hours, sailing up and down the coast—you and I! We will buy raw wool from the peasants. And wine. And cheeses. In exchange we will sell them woolen cloth. What do you think, Christopher? Does it not sound like the way to riches and happiness?

CHRISTOPHER: It sounds like every dream come true, Papa. Sailing a boat! (*Hesitates*) But Bartholomew . . . ?

DOMENICO: When he is a little older, he shall come too.

(*Beaming*) "Domenico Columbus and Sons—Master Clothiers, Wine Dealers, Cheesemongers."

CHRISTOPHER: And sailors! Don't forget sailors.

DOMENICO: Of course. Does it not sound beautiful?

CHRISTOPHER: The most beautiful punishment in the world, Papa. But . . . what will Mama say?

DOMENICO: She has a good head for business, your mother. She will see the good business of it, I am sure, after I talk to her. I will bring her to our way of thinking. Did you not hear her say I am a bee who never misses the way to a flower? I shall fly to her as directly . . . as a boat in the wind, Christopher! I promise you.

CHRISTOPHER: And I promise you something too, Papa. I will become the best sailor on the Ligurian coast. And after that, the best sailor on the Tyrrhenian Sea. And after that, the best sailor on the Mediterranean. And after that . . . who knows? But I can dream of it.

DOMENICO: Ah, Christopher, I can see you are a weaver's son, after all. I can see you are a weaver . . . of dreams.

THE END

Day of Destiny

Characters

COLUMBUS
YOUNG PEDRO, *his page*
PEDRO DE TERREROS, *his steward*
FIVE SAILORS
DOMINGO, *able seaman and cooper*
SHIP'S BOY

TIME: *Late afternoon of October 10, 1492.*
SETTING: *On board the Santa Maria.*
AT RISE: COLUMBUS *and his* PAGE *are at one side of the stage, looking out as if over the sea.* PAGE *holds a book. A group of muttering* SAILORS *are on the other side. Their looks and gestures directed toward* COLUMBUS *suggest they are on the verge of mutiny.*

COLUMBUS: This weather is like April in Andalusia, Young Pedro. The only thing wanting is to hear nightingales!

PAGE: Yes, Captain. It would indeed be good to hear nightingales . . . in place of some of the sounds that come to our ears. (*He glances furtively at the* SAILORS).

COLUMBUS: The tenth of October, and such warm fragrance in the wind!

PAGE: More than fragrance in the wind, Master, (*Looks toward* SAILORS) I am sorry to say.

COLUMBUS: Boy, you could not know, but lately I had a birthday. I stood on deck many hours, looking out upon the sea, thinking. Let me tell you it is a rare thing to end one's fortieth year sailing, so close to the fulfillment of a dream.

PAGE: So close to the fulfillment? You still think . . .

COLUMBUS: For thirty years, lad, I have been waiting for these days. Waiting, waiting. When I was a boy of ten I used to sit on the docks in Genoa watching the ships come and go. Always the mast tops appeared first over the curving expanse of sea. Always the mast tops disappeared last. What, I wondered, lay out there leagues away, beyond the unknown? Japan? India?

PAGE: Still the unknown, my Captain.

COLUMBUS: I was a weaver's son, but I wove dreams instead of woolen cloth. And all these years I have waited for the pattern to come clear. You cannot believe how long the years of waiting were in Spain, Young Pedro. (*Sighs*) Six years . . . before the Sovereigns gave their consent. Yet I did not give up. Life is a river, lad. For some it twists and turns and doubles back upon itself. But my river flows straight ahead. Straight ahead.

PAGE: Yes, Sir, I know. And always to the west!

COLUMBUS (*Smiling*): You learn well. Now let me see the book you have brought. Today I have need of it, with doubts and fears lurking behind my back like tigers. (*Glances at* SAILORS *as he takes the book*) Seneca's *Medea*. The words are fourteen centuries old, Young Pedro, and now, at last, on the verge of proof. (*Finds place*) Listen, then. "An age will come after many years when the Ocean will loose the chains of things, and a huge land lie revealed . . ." (*With assurance*) The chains are loosening. The new land will soon lie revealed.

PAGE (*Straining eyes into distance*): Soon? Today, Sir, is the thirty-first day since we left the Canary Islands behind us. The thirty-first day we have been out of sight of land.

COLUMBUS: You have been listening to the grumblings of the crew! Confess it.

PAGE: Well, it is hard not to listen. Perhaps I should tell you, Master . . .

COLUMBUS (*Shrugging*): No need. (*Glancing at* SAILORS) I know without being told. One does not have to *listen* to know what a Spaniard thinks. I have smelled the vinegar on those Spanish breaths for many days. I have seen the sourness of their thoughts. But my river flows straight! Go, bring me a cup of fresh water, boy. (PAGE *exits.* COLUMBUS *looks at book.* SAILORS' *mutterings grow louder.*)

1ST SAILOR: First he takes us through the seaweed—days of seaweed, leagues of seaweed. Was ever a ship expected to sail through meadows of green and yellow, I ask you? Not an inch of open water! We might be there yet, but for a good wind at our backs. And how can we get home again with the wind in our faces?

SAILORS: Aye, that will be another matter. (*Angry muttering*)

1ST SAILOR: I say we will stick in the seaweed till we rot, if we don't starve first, or perish of thirst.

2ND SAILOR: The farther we go, the less sure we are of the way back. Don't forget the compass. (*Looks maliciously at* COLUMBUS) I tell you I do not trust his bearings. Why did the compass last month vary to the Northwest of the polestar by night, and vary to the Northeast by morning? Why? The compass is bewitched.

SAILORS (*Shaking fists at* COLUMBUS): Not only the compass.

3RD SAILOR: You notice how he keeps pointing out the birds. "Look at the birds," he says. "Land is near," he says. "With birds flying overhead land cannot be far away," he says. Ha! Have we not been seeing birds for weeks? And still no sight of land. Who knows these are not *sea* birds we have been seeing, with no need of land save at nesting time? (YOUNG PEDRO *returns with cup of water.* COLUMBUS *drinks, paying no attention to* SAILORS' *grumblings.* YOUNG PEDRO *exits.*)

2ND SAILOR: Have you noticed? He is varying his course to follow the birds that pass overhead. I do not trust his reckoning.

SAILORS: Foreigner! Genoese!

3RD SAILOR: "Land is near," he says. How many oceans away does he call near? For a month we have not seen land.

4TH SAILOR: And the soundings. Do we have a sounding line long enough to reach the bottom of this unknown sea? No. The sea here is bottomless. And endless. And that's a combination for you!

SAILORS: Aye, bottomless. Endless.

5TH SAILOR: How much longer must we put up with it then? Sailing into nowhere. He is only one. At the most a handful are with him. We are thirty, at the least. Why do we sail on? We must turn back at once, or the food will run out. And the water. Does it ever rain here in this bitter desert of sea? Have you seen a single drop of rain in the last week?

SAILORS: True, true. The sea is a desert here.

1ST SAILOR: This foreigner from Genoa is seeking to make himself a rich lord, a great Admiral . . . at our expense. King Ferdinand and Queen Isabella are *our* sovereigns, not his. Why should we take his orders? (PEDRO DE TER-REROS *comes in with a bird in his hand. He slows up as he passes* SAILORS, *though pretending not to listen.*)

SAILORS: Aye, why?

3RD SAILOR (*Slyly*): Who would know . . . I say . . . who

would know how it happened . . . if the Captain should
fall overboard tonight while observing the stars? An accident, of course!

SAILORS: Of course. An accident.

3RD SAILOR: It would be dark. His foot would slip on the
deck. Or he might lose his balance, you know.

4TH SAILOR: Ha—let him swim to land, then, if it is so close!

5TH SAILOR: Tonight, eh? An accident. Then assuredly we
will have to sail back to Spain immediately to report the
accident. (PEDRO DE TERREROS *has returned to* COLUMBUS
and holds the small bird out to him.)

COLUMBUS (*Nodding to* PEDRO *briefly*): It is you, steward.

PEDRO: Captain . . .

COLUMBUS: Stand here quietly a moment and breathe this
air. Is it not soft and fragrant as April in Seville?

PEDRO: Yes, Captain, but . . .

COLUMBUS (*Seeing the bird*): Ah, another bird. (*Takes it*)

PEDRO: One of several that alighted on the ship, Sir. Quite
different from the others, it seems.

COLUMBUS: Yes, yes. Smaller. More frail. (*Glances at* SAIL-
ORS, *then confidentially*) You know, Pedro, I have con-
cluded the others must be sea birds. They have been with
us so many days. But this—it resembles a warbler, don't
you think?

PEDRO: Yes, Captain. It seems somewhat like a warbler.

COLUMBUS: That means land, surely in a day or two.

PEDRO (*In low voice*): If meanwhile you should not accidentally slip tonight while observing the stars! If you should
not accidentally lose your balance tonight in the dark!

COLUMBUS: Is that what they are talking now, Pedro? As
bad as that?

PEDRO: I heard them as I passed just now. "Who would ever
know how it happened?" they said.

COLUMBUS: Only a day or two more. That is all I ask—only a day or two. Now is not the time to turn back, when the ripe fruit is little more than arm's length away. I *know*, Pedro. Here, inside, I know it is not far now.

PEDRO: I believe it. But we who believe are few. *They* are many.

COLUMBUS: I have dampened their fears before, smothered their doubts, soothed their tempers. I must do it again.

PEDRO: This time it will take more than soft words, Captain, I am afraid.

COLUMBUS: Then, Pedro, that is what they shall have. Soft words. And more! (COLUMBUS *walks toward sullen* SAILORS, *carrying bird.* PEDRO *follows.*) Here is a song for your hearts, men, on a beautiful day. Here is a good omen. This bird has just alighted aboard the Santa Maria. You will see he is smaller than the others we have caught. (SAILORS *mumble.*) Like a warbler, would you not say? (SAILORS *mumble.*) Surely so small a bird cannot be far from land.

1ST SAILOR (*Gruffly*): We have seen your birds before. But we have seen no land since we left the Canaries on the 9th day of September. A month and a day ago!

COLUMBUS: I cannot think a bird this size, like a warbler, could be more than a day or two from land. Three days at the most. (SAILORS *mumble.*)

2ND SAILOR: Who knows the habits of birds in this uncharted desert? We must turn back at once. Otherwise we will starve. We will starve, or perish of thirst, if we do not turn back . . . today.

COLUMBUS: Starve, you say? Come, now. My steward here, Pedro de Terreros, will know about the food supplies. (*Turns to* PEDRO) Would you say, Pedro, that we are in danger of starvation?

PEDRO: As everyone knows, we left Palos, Spain, on the third day of August. That was two months and a week ago. And we were stocked for a twelvemonth, Sir . . . as everyone knows.

COLUMBUS: So you think you will starve, if we are gone a little over two months, on twelve months' supplies! And perish of thirst? Fetch me the cooper, Pedro. He will know the condition of the wine and water casks. (PEDRO *exits.* SAILORS *grumble menacingly.*)

3RD SAILOR: There is still the matter of the compass.

COLUMBUS: Still the matter of the compass! Did I not explain it to you, in great detail? Did I not tell you it was the Pole Star that varied in its rotation, not the compass needle? Besides, the variation is over now.

4TH SAILOR: The seaweed. How can we get back through the seaweed?

COLUMBUS: You saw how it was. The thin layer of weed parted easily before our ships. The worst fear was, as always, the unknown. But now you know, now you have seen the green and yellow meadow part neatly before us, what is the worry?

5TH SAILOR: The wind, that is the worry. The wind continually blows west, away from home. Not east, toward Spain.

COLUMBUS: A good sailor knows how to use the wind, man, however it blows. (PEDRO *returns with* DOMINGO) How now, Domingo Vizcaino, have you been seeing to the casks?

DOMINGO: Yes, Captain. Is anything wrong?

COLUMBUS: Tell us, are the casks leaky or tight?

DOMINGO: As tight as a cooper can make them.

COLUMBUS: And lashed so they can not roll?

DOMINGO: Aye, Sir. Safely lashed and stowed.

COLUMBUS: And the wine and water will last . . . how many months would you say?

DOMINGO: Oh, many months, Sir. Even without rain. We are well stocked with water and wine.

COLUMBUS: Good, Domingo. (*Nods to him in dismissal*) You will be rewarded one day. (DOMINGO *exits.* SAILORS *are still defiant.*)

5TH SAILOR: Rewarded? With what? The bottomless sea and the endless horizon?

COLUMBUS: Surely you have heard of the wealth of the Indies, of the great Khan . . .

5TH SAILOR: Aye, we have heard. But no one has ever reached the Indies by sailing west. We must return to Spain and sail south and east.

SAILORS: Tonight. We turn back tonight.

COLUMBUS: A little more time, men. I beg you. Land is so near now, would you throw to the winds all these days of sailing? Would you fail your King and Queen?

SAILORS: Tonight!

COLUMBUS: Come, I can understand your feelings. And do you think my heart is closed to your longings? Never have you been so long from land on uncharted seas. Of course, you are tormented by doubts. But have you suffered on the journey? Has not the wind been favorable and the sea well-behaved? Have not your tasks been light? To turn back now would be to let the riches of the Indies slip through your fingers.

1ST SAILOR: You have said that before.

2ND SAILOR: And still no sign of land.

SAILORS: Tonight.

COLUMBUS: Today is the tenth day of October. Give me until the thirteenth. Then, on my word, if we do not reach land, I will take you back to Spain. Safely. And without bitterness.

SAILORS: No. No.

COLUMBUS: Consider well what you are saying to your Captain, men. (SAILORS *withdraw a little, talking together.*)

PEDRO: As I said before, I am afraid it will take more than soft words, my Captain.

COLUMBUS: And as I said before, they shall have their soft words . . . and more.

SAILORS (*Turning back*): Three days is too long. We turn back tonight.

COLUMBUS (*Getting angry*): I have come on this journey of exploration under the flag of two great Sovereigns to find the Indies. I shall not turn back until I am satisfied that I have been mistaken. I am not yet satisfied! So far all is well. Land is near. I have no doubt of it in my heart. As long as I am Captain of the Santa Maria . . .

1ST SAILOR (*Mockingly*): Aye, as long as you are Captain!

2ND SAILOR: You are only one. At the most, you have a handful of men with you.

3RD SAILOR: We are thirty strong.

COLUMBUS: Enough. I know what thoughts you are thinking. The words are written on your faces for me to read, and in your gestures. You are thinking: "How easy it will be. How simple. The Captain's foot will slip accidentally while he is observing the stars tonight. The Captain will lose his balance tonight in the darkness and fall overboard." I know your thoughts. But let me tell you it is not so easy! It would do you no good to kill me. Do you hear what I am saying? It would do you no good to kill me! The Sovereigns have already been warned what might happen on such a voyage as this. (COLUMBUS *measures his words*) I tell you . . . if you return without your Captain, the King and Queen will have you hanged . . . the whole lot of you. It is already agreed. (SAILORS, *mumbling, huddle again for consultation.*)

PEDRO: That will give them something to chew on, Sir.

COLUMBUS: "He deserves not the sweet that will not take the

sour." (*After a few moments,* SAILORS *reach a decision, turn to* COLUMBUS)

4TH SAILOR: We are willing to sail on . . . for two more days.

5TH SAILOR: Only two.

SAILORS: Two days. If your land is so near, we should see it in two days.

COLUMBUS (*Looking at the bird*): A little bird like a warbler would not be far from land. (*To* SAILORS) Two more days? That is enough. It will be a compact, then, on both sides. And let us hear no more grumbling. Tell the others. Two more days, and no grumbling! (SAILORS *exit.*) As I told you before, Pedro, I need only a day or two more. It is the voice of destiny telling me.

PEDRO: Your faith is wondrous to behold, my Captain. (*There is silence for a moment as the two look out over the sea.* SHIP'S BOY *comes in with an unlit lantern, chanting.*)

SHIP'S BOY: "Amen and God give us a good night and good sailing; may the ship make a good passage, sir Captain and master and good company."

COLUMBUS: My faith burns in me like a fire, Pedro. Like an unquenchable white light. Two days are enough. Look, Pedro, the sun is setting in the western sea, toward the land of promise. And we sail toward it!

THE END

Light in the Darkness

(October 11, 1492)

BOYS: "I saw a light," Columbus said,
straining his anxious eyes.
"There in the darkness, straight ahead,
seeming to fall and rise.
The waxen gleam of a candle beam,
seeming to fall and rise!"

GIRLS: Was it a light from far away?
Was it a wind-blown star?
Twelve leagues ahead the islands lay!
Nothing could show so far.

BOYS: "I saw a light," Columbus cried,
tense as a tightened wire.
"There on the wave it seemed to ride,
flashing its waxen fire.
Yellow-bright as a taper's light,
flashing its waxen fire!"

GIRLS: Was it a light the Captain saw?
Was it but fancy's wraith?
The only light that could show so far,
bright as the brightest guiding star,
was the light of the Captain's faith.

ALL: The light of the Captain's faith!

Boy in Genoa

GIRLS: What are you watching, lad,
      shading your pale blue eyes?

BOYS: The mainmast tips
      of the sailing ships
      where the curving distance lies.

GIRLS: What are you thinking, lad—
      Christopher is the name?

BOYS: That a ship at sea
      is the place to be
      and a weaver's life is tame.

GIRLS: What are you dreaming, lad,
      smile on your freckled face?

BOYS: That the sea is wide
      and the waves still hide
      secrets for ships to trace.

GIRLS: What are you hoping, lad,
      scanning the sweeping shore?

BOYS: That I'll sail away
      in a ship some day
      where nobody sailed before!

Across the Unknown

(1492)

Three little ships, well-built, well-manned,
set sail one day in search of land,
into a mystery of space . . .
and faith was in the Captain's face.

Three little ships sailed long and far,
checking the compass with the star,
till fearful sailors scorned the prize . . .
but faith was in the Captain's eyes.

Three little ships reached land at last,
after the anxious weeks crawled past.
Three little vessels found their goal—
for faith was in the Captain's soul.

HALLOWEEN

Ghosts on Guard

Characters

MRS. BRIGGS, *who doesn't want her windows soaped*
MR. BRIGGS, *her long-suffering husband*
TOM
PEGGY
DONNA } *out for Halloween fun*
DICK
HARRY, *younger brother of Donna and Dick*

SCENE 1

TIME: *Early evening, Halloween.*
SETTING: *The living room of the Briggs's home*
AT RISE: MRS. BRIGGS *is dressing her husband in an old white shirt and sheets, making him into a ghost.* MR. BRIGGS *is very unhappy about it.*

MRS. BRIGGS (*Pinning and fixing*):
　To dress a ghost requires some skill.
　Clarence Briggs, will you stand still?
MR. BRIGGS (*Giving a jump*):
　Ouch!
MRS. BRIGGS: Well, *now* perhaps you will!
MR. BRIGGS: What a wife—to prick her spouse.

MRS. BRIGGS:
Stand as quiet as a mouse.
Tonight you must protect our house.
Tonight the children will be mean,
And *you* must keep our windows clean.
Who ever thought of Halloween! (*Sighs*)

MR. BRIGGS (*Looking at costume*):
I feel silly.

MRS. BRIGGS:
Don't you mope.
You'll scare the children off, I hope.
For every windowpane they soap
I'll hide your pipe for one whole day.

MR. BRIGGS (*Horrified*): Hide my precious pipe away?

MRS. BRIGGS:
That's the price you'll have to pay
If you permit the Toms and Dicks
To play their silly stunts and tricks.

MR. BRIGGS: Ouch! That safety pin . . . it pricks.

MRS. BRIGGS (*Standing off to survey him*):
You make a lovely ghost, my man.
These sheets are old, but spick and span.

MR. BRIGGS:
Oh, Maggie, if the truth were told,
I'd rather *play* with kids than scold.

MRS. BRIGGS:
You'd think you were a 10-year-old!
(*She takes an extra sheet and drapes it around his shoulders.*)
Now, keep this sheet on for a shawl
To shut away the cold and all.

MR. BRIGGS (*Trying to walk*):
These skirts will surely make me fall.
Let the youngsters have their fun!

Mrs. Briggs:
> My windows shan't be soaped—not one!
> You go and make the hoodlums run.

Mr. Briggs:
> I'd rather give them little treats . . .
> You know, an apple or some sweets.

Mrs. Briggs:
> Give away our hard-earned eats?
> Well, I guess not. And now, be gone:
> Go slink around the yard and lawn,
> And don't you dare to nod and yawn.

Mr. Briggs: No youngsters will appear, I hope.

Mrs. Briggs:
> Better take this piece of rope
> To tie the hands that hold the soap.
> (*She hands him a piece of clothesline.*)

Mr. Briggs (*Sighing*): I think this being a ghost is silly.

Mrs. Briggs: Well, go and be one, willy-nilly. (*She leads her husband out.*)

CURTAIN

*   *   *

Scene 2

Setting: *In front of the Briggs's home.*

At Rise: Tom *and* Peggy *come in dressed in old clothes and masks. They carry paper bags for their treats. They also carry laundry soap for windows, if they don't get treats.* Tom *has a tick-tack and* Peggy *a noisemaker which she shakes every now and then.*

Peggy: I wonder if we'll get some treats.

Tom: If not, we'll do some tricks.

PEGGY:
  Mrs. Briggs won't give us sweets—
  Her heart is hard as bricks.

TOM:
  We'll have to soap her windows, then.
  We promised Mom and Dad
  We'd never do *mean* tricks again . . .
  And soaping isn't bad.

PEGGY:
  It's worse than making doorbells go,
  Or making tick-tacks rattle.

TOM:
  Mrs. Briggs deserves it, though:
  She's always set for battle.

PEGGY: *Mr.* Briggs seems nice and kind.

TOM:
  If we could know him better
  I think we'd like his type of mind.

PEGGY:
  His wife is such a fretter. (*Appeals to* TOM)
  Could you make my mask hold tight—
  It wiggles on my nose.
  (TOM *adjusts* PEGGY'S *mask, then looks up and down the street.*)

TOM: Dick and Donna aren't in sight.

PEGGY:
  They had to change their clothes
  And find the masks they wore last year.
  I only hope their mother
  Will let them come and meet us here
  Without their little brother.

TOM:
  Harry? Oh, he's much too small.
  He'd make our plans go wrong:

He'd fall, and slow us up, and all!
We can't have *him* along.

PEGGY: We can't? (*Points*)
Well, look, they're coming now—
Donna, Dick, and Harry.
Tom, you mustn't make a row . . .

TOM (*Obviously displeased*):
I hope my mask is scary,
Enough to send him home, and quick!

DICK (*Calling*): Hello. I'm sorry, Tom . . . (DONNA *and* DICK, *dressed in Halloween costumes and wearing eye-masks, come in.* HARRY, *a rather pathetic little fellow, tags behind.*)

DONNA (*Indicating* HARRY):
I think it is a mean old trick.
They *made* us, Dad and Mom.
(*As the children talk,* MR. BRIGGS, *the ghost, tiptoes in behind them, cocks his ear, hides behind a bush and listens. The children, of course, do not see him.*)

DICK:
They said that they were going out.
They said we had to take him.

TOM:
Perhaps if we should run about
We'd . . . accidentally . . . shake him.

DICK:
Let's leave him here at Briggs's gate
While we go up the street. (*To* HARRY)
Now you be good and sit and wait,
And we may bring a treat.

HARRY: It's dark.

DONNA: Perhaps I ought to stay.

DICK (*To* HARRY): If you get scared, just yell.

TOM:
Or, if you'd rather run away,

Start home . . . you might as well.
But if you're here when we get back,
We'll let you watch the fun.
(*Boastfully points to Briggs's house*)
We'll cross that hedge, and then attack
Those windows, one by one.
(*Gestures as if soaping windows*)

PEGGY:
Just make a face and you will scare
A ghost, if any comes!

HARRY: I'd rather go along . . .

TOM: No fair.
You sit and twirl your thumbs.
(*The children run off and leave poor* HARRY *alone. He is forlorn and a bit frightened. At first he starts after the children, then turns back slowly.*)

HARRY (*Almost crying*): Donna! Dick!
(MR. BRIGGS *pops up from behind the bush.*)

MR. BRIGGS: Sh! Listen here,
Cross my heart, I'm not a ghost.
There's not a thing for you to fear.

HARRY: I'm not . . . a bit afraid . . . almost. . . .

MR. BRIGGS: I'm only Mr. Briggs, you see.

HARRY: Are you dressed up for Halloween?

MR. BRIGGS: My wife rigged up these sheets on me.
It wasn't *my* idea, I mean.

HARRY: I'd like to be a ghost.

MR. BRIGGS: You would?

HARRY: I'd love to be a ghost.

MR. BRIGGS: Why not?
Between us we might do some good,
We might accomplish quite a lot.

HARRY: They wouldn't let me go along . . .

MR. BRIGGS:

I know. I hid and heard it all.
When they come back, if I'm not wrong,
They'll find *two* ghosts, one big, one small.
Stand up and see how this will fit . . .
(MR. BRIGGS *takes off his extra sheet and begins to drape it over* HARRY.)

HARRY: They're going to soap your windowpanes.

MR. BRIGGS:

They *think* they are. I question it.
We ghosts are noted for our brains.
(*Works over costume*)
I'll have to make two slits for eyes—
It's good these sheets are old and thin. (*Fixes hood*)
There! As a ghost you'd take a prize . . .
You even give *me* prickly skin. (*He shivers, and* HARRY *giggles.* MR. BRIGGS *looks over the situation.*)

HARRY:

They said they'd cross the hedge right there . . .
And soap your windows, one by one.

MR. BRIGGS:

They made you stay. It wasn't fair!
If they could see you now, they'd run.

HARRY: They'll run a mile when we say, "Boo."

MR. BRIGGS:

But what about those treats they've got?
We wouldn't want to lose them too.

HARRY: Oh, no.

MR. BRIGGS: I have a plan. Here's what:

You hide behind that little tree,
I'll hide behind the bigger one,
We'll stretch this rope between us, see?
And trip them gently, just for fun,
And then we . . . listen! here they come.

Careful. Hide yourself. Keep mum.

(MR. BRIGGS *and* HARRY *hurry and hide behind the "trees," holding the rope between them. In a moment the four children come in, looking at each other's treats.*)

TOM: I got a doughnut.

DONNA: I got *two*.

DICK: Some apples and some candy.

PEGGY: And see these peanuts—quite a few.

TOM: They'll surely come in handy!

DONNA (*Looking around for* HARRY):
Harry must have got a fright—
He isn't at the gate!

TOM:
Don't worry—he will be all right.
He didn't want to wait.
Let's soap the Briggs's windows first,
Then hustle home and eat.

DICK:
I bet that Mrs. Briggs will burst
When we have left the street:
Her precious windows full of soap!

PEGGY: She'll fuss to all the neighbors.

DICK:
When we go by tomorrow, I hope
We'll see her at her labors.

DONNA:
Her husband must have quite a time—
No fun at all, I bet.

TOM:
His wife thinks having fun a crime.
Well, here we are. All set?

(*The children approach the hedge and jump over. As they begin to move stealthily toward the house, they trip over the rope* MR. BRIGGS *and* HARRY *hold. They fall, clutching their*

treats. The ghosts begin to make weird noises. Quickly MR.
BRIGGS *loops the rope around the captives.*)
MR. BRIGGS (*In a quavering, ghostly voice*):
Villians . . . rascals . . . mischief-makers . . .
Scoundrels . . . bullies . . . child-forsakers . . .
Give a treat, or stand a trick
For every evil deed. Be quick.
TOM: W-w-we didn't d-d-do a thing unlawful.
PEGGY: Eek! I think that ghosts are awful.
MR. BRIGGS (*Threateningly*):
For every piece of wickedness
We'll play a trick on you, unless
You give a treat, as you confess!
DICK:
B-b-but, Sir, wh-what damage did we do?
Wh-what evil d-d-deeds did we pursue?
MR. BRIGGS:
First. You planned on playing some jokes
On innocent, hard-working folks:
Soaping windows, for example.
(*Picks up soap*)
See, this bar is just a sample.
DICK (*Nodding in the direction of Briggs's house*):
With *her* there wasn't any use
To ask for treats . . .
MR. BRIGGS: That's no excuse.
You planned to give those panes a soaping.
DICK (*Pushing his bag of treats toward* MR. BRIGGS): This
treat will help us out, I'm hoping. (MR. BRIGGS *picks up
the bag and peeks in, nodding happily.*)
MR. BRIGGS:
Next. You left a child alone
This night when ghosts and witches groan.

You left a child . . . that takes explaining!

There's just a *ghost* of him remaining.

DONNA (*Thoroughly frightened, feeling guilty*):

Just a ghost! The little dear . . .

We never should have left him here.

Just a . . . oh, I can't repeat it!

Take this treat . . . I couldn't eat it.

(*She pushes her bag toward* MR. BRIGGS, *who takes it with pleasure.*)

MR. BRIGGS:

Third. You boasted—shame on you—

How smart you were, and what you'd do.

Boasting is an evil habit.

TOM: Guilty! There's a doughnut—grab it. (*He shoves his bag toward* MR. BRIGGS.)

MR. BRIGGS:

Fourth. You know it's very wrong

To trespass where you don't belong.

You did a thing that's bad and vicious.

PEGGY: Yes. (*Guiltily gives up her treat*)

These peanuts are delicious!

Now you have our treats, please say

That we can run a mile away!

DICK: We promise to be nice to Harry.

DONNA (*Tearfully*): If we find him. Oh, how scary.

PEGGY: We'll never soap those panes, or boast. (*Nods at house*)

TOM: Or jump the hedge again, Sir Ghost.

ALL:

So, please, just let us go—untie us.

We promise to be good. Just try us.

MR. BRIGGS:

I'll have to ask my pal. (*To* HARRY) What say?

Do they deserve to get away?

HARRY: Yes. They all sound sorry—very.

DICK: Hear that voice?

DONNA (*Excitedly*): It sounds like Harry!
Harry! Harry! Is it you?
(HARRY, *laughing, takes off his ghost hood. So does* MR.
BRIGGS.)

MR. BRIGGS: I guess our little game is through.

TOM: Mr. Briggs!

MR. BRIGGS: I thought you'd guess it.
Now, my friends, I must confess it:
My wife insisted I must be
This frightful ghostly ghost you see,
And though I seriously objected,
I've had more fun than I expected—
More fun than I have had for years.

TOM: I'm glad of that. I say, "Three cheers."

MR. BRIGGS:
And, thanks to you, it now appears
That we are going to have a party.
(*He holds up the bags of treats.*)

DICK: Our appetites are pretty hearty.

MR. BRIGGS:
It's been an age since I have seen
Such special treats for Halloween.
Let's sit around and all be merry.
(*He passes the bags around, and everyone joins in the fun.*)
I know some stories that are scary.

CHILDREN:
Tell them! That will be just right
For such a scary sort of night.

MR. BRIGGS: I'll tell you all you want to hear . . .
If you will come again *next year!*

THE END

On Halloween

(A skit for many boys and girls)

AT RISE: TWO GIRLS *in Halloween costumes enter and look around timidly.*

1ST GIRL: This is the night
               that is dark and scary.

2ND GIRL: *Much* more scary
               than ordinary.

1ST GIRL: Witches loom
               through the eerie gloom
               as they zip and zoom
               on a magic broom.

2ND GIRL: Their voices boom
               with the sound of doom.

BOTH: And oh, but we must be wary. (*They shrink back as they see* WITCHES *approach on broomsticks.* WITCHES *chant and dance around weirdly.*)

WITCHES: Swish . . . swish . . . swish,
            Tonight is so spooky-ish,
            We feel right at home wherever we roam.
            Swish . . . swish . . . swish.

(*The* GIRLS *watch the dancing for a few minutes, then begin to clap.* WITCHES, *startled, swish to sides of stage and crouch there.*)

1ST GIRL: This is the night
that is dark and scary.

2ND GIRL: Much more scary than ordinary.
But don't you feel merry?

1ST GIRL: Very! (*They sit down with* WITCHES)

(TWO BOYS *in Halloween costumes enter and look around nervously.*)

1ST BOY: This is the night
when ghosts are stary.

2ND BOY: Much more stary
than *necessary.*

1ST BOY: They glide in view
on the avenue,
and clutch at you
with a wailing "Woooo."

2ND BOY: Or pierce you through
with a fearful, "Boo!"

BOTH: And oh, but we must be wary. (*They shrink back as they see* GHOSTS *glide in.* GHOSTS *dance in slow motion as they wail.*)

GHOSTS: Wooooo . . . wooooo . . . woooo,
Tonight we have things to do:
We'll make folks shake and quiver and quake.
Wooooo . . . wooooooo . . . woooo.

(*The* BOYS *watch the dancing a few minutes, then begin to clap.* GHOSTS, *startled, glide behind the* WITCHES.)

1ST BOY: This is the night
            when ghosts are stary.

2ND BOY: Much more stary
            than necessary.
            But don't you feel merry?

1ST BOY: Very! (*They sit down with* GIRLS, WITCHES *and*
         GHOSTS. *A* BOY *and a* GIRL *come in with jack-o'-lanterns.*)

BOY: This is the night
            that is legendary.
            Pumpkin-lanterns
            are gay and glary.

GIRL: Cats are seen
            with their eyes of green.

(BLACK CATS *come in meowing and meowing. They stalk
around, then take places with the others.*)

BOY: Spooks convene
            on the ghostly scene.

(*Various* SPOOKS, GOBLINS, SCARECROWS *and other Halloween
characters come in trying to frighten each other. Then they
take their places with the others.*)

BOTH: But pleasure is keen
            for it's . . .

ALL (*Shouting gaily*): H A L L O W E E N !
            And everyone's merry.
            Very!

THE END

Jack-o'-Lantern

BOY: Who wears a grin
from ear to chin?

ALL: Jack-o'-lantern.

GIRL: Whose teeth are few
and jagged, too?

ALL: Jack-o'-lantern.

BOY: Who shows a light
all orange-bright
that makes his face a jolly sight?

ALL: Jack-o'-lantern.

GIRL: Who has a pair
of eyes that stare?

ALL: Jack-o'-lantern.

BOY: Whose nose is flat—
no doubt of that?

ALL: Jack-o'-lantern.

GIRL: Who sports a smile
that shows a mile,
and once a year is all in style?

ALL: JACK-O'-LANTERN.

Black and Orange

BOYS: Black for cats
and black for bats
and black for witches' cloaks and hats.

GIRLS: Orange for the harvest moon
rising like a bright balloon.

BOYS: Black for shadows,
black for shades,
black for masks at masquerades.

GIRLS: Orange for a pumpkin—bright
with orange eyes or orange light.

ALL: Black and orange, side by side,
on the night that witches ride—
black and orange always mean
heaps of fun on Halloween,
heaps of fun on Halloween!

Halloween Concert

BOYS: "It's cold," said the cricket,
"my fingers are numb.
I scarcely can fiddle,
I scarcely can strum.
And oh, I'm sleepy,
now summer has gone."

ALL: He dropped his fiddle
to stifle a yawn.

GIRLS: "Don't," said the field mouse, "act so sober.
You can't stop *yet*, when it's still October."

BOYS: "I've played," said the cricket,
"for weeks and weeks.
My fiddle needs fixing—
it's full of squeaks.
My fingers need resting . . ."
He yawned. "Ho, hum,
I'm quite . . . (*Yawn*) . . . ready
for winter to come.
I've found me the coziest,
doziest house . . ."

GIRLS: "You can't stop *now*," said his friend the mouse.

BOYS: "No?" yawned the cricket,
      and closed his eyes.
      "I've played so much
      for a chap my size.
      It's time (*He yawns*)
      for my winter snooze:
      I hear the creak
      of November's shoes."

GIRLS: "You *can't* . . ." said the mouse in a voice of sorrow,
      "you can't desert us until tomorrow.
      Tune up your fiddle for one last scene . . .
      don't you remember it's HALLOWEEN?"

BOYS: "What!" cried the cricket.
      He yawned no more.
      "You should have mentioned
      the fact before!
      Is everyone ready?
      And where's the score?
      What in the world
      are we waiting for?"

ALL: The cricket fiddled,
      the field mouse squeaked,
      the dry weeds twiddled,
      the bare twigs tweaked,
      the hoot-owl hooted,
      the cornstalks strummed,
      the westwind tooted,
      the fence wires hummed:

Oh, what a concert all night long!
The fiddle was shrill, and the wind was strong.
"Halloween, Halloween, crick, crack, creak.
Halloween, Halloween, scritch, scratch, squeak."

Pumpkins

Cinderella's pumpkin
is not the only one
that turned to something magic—
when all is said and done.

Our October pumpkin
felt a magic knife,
turned into a smiling face
with teeth as big as life.

And its orange insides
under Mother's eye
turned into a luscious,
    squishious,
     spicy pumpkin pie!

ELECTION DAY

The Voice of Liberty

Characters

MR. DAWSON
MRS. DAWSON
GRAM
JOEL
ISAAC
WILLIAM
STEPHEN
A YOUNG WOMAN
A MAN
AN OLD WOMAN

TIME: *The present, with flashbacks to the past.*
SETTING: *The Dawson living room.*
AT RISE: MR. *and* MRS. DAWSON *and* GRAM *are seated in the living room.*

MR. DAWSON: There's not much use to vote. Such candidates!
   Why bother to go down to vote at all?
   Why make the effort?
MRS. DAWSON: That's the way I feel. What good is it?
   Besides, it breaks my morning work time up,
   Having to stand in line for half an hour.
   The men we like the most don't have a chance!

GRAM: If folks like you stay home,
The peoples' candidates are sure to lose.
I think you ought to go.

MRS. DAWSON: Now, Gram, you know *you* plan to stay at
home
And lose your vote again!
Why don't you vote yourself?

GRAM: With all this rheumatism in my bones?
Besides, I'm not much hand at politics,
And I'm too old.
Ten years from now I won't be here to care
Who's President or Senator or Judge
But you'll be here, and so you ought to vote
And let your voice be heard.

MRS. DAWSON: The weather's so uncertain.
Why did they pick this month as election time?
The chances are there'll be a blizzard on.

MR. DAWSON: As like as not.
Besides, there's not much chance that folks like us
Can do a bit of good, filling a ballot in.

JOEL (*Entering excitedly*): I've just been reading of a resident
Of Philadelphia since way back when,
Who hasn't said a word for—let me see—
More than a hundred years,
And yet whose voice is heard from coast to coast,
From North to South, across the U.S.A. . . .

MR. DAWSON: What's that you say?

MRS. DAWSON: Don't talk such nonsense, son.
How can a voice be heard when it is still?

JOEL: Well, here's a hint:
If you should go to Independence Hall, in Philadelphia,
You'd see it for yourselves—
A great American, still holding open house
And drawing quite a crowd year after year!

GRAM: A great American?

JOEL (*Laughing*): Yes. Three feet high. A good big ton in
　　weight.

　And slightly cracked!

MRS. DAWSON: You sound that way yourself.

JOEL: There's something masculine about the size,
　　The crudeness of the finish, and the strength.
　　The shape is classic, though—quite feminine . . .

MR. DAWSON (*Impatiently*): Come, come, my boy.

JOEL: It's really quite a bell!

MRS. DAWSON: What's that?

GRAM: A bell!

JOEL: The story is a thriller any day
　　But now *especially*—around election time.
　　I wish that I could vote!
　　Well, want to hear?
　　It's all about a bell called Liberty . . .

MRS. DAWSON: Of course, we want to hear.

JOEL: You have to start way back to set the scene.
　　You start with Philadelphia, the town
　　That William Penn laid out on a peninsula
　　Between the Schuylkill and the Delaware.
　　The colonists put up a State House there—
　　Began the year Ben Franklin started publishing
　　His old Gazette. 1729, to be exact.
　　Well, they had quite a time, those colonists,
　　Getting the State House up
　　With all their ties to Britain's apron strings.
　　The British wanted trade:
　　They forced their products on the colonies.
　　They made them pay.
　　Some colonists approved—the tie was strong
　　Between them and the mother-country still.
　　But others fumed,

And even children had their dander up.

(*Flashback to* ISAAC *and* WILLIAM, *two colonial boys*)

ISAAC: My father calls them blasted British nails!
Why can't we make our own?
When I grow up, I'm never going to pound a British nail!

WILLIAM: They *had* to use them in the State House here.
It makes my father mad.
That building should have been American
From start to finish—that's what Father said.
When I grow up, I'm going to make some nails!

ISAAC: Let's both make nails when we grow up, what say?
I'd like to work with iron.
Let's hang around at Pass and Stow's and watch,
So we'll know how to handle it.

WILLIAM: They used good native lumber though, at least,
To build the State House of,
And Uncle Edward says we kilned our bricks.
He helped to lay them up.

BOTH: But British nails! (STEPHEN *enters*)

STEPHEN: Say, wait—
I bet you haven't heard the latest news
Or you'd have something sharper than a British nail
To bother you!
I've hung around the State House, and I know . . .

ISAAC: Know what?

STEPHEN: The Superintendents plan to buy a bell . . .

ISAAC: That's good. It's time the State House had a bell.

WILLIAM: I hope it's big and loud.

ISAAC: My father says we need a good strong bell
That can be heard across the countryside,
Way out past Germantown.
Who'll make it? Pass and Stow?
They're good at iron. We've watched them lots of times.

STEPHEN: Huh! Pass and Stow!

The Superintendents never even thought of them.
They've ordered us a *British* bell, my lads!
If you've been fussing over British nails,
What do you say about a bell, I ask?

ISAAC: You're sure that's right?
I bet my father hasn't heard it yet . . .
He'd say a bell like that would never ring!

STEPHEN: Of course it will.
The British know their bells . . .
That's why a firm in London got the job.

WILLIAM: But if it doesn't ring . . .

STEPHEN: No chance at all.
They've made a lot of bells, the British have.

ISAAC (*Belligerently*): There must be someone in the colonies
Who'd know the way to cast a metal bell.

WILLIAM: A British bell will never ring, I say.
We'll bet on that!

STEPHEN: I'll bet a shilling's worth of British nails
The bell will ring.

ISAAC: We'll take you up.
You'll buy the shilling's worth, because we'll win!

STEPHEN: What difference does it make who casts the bell?
Just so it's good.
Just so it rings, I say. (*Shrugs and goes out*)

WILLIAM· When we grow up
Let's learn to turn out bells as well as nails. (*They go out.*)

GRAM: And how did it turn out, about the bell?

MR. DAWSON: They got an English one?

MRS. DAWSON: And did it ring?

JOEL: The bell was cast by Englishmen all right,
And at a bargain, too.
It came in August of the following year—1752,
Across the sea from London, up the Delaware,
Suspended from the hardwood beam that still supports

Our bell in Independence Hall.
It had these words around the top of it,
According to the order that went in:
"Proclaim Liberty throughout all the land and unto all
   the inhabitants thereof."
Folks didn't rush it to the belfry though.
They swung it on a temporary frame
Inside the State House yard, to try it out.
A crowd turned out to watch . . .
A few were certain that the bell would fail,
Being British made;
But, by and large, the crowd was confident.
Of course, the bell would ring.
Why shouldn't it?
That's what a bell was for.

MRS. DAWSON: Of course. Of course.

JOEL: But when the rope was pulled . . .

*(There is an abrupt clang offstage, stopping almost as soon as
it starts. In a minute* ISAAC *and* WILLIAM *come in excitedly.)*

ISAAC: We heard it start to ring, and then it stopped!
The woman next to me
Was sure the sound would carry miles and miles.
But, say, it didn't even ring one round!

WILLIAM: It cracked . . . it broke!
The bell split up the side. We won our bet.

ISAAC: I never thought we'd get some British nails
And feel so glad about it.
British nails!
Let's throw them in the river, one by one.

WILLIAM: I wonder if they'll throw the bell in too.
It's not much good like that, with such a crack.

ISAAC: The first clap of the knocker and it split.
My father said it would.
Now will they let us make one in the colonies?

WILLIAM: I heard John Pass and Charley Stow suggest
   They'd like a try.
   They'd make a bell that wouldn't crack, I bet.
ISAAC: They never made a bell but they can try.
   They know their iron.
   We'll have to watch them every chance we get. (*They
   go out.*)
JOEL: Pass and Stow, two eager colonists,
   Turned out a bell.
MR. DAWSON: What happened to the English one that
   cracked?
JOEL: They broke it up, and then they melted it
   With native copper ore, to make it strong.
   They tried a formula:
   For each ten pounds of broken British bell,
   Not quite one pound of copper.
MR. DAWSON: Did it work?
JOEL: They tried it out on little bells at first,
   To test the strength and sound,
   And then they made a mould and cast the bell!
   It looked quite good when taken from the mould.
   The size and shape were pleasing . . .
GRAM: And the words? The words around the top?
JOEL: The lettering was better than the British,
   People said.
   The words were still the same:
   "Proclaim Liberty throughout all the land and unto all the
   inhabitants thereof."
MRS. DAWSON: And did it ring?
JOEL: Just wait!
   It's spring in Philadelphia this time, 1753.
   The trees aren't yet in leaf, but swelling at the tips;
   And farmlands greening off beyond the town.
   Another day for hanging up a bell,

For crowds to gather in the State House yard . . .
(ISAAC *and* WILLIAM *come in.*)

ISAAC: It's *got* to ring. It musn't fail to ring.

WILLIAM: There's Stephen coming. Shall we make a bet?

ISAAC: We'll bet *this* time the bell will ring, not fail. (*Calls*)
Say, Stephen, wait. You think the bell will ring?

STEPHEN (*Coming in*): Well, even if it does, it won't be good.
You can't make music in a blacksmith shop!

WILLIAM: You'll bet on that?

STEPHEN (*Hurrying off*): There isn't time. I want to find a
place. (WILLIAM *and* ISAAC *exit.*)

JOEL: The crowd is waiting, and the moment tense.
The rope is pulled amidst a mighty cheer.
The second bell is swung . . .
(*There is a discordant crash offstage, like a crash of kitchen
pots and pans.*)

A YOUNG WOMAN (*Offstage*): You call that thing a bell?
A noise like that?
We'd be a town of deaf mutes in a year
If we were forced to listen to that din!

A MAN (*Offstage*): Let's Pass it up and Stow the bell away.
Aye, Pass and Stow!
They deal in iron, not bells. We might have known.

AN OLD WOMAN (*Offstage*): You'd think they caught a thou-
sand cawing crows
And made a bell of them.
We'd hear it, heaven knows. But what a sound!
(*Colonists' voices trail off, as* WILLIAM *and* ISAAC *come on.*)

WILLIAM (*Trying to be cheerful*): It didn't crack at least. It
made a noise.

ISAAC (*Sorrowfully*): A noise is right . . . but not the noise
of bells.
It's just as well we didn't make that bet.

WILLIAM: There's something wrong . . .

They put in too much copper, someone said;
They melted too much copper with the iron.
They'll know next time.

ISAAC: You think they'll break it up and try again?

WILLIAM: Of course they will.

ISAAC: But people made some pretty mean remarks
About poor Pass and Stow.
You heard them, standing near us in the crowd.

WILLIAM: I wouldn't care. I'd want to try again.
And so would you.
And so will Pass and Stow. (*They go out.*)

MR. DAWSON: And did they try?

GRAM: Of course they did! They couldn't wait to try.

JOEL: They broke the bell and changed the formula:
They cut the copper down, and made a mould,
And cast another bell.
It didn't take so long—a couple of months—
And it was ready to be swung again.
Summer. 1753.
Three times and out, you know!
The crowd is sober now, and questioning,
Not jubilant, expectant as before.
This time the crowd is on the anxious seat:
Two bells have failed, is this a blunder too?
(ISAAC *and* WILLIAM *appear*.)

WILLIAM: My father still is full of confidence.
Three times and out, he says.
This time it works!

ISAAC: We'd better climb the fence so we can see. (*They go out.*)

JOEL: A little ritual, and the rope is grasped.
The bell begins to swing . . .
And then it sounds . . .
(*Sounds of a clear bell ringing offstage.*)

MRS. DAWSON: I'm glad of that! The trouble those folks had.

JOEL: The bell rang strong and clear—
Over the town, over the fields, it rang,
Into the hills along the Delaware,
All up and down the rich green countryside.

MR. DAWSON: At last, at last.
Those fellows made a fight, by Jove, and won.
They didn't just sit back . . .

JOEL: For years the big bell rang:
For meetings, celebrations, deaths,
For summoning the Philadelphians to hear
(July the fourth, 1776)
The Declaration from the State House yard.

GRAM (*Remembering, slowly*): "We hold these truths to be self-evident—that all men are created equal; that they are endowed by their Creator with certain inalienable rights; that among these are life, liberty, and the pursuit of happiness . . ."

MRS. DAWSON: Why, Gram, how you remember! Every word.

MR. DAWSON: I learned it, too, but not as well as that.

JOEL: And then it rang of war.
The colonists against the Britishers!
It rang of Washington—the day he took command,
And early victories.
And then the British marched on Philadelphia!

GRAM: They didn't get the bell—don't say they did!

MRS. DAWSON: They couldn't have . . .

MR. DAWSON: Their fingers itched to melt it down, I bet,
For cannon balls, to shoot the rebels with!
And was it safe?

JOEL: The Continental soldiers saw to that.
They moved the bell away,
Just put it in a wagon, one of those
For hauling troop supplies.

And carted it away to Allentown—
A creaky, bumpy ride of fifty miles—
To hide it safely there inside a church.

GRAM: I'm glad of that.

JOEL: Next year the bell was back,
Rehung, and going strong in Independence Hall.

MRS. DAWSON: In Independence Hall? The State House, then,
Was harmed perhaps?

JOEL: Oh no, it's standing yet, it's still the same.
You see, with victory, they changed the name . . .
To Independence Hall.

MR. DAWSON: And what about the bell?

JOEL: It rang for more than eighty years. Then cracked.
It's in the Hall on exhibition now.

MRS. DAWSON: Too bad it had to crack.

JOEL: Well, strange to say, that crack has made the bell
More famous than it ever was before:
It's down where folks can look at it these days,
And looking makes them think,
It makes them pause . . .

MR. DAWSON: It makes me pause, myself.
They fought for things I take for granted now,
Those colonists.
My liberty has come the easy way.
They took a stand. They saw a problem through—
By Jove, they did.
I must confess the story makes me blush . . .
I wasn't going to vote!
Oh, what's the use? I said. What good is it?
We'd still be pounding British nails, I guess,
If *they'd* said things like that, and just sat back.

MRS. DAWSON: They had to *work* for liberty, and I
Felt taking time to vote would be a chore.

GRAM: I'm guilty too.

Perhaps I will be gone in ten more years—
But that's no reason for being silent now!
I ought to care what kind of world there'll be
For you folks left behind.
My rheumatism—fiddlesticks! I'll vote.
Why, even with the crack, the clapper dead,
That bell still speaks to me
I still can hear it with my inner ear.

JOEL: The voice of liberty is more than just a weight
Of iron and copper in a cracked old bell:
It's still alive,
It still has things to say . . .

MR. DAWSON: I know. We can't stop now.
We can't stop here.
If I lived where I wasn't free to vote,
Where liberty and voting were a farce,
I'd realize then, by Jove . . .
I'd prize these free elections we have here!
The only way to keep democracy
Is taking part in it. No other way!
There still is work to do, for all of us.

JOEL: Those words around the bell . . .
We've got to keep on hearing what they say.

ALL: "Proclaim Liberty throughout all the land and unto all
the inhabitants thereof."

THE END

Voting Day

A group of boys and girls are looking at a large sign (tacked to a screen or desk) which says VOTING DAY. *Behind the screen hide three girls and three boys, each holding a placard with a letter of the word* VOTING.

1ST GIRL (*Looking at sign*): Today, they say, is Voting Day,
with posters everywhere.
But all the fuss is not for *us*—
we're much too young to care.

1ST BOY: We cannot vote, it's sad to note,
until we're twenty-one,
so why should we care one-two-three
what voting-things are done?

2ND GIRL: Today, they say, is Voting Day-
for grownups. Some are keen,
but some stay home and sigh and groan:
"Huh, what does voting mean?"

2ND BOY: The posters shout, "Turn out, turn out
and vote! It's up to you
what laws get passed." But, first and last,
I wonder if that's true.

ALL: Today, today, is Voting Day.
Before the day is spent,
we wish we'd hear, as clear as clear,
exactly what is meant!

(*Boys and girls behind the sign run out in order, so the letters they hold spell* VOTING.)

ALL SIX: You wish to know what's thus and so
in VOTING? Listen well,
and we will try to clarify
just what our letters spell.

BOY WITH V: V for vision of the kind
of life that's worth foreseeing.
Voting is the way to bring
that vision into being.

GIRL WITH O: O for obligation
on the part of you, and me,
to keep Old Glory waving
in a land of liberty.

BOY WITH T: T for thought and teamwork
in choosing right from wrong.
And no one is too young or old
to help that cause along!

GIRL WITH I: I for international—
applied to point of view,
for insight into others' needs,
ideas of what to do.

BOY WITH N: N for nation that we love;
and need of serving, giving.
If we cannot vote, we still
can serve by friendly living.

GIRL WITH G: G for government in gear
to serve the greatest good,
government not based on force,
but faith and brotherhood.

ALL SIX: That spells VOTING. You'll agree
that a simple word can be
mighty big, although it's small—
full of meaning for us all.

(Boys and girls of first group summarize the meaning of VOTING, *as each member of the letter-group steps forward in turn and holds his letter high.)*

1ST GIRL: *V*ision!

1ST BOY: *O*bligation
to keep our country free.

2ND GIRL: *T*eamwork!

2ND BOY: *I*nsight!

1ST GIRL: *N*ation
in need of you and me.

1ST BOY: *G*overnment in gear to serve
the greatest good . . .

ALL: It's clear
all of us have parts to play,
today . . . and all the year!

Veterans Day

BOYS: Eleventh month. Eleventh day.
GIRLS: Eleven in the morning.
BOYS: A solemn bell begins to sway
and ring its solemn warning:
ALL (*Softly*): "Silence . . . silence . . . face the east.
Silence . . . think upon the men
who supposed, when fighting ceased,
war would never come again."

GIRLS: Eleventh month. Eleventh day.
BOYS: Eleven, on the hour.
GIRLS: The silent soldiers seem to say
that faith is still a tower:
ALL (*Softly*): "Listen . . . listen . . . can you hear?
We who battled and were killed
know the dream that we held dear
some bright day will be fulfilled."

BOYS: Eleventh month. Eleventh day.
GIRLS: Eleventh hour. A prayer
sent by voices far away
is hanging in the air:
ALL (*Softly*): "Onward . . . onward . . . do not flinch,
now the task is up to you,
push the vision, inch by inch,
make our dream of peace come true."

To an Unknown Soldier

1ST BOY:	We do not know your age, or name,
2ND BOY:	or how you looked, or what you thought,
3RD BOY:	or from what town or farm you came—
ALL THREE:	we only know how well you fought.
1ST GIRL:	We do not know what books you read,
2ND GIRL:	what gave you pleasure and release,
3RD GIRL:	what poems you thought but never said—
ALL THREE:	we only know you died for peace.
ENTIRE GROUP:	We do not know so many things,
	but you must know (somehow, somewhere)
	your dream of peace still spreads its wings
	above our heads and hovers there.

Prayer for Peace

Swing out, oh bells,
sing out, oh bells,
our prayer that strife be ended,
that guns be still
on plain and hill
and all our discords mended.
Let weapons turn to plowshares **now**
and fighting planes be grounded
as through the air of Everywhere
the words of peace are sounded.

Ring out, oh bells,
swing out, oh bells,
sing out from every steeple
the burning hope
the yearning hope
for peace by weary people.
Let understanding be our aim,
the goal for which we're heading,
as through the earth a strong **rebirth**
of brotherhood starts spreading.

BOOK WEEK

Once Upon a Time

Characters

READER
OLD WOMAN
HER CHILDREN
BAKER'S MAN
WHIZZER, *a young magician*
GEORGIE
PETER RABBIT
THE HARE
THE WHITE RABBIT
THE MARCH HARE
ALICE
PINOCCHIO
HEIDI
MR. POPPER
CHRISTOPHER ROBIN
MARY POPPINS
ROBIN HOOD
CINDERELLA

SETTING: *Inside the Old Woman's shoe.*
AT RISE: *The* READER, *with nose in book, comes on stage and begins to read aloud. The* READER *soon curls up in easy chair and remains there throughout play. Throughout the play,*

while the READER *reads, the* OLD WOMAN *and the* CHILDREN
should pantomime as much as possible.

READER: Once upon a time . . . there was an old woman
who lived in a shoe. She had so many children she didn't
know what to do. (*The* OLD WOMAN *comes in shaking her
head. Her* CHILDREN *swarm around her, hopping, skipping,
dancing, turning cartwheels, etc.*)
She had fat children, and lean children,
And frumpy children, and clean children,
And sort-of-in-between children,
And big children, and small children,
And short children, and tall children,
And nothing-to-do-at-all children.
And since it is often upsetting to have even one child in a
family, or two . . . (*A* CHILD *almost upsets the* OLD
WOMAN.)
No wonder the poor Old Woman didn't know what to do!
OLD WOMAN (*Holding her head*):
They get underfoot
Wherever I stand.
They never stay put,
They get out of hand,
They occupy all the available inches.
Oh dear, when you live in a shoe, how it pinches!
(*She sits down on a stool, her head in her hands.*)
I must think of something before it's too late . . .
The day is approaching . . . the King will not wait.
I wish I could gather my thoughts in a cup
Like berries or cherries. The time's almost up.
READER:
But, unfortunately, before the Old Woman could gather a
single thought,

Her children began asking many more questions than they
ought,
Or else they came up with an adventure to tell, or two,
So . . . no wonder the poor Old Woman didn't know what
to do!

A GIRL: Mama, when I asked the little red hen for a kernel of
corn, she gave me a *peck*.

A BOY: Mama, what is the difference in size between a bird
and a beast? (*He waits a moment, then shouts.*) *Two feet.*

A GIRL: First I was in a jam, then I was in a pickle, then I
was in a stew, and now I'm in the soup.

A BOY: Mama, who has four eyes but cannot see? (*Calls
over his shoulder as he hops away*) *Mississippi.*

A GIRL: Mama, when I went to the orchard, they told me to
sleep on an apri*cot*, but I'd much rather lie on a rose-bed.

A BOY: Mama, if you want to pick a flower that's good to
eat, what do you do?

SEVERAL CHILDREN: Picc-a-lilli!

READER:
And so it went from morning till night,
Until the Old Woman who lives in a shoe
With so many children so lively and bright
Simply didn't know what to do!
And all the time it was becoming very important for the
Old Woman to determine
How she was going to entertain the King, in his robe trimmed
with ermine,
For, you see, everyone had to take turns entertaining the
King for one whole day,
And the Old Woman's turn was only a few (*three*, to be
exact) days away.
But how could she think—with so many children crammed
into the shoe?

No wonder she couldn't decide what to do, what to do,
   what to do.

OLD WOMAN (*To the tune of "Three Blind Mice"*):
   Three more days. Three more days.
   Oh, how they race. Oh, how they race.
   If I don't think of a plan at once,
   The King will call me a frightful dunce—
ALL: Three more days!
OLD WOMAN:
   Oh, hum. Hum, ho,
   What's to come, I don't know.
   All my thoughts have taken wing—
   I cannot think of *any*thing
   To entertain his Nibs, the King.
A BOY: Mama, you could throw a party, if you didn't throw
   it too far.
A GIRL: Mama, you could *spring* a surprise . . . if it weren't
   fall.
READER:
   And so the *first* day came, and went,
   Till every single hour was spent,
   And still the Woman in the shoe
   Had not a thought of what to do
   To entertain the King.
OLD WOMAN: Boo, hoo!
   If I could think . . . if I were wise . . .
   I might receive a royal prize:
   A ten-cent pearl, or even ruby.
   But, as it is, I'll get a *booby*.
READER:
   Now, a booby, as you know, is a dumb and witless bird
      from tropical isles,
   And everybody getting a booby is the object of lifted eye-
      brows and smiles,

Especially since people receiving a booby from the King
    are ordered to tie it
Right out in the front yard where everybody passing by
    can spy it.
So . . . is it any wonder the poor Old Woman who lived
    in a shoe
Wanted her children to be quiet so she could figure out
    what to do?

OLD WOMAN:
    Ho, hum. What's to come?
    Hum, ho. I don't know.

READER:
    There she sat, leaning her head on her hand and using her
        arm for a bracket,
    Not knowing what she could do in the midst of the muddle
        and racket.

A BOY: What can we do?

A GIRL: What can we play?

A BOY: Give us a clue, and we'll go away.

READER:
    But their mother wasn't able to think of a single pastime,
        or a single clue,
    Because she had come to the end of her shoelace, and didn't
        know what to do.
    Then the Eldest Boy, who was always hungry because he
        was always growing,
    Thought of a plan that set all the other children to ah-ing
        and oh-ing.

ELDEST BOY: Mama, why don't you get in touch with the
    Baker's Man? Have him cook up a great big special kind
    of pie. Then when we are all busy eating, with our mouths
    full of pie, we will be so quiet you will be able to think.
    Then you can figure out how to entertain the King.

READER:

> That seemed like a wonderful plan indeed.
>
> If only . . . if only it would succeed!
>
> So the Old Woman called up the bakery and put in a hurry-up order
>
> For a special kind of pie with goodies in the middle and a crusty border,
>
> And that very evening the Baker's Man set foot in the shoe before dinner
>
> With a pie that was certainly a great deal *thicker* than it was thinner.

BAKER'S MAN (*Coming in with big platter*):

> I've baked them big, and I've baked them little,
>
> I've baked them soft, and I've baked them brittle,
>
> I've baked for many a man and miss,
>
> But I *never* have baked such a pie as this.

A BOY: Can you put in your thumb and pull out a plum?

> (BAKER'S MAN *sets the pie down on the table, smiles and bows, then hurries out.* CHILDREN *rush to the table in great excitement.* OLD WOMAN *makes believe she is cutting the pie and passing it around.*)

READER:

> My, but it was a wonderful pie—
>
> Big and broad, and deep and high!
>
> Every son and every daughter
>
> Felt his mouth begin to water.
>
> Oh, the filling! Oh, the batter!
>
> One thing only was the matter:
>
> The pie, unfortunately, was so *very* special, and so very nice,
>
> So unusually full of raisins and cocoanut and spice
>
> That the children, instead of keeping quiet, kept repeating
>
> "Yummy, yummy, yummy," *all* the time they were eating.

CHILDREN: Yummy, yummy, yummy.

READER:

And so the poor Old Woman saw all of her hopes take wing,

Because she hadn't time to think about the King, the King.

OLD WOMAN: Boo, hoo, hoo. What shall I do?

READER:

And thus the *second* day slipped past—

The time was going very fast!

The poor Old Woman wiped her eyes—

She'd lost all hope of any prize

(A trinket or a red-glass ruby)

But still she *didn't* want a booby.

And then the Youngest Girl, who liked to look out of the window and dream,

Thought of—at least, so it seemed to the Old Woman— a wonderful scheme.

YOUNGEST GIRL: Mama, if only you knew someone who could make *magic*, instead of a pie! Then maybe you would be able to figure out what to do.

OLD WOMAN:

Magic! My dumpling, that's just what we need.

I'll hire the Wizard of Oz. Yes, indeed. (*She goes to the phone.*)

READER:

But, unfortunately, when the Old Woman called up the Employment Agency in the city,

She learned that the Wizard of Oz was booked for a good long time. What a pity!

And when she asked if the Agency could supply some other magician,

The man-at-the-other-end said they had only one person for the position.

OLD WOMAN (*Holding hand over phone to talk to the children*):

It seems that the best they can do after dinner

Is send a magician who's just a *beginner.* (*Speaking into phone*)

Well, send him on over. I'm in such a fix

Perhaps a beginner can pull enough tricks.

READER:

So Whizzer, who was just learning to be a magician, whizzed into the shoe. (WHIZZER *swoops in to the sound of a slide whistle.*)

With his wand and his stiff black hat and great big how-do-you-do.

WHIZZER: How do you do! Hocus . . . pocus . . . dominocus.

CHILDREN (*Excited*): Play your tricks, but do not joke us.

OLD WOMAN:

Do you know the clever magician's habit

Of reaching into your hat and pulling out a rabbit?

WHIZZER (*Consulting a little book of instructions, which he has tied around his neck on a string for easy reference*):

Rabbit? Rabbit? Why, yes, I can bring you so many

You may, in the end, be sorry you asked for any.

(*He moves to the door, waves his wand over his hat, and chants*)

Abra . . ca . . dabra . . . and other such words as that!

Come, little magical rabbits, jump out of my hat!

(*He sweeps his hat near the door, and a boy hops into the room like a rabbit.*)

GEORGIE: New folks coming, oh my! (*Hops toward other exit*)

Hi, Uncle Analdas, new folks coming! Hi, Phewie Skunk, new folks coming! (*He goes out.*)

CHILDREN: Who in the world was that?

WHIZZER:

Why, that was Georgie from *Rabbit Hill.*

Abra . . ca . . dabra . . . look your fill!

(*He goes through the motions again and another small boy hops in like a rabbit. He seems very excited.*)

PETER RABBIT: I lost one of my shoes among the cabbages in Mr. McGregor's garden, and the other shoe among the potatoes. And my little blue jacket with brass buttons got caught on a gooseberry net. What will Mama say! (*Exits*)

A GIRL:
Who was that, and how did he lose
His little blue jacket and both his shoes?

WHIZZER:
That was Peter Rabbit, and he didn't mind his mother.
Presto . . . jesto! Here come another!
(*He goes through his gestures again, and another boy hops in quickly. He seems very sure of himself.*)

THE HARE: Imagine that slow old Tortoise thinking he can beat me. I can run like the wind . . . I can run like the wind! I can beat him all to pieces in a race. (*He hurries out.*)

A BOY: Of course, he can.

WHIZZER: Oh, no—you'll find
That boastful Hare gets left behind!
(*He goes through his motions and another rabbit hops in, this time with a pair of white gloves and a fan. He is in a hurry.*)

WHIZZER:
Here's a rabbit in a hurry,
Wrinkling up his nose with worry.

WHITE RABBIT: Oh, the Duchess, the Duchess. Oh, won't she be savage if I've kept her waiting! Oh, my fur and whiskers. (*Exits*)

A GIRL: What's the matter? And who was that?

WHIZZER:
I pulled the White Rabbit out of my hat.
And, while I'm at it, the March Hare, too,
To show what Wonderland rabbits do. (*Gestures. The MARCH HARE, yawning, hops slowly across the stage. Stops in the middle and yawns.*)

MARCH HARE: Suppose we change the subject. (*Yawns again*)
I'm getting tired of this. (*Exits slowly, mumbling under his breath.*)

WHIZZER (*Consulting his little book*):

Had enough rabbits? I see there are more.

In fact, it appears there are rabbits galore.

A BOY: Are they all wild ones or are they all tame?

A GIRL: How do you happen to know each one's name?

A BOY:

Can you, instead, pull a dog or a cat

Or maybe an *elephant* out of your hat?

WHIZZER:

Goodness, the questions! Be patient a minute.

My hat, as you noticed, has magic within it,

But since I am not yet a full-grown magician,

The things I pull out must fulfill *one condition:*

I can't pull out someone by hook or by crook

Unless he is written about *in a book!*

READER:

Well, you can imagine how the Old Woman and her children
gasped at that information,

Because they hardly ever got around to read books—not
even in vacation,

And so they knew very little about books and all the magic
that hovers

On black and white sheets under yellow, and red, and green
covers.

That is the reason their eyebrows went up, and their chins
went under

And they stared and stared with their mouths wide open in
wonder.

And it was in that moment of quiet, when the air was as
still as a feather

That the Old Woman was able to gather a few of her
thoughts together.

OLD WOMAN:

Wait, I think I have a plan!

May I speak to you, my man? (*She beckons to* WHIZZER.)

READER:

Then the Old Woman whispered something into the magician's right-hand ear,

Something to the effect that—if he could make all those
magical rabbits appear—

Why couldn't he pull some magical *people* out of his hat
as well?

Some who would entertain the children by the stories
they had to tell?

Then they would be quiet, and there would be peace in the
Shoe,

And then the Old Woman could think what to do, what
to do.

WHIZZER (*To* OLD WOMAN):

As long as folks are *in a book*

My magic works on them, but look,

(*Shows his little book*)

There are so *many* I can use

It will be hard to pick and choose.

I guess I'll close my eyes, and go

"Eeny, meeny, miney, mo."

(*He closes his eyes and finds a place in his book. Then he
moves over near the door and waves his wand over his hat.*)

Twinkle, twinkle, little hat—

Who's a girl to wonder at? (ALICE IN WONDERLAND *comes
running in, with something small in her hand. When
she sees the* OLD WOMAN, *she curtsies.*)

ALICE: My name is Alice, so please your Majesty. (*Looks at
what is in her hand.*) This little cake says EAT ME. Well,

I'll eat it, and if it makes me grow larger, I can reach the
key; and if it makes me grow smaller, I can creep under
the door; so either way I'll get into the garden.

A GIRL: Will you let me go along?

ALICE: Of course. Come on! (*Starts to exit and* GIRL *follows*)
Dear, dear! How queer everything is today. And yesterday
things went on just as usual. (*They exit.* NOTE: *If more
than eight boys and girls have been used for the* OLD WOMAN'S
CHILDREN, *more than one should exit with each book character, so that by the time the eight book characters have left
the stage, all the* CHILDREN *are gone.*)

WHIZZER (*Making more magic, after finding another name in
his book*):
Twinkle, twinkle, my chapeau—
Where's that scamp Pinocchio?

(PINOCCHIO *walks in stiffly, because he is made of wood.*)

PINOCCHIO: I may be made of wood, but I hope I'm not a
blockhead. Jacket of wall paper, shoes of wood, hat of
bread crumbs—that's me, Pinocchio. Oh, I'm a very unusual fellow. (*Looks at* CHILDREN) Who'd like to sit in the
front row with me at the marionette show? You'll be surprised at what will happen—me, coming out with five gold
pieces as a reward for valor!

A BOY: Let's go, Pinocchio. (*Exits with* PINOCCHIO)

WHIZZER (*Finding another name in his book and making magic*):
Twinkle, twinkle, who is this?
Hmmm . . . she looks a little Swiss.

(HEIDI *comes in.*)

HEIDI: Oh dear, I mustn't stay away from grandfather so
long. I must go back to the fir trees and the goats. I must
climb up to the rocks where the sun paints the mountains
with his most beautiful colors before he goes to bed . . .
so they won't forget him before morning.

A GIRL: Who are you?

HEIDI: I'm Heidi. Would you like to go to the mountains with me?

GIRL: Oh, yes. (*Goes out with* HEIDI)

WHIZZER (*Finding another name and going through his gestures*):
Twinkle, twinkle, little topper—
Where's that funny Mr. Popper?
(MR. POPPER *comes in.*)

MR. POPPER: Who'd like to take a look at the penguins? Popper's Performing Penguins! Seems a long time since I got those holes drilled in the refrigerator so Captain Cook . . . that was my first penguin . . . could live there. Now you ought to see them. You just ought to see them!

A BOY: *I'd* like to see them, Mr. Popper.

MR. POPPER: Come along, then. (*Exits with* BOY)

WHIZZER (*Going through the motions again*):
Twinkle, twinkle, hat to wear,
Halfway isn't *any*where—
Not the bottom, not the top . . .
Who's that coming hop, hop, hop?
(CHRISTOPHER ROBIN *hops in.*)

CHRISTOPHER ROBIN: Christopher Robin goes hoppity, hoppity. (*Stops hopping and begins to remember*) Silly old Bear, getting his head stuck in a honey jar so Piglet thought he was a Heffalump! Silly old Winnie-the-Pooh. Remember the time he went down the hole to call on Rabbit? He couldn't get out again—at least, not all of him could. Only his head and shoulders. Remember what happened?

A BOY: No. What?

CHRISTOPHER ROBIN: Come with me and I'll show you. (*Starts to hop out, followed by* BOY.) Nice, silly old Bear!

WHIZZER (*Making his magic again*):
Twinkle, twinkle, little bonnet,
With a wizard's magic on it,
Bring us from the windy sky

Mary Poppins—on the fly.

(MARY POPPINS *comes in hanging on to an open umbrella and a carpet bag.*)

MARY POPPINS (*Tossing her head*): Know there is a Red Cow out in the yard, looking for something? I think it was a mistake for the King to tell the Red Cow how to get that fallen star off her horn. Now she can't dance any more. (*Sniffs the air*) Humph, wind's right for adventures. Anybody want to come along and have tea on the ceiling with my uncle, Mr. Wigg?

A GIRL: I do! (*She hurries out after* MARY POPPINS.)

WHIZZER (*Making more magic*):

Twinkle, twinkle, little hat,

Now who's there to marvel at?

(ROBIN HOOD, *with bow and arrow, comes in with great gusto.*)

ROBIN HOOD: Who would like to speed a gray goose shaft from a longbow? Who would like to fool the Sheriff of Nottingham by going to the archery contest in disguise . . . and winning the golden arrow? Come along, then, to Sherwood Forest where my merry men are waiting. Come along with Robin Hood.

A BOY: I'm coming! (*Runs after* ROBIN HOOD *as he exits*)

WHIZZER (*Going through his gestures again*):

Twinkle, little hat, once more.

One more magic visitor!

(CINDERELLA *comes in.*)

CINDERELLA: My stepsisters used to make me sleep in the ashes on the hearth. That is why they called me Cinderella. Then, one night everyone went to the ball and left me home alone. Oh, how I wanted to go to the ball! But I had only an ugly old dress and heavy shoes. Then something happened—and I went to the ball in a gown of gold-colored cloth.

A GIRL: What happened?

CINDERELLA: Come with me and I'll tell you all about it. (GIRL *exits with* CINDERELLA. *All the* CHILDREN *have now left the stage, and the* OLD WOMAN *is alone with* WHIZZER. *The Shoe seems very quiet.*)

OLD WOMAN:

Well! I never knew such peace
Inside the Shoe, in every crease.
Now I'll think from A to Izzard.
Thank you, Whizzer. You're a wizard.
I only hope it's not too late
To keep that booby from my gate!

READER:

And so the Old Woman collected her thoughts in a hurry,
For now that the shoe had stopped pinching, she lost every worry.
And before you could say "Tra-la-la" like the birdies in spring,
She thought of a way to entertain the King, the King, the King!

OLD WOMAN:

With such a life as the King is leading
He can't have very much time for reading—
For every day is filled to the brim
With teas and parties to honor him.
So how can he meet, in his marble palace,
Georgie, and Winnie-the-Pooh, and Alice,
And Mary Poppins, and folks like that?

WHIZZER: He couldn't, Madam, I bet my hat. (*Taps his hat*)

OLD WOMAN:

So I have decided when my turn comes,
The King shan't sit and twiddle his thumbs,
Because my children and I will bring
Our book-friends over to visit the King,

And with their magical gifts and powers
They'll entertain all of the Court for *hours*.
WHIZZER:

That's an excellent thing to do.

Madam, I take off my hat to you.

(*He bows with a sweep of his hat, then exits.*)
READER:

And so the Old Woman began to dance and to sing "Toodle-oo, toodle-oo,"

Because she was no longer a woman who didn't know what to do.

OLD WOMAN (*Dancing*): Toodle-oo, toodle-oo.

READER (*As* CHILDREN *start coming in*):

And now, as we come to the end of this tale, it is fitting and proper

To say that the King was *so* pleased with the penguins and Mr. Popper,

And Christopher Robin, and Winnie, and Alice, and Heidi,

He wanted them all to remain—at least till next Thursday or Friday!

In fact, he thought *every* new book-friend worth more than a ruby,

Which means that the Old Woman *didn't* get given a booby.

Instead, as a special reward . . . for the red-letter day of the year,

The King had the high-uppy-ups of the Shoemakers' Union appear,

And told them to make the Old Woman a much bigger Shoe,

And to line the old one with bookshelves . . . so there would be *two*.

CHILDREN: Goody *two* shoes! Goody *two* shoes!

READER:

And so, with more room underfoot (without hanging from ceiling or rafter),

And with shelves full of magical books, and with hearts
full of laughter,
The Old Woman lived with her children . . . happily . . .
ever after!

THE END

Treasure Hunt

Characters

ALICE
DODO } *from "Alice in Wonderland"*
MOUSE

TOM SAWYER
HUCKLEBERRY FINN } *from "Tom Sawyer"*

MEG
JO
BETH } *from "Little Women"*
AMY

MICHAEL BANKS, *from "Mary Poppins"*
HEIDI
ROBIN HOOD
CHRISTOPHER ROBIN
FERDINAND
MISS BROOKS, *the teacher*
FIVE BOYS
FOUR GIRLS

SCENE 1

SETTING: *A sidewalk in front of the school, or a corridor where children pass back and forth.*

AT RISE: *The girls come in talking excitedly.*

1ST GIRL:

She says there's a treasure—a treasure to find.

2ND GIRL:

She says it is priceless, and more than one kind.

3RD GIRL:

Where is it, I wonder?

4TH GIRL:

Look up, and look under,

Look sideways, and frontwards, ahead and behind!

(*They all look around, baffled.*)

1ST GIRL:

I can't think what treasure Miss Brooks has in mind.

(*A group of boys, talking, come in from the other direction.*)

1ST BOY:

She says if we guess it, we all can take part

In a play for the school . . .

2ND BOY:

Let's hurry. Let's start.

3RD BOY:

She says it's a treasure

Too mighty to measure.

4TH BOY:

Can't *somebody* guess it? (*He notices one of the girls and nods
at her.*)

                     Alberta, you're smart,

You surely must know all the treasures by heart.

ALBERTA (*One of the girls*):

Well, money's a treasure—like silver and gold,

And emeralds and rubies and pearls you can hold,

And bracelets and lockets,

And coins in your pockets,

And all kinds of valuable things that are sold,

And bonds are a treasure—or so I've been told.

1st Boy:

Miss Brooks says this treasure is found everywhere.

1st Girl:

She says it is riches all people may share.

Boys:

Look hither and thither. (*They look.*)

Girls:

We're all in a dither. (*They look.*)

2nd Boy:

I can't see a treasure, wherever I stare.

2nd Girl:

And, goodness, there isn't a moment to spare!
(*Another boy,* Nathaniel, *comes in hurriedly and eagerly. He calls to the others.*)

Nathaniel:

Listen, I've thought what the treasure might be!

I've just had a hunch, and I hope you'll agree . . .

Boys: Tell us, and hurry.

Girls: We're wasted with worry.

Nathaniel: It seems like a pretty good treasure to me.
(*The children go into a huddle around* Nathaniel. *There is much whispering and giggling.*)

All: Let's bring some to Teacher tomorrow, and see!

1st Girl: I'll bring her some slippers.

1st Boy: I'll bring a dead cat.

2nd Girl: I'll bring her some rolls that are crusty and fat.

2nd Boy: A bow and an arrow.

3rd Boy: A tail—long and narrow.

3rd Girl: A thimble.

4th Boy: A compass.

Nathaniel: Some flowers for her hat.

All (*Merrily*): We'll make her guess *what* kind of treasure is
that! (*Laughing and excited, the children exit.*)

*   *   *

SCENE 2

SETTING: *A classroom.*

AT RISE: *The children, dressed in costumes, are sitting in the classroom showing each other their "treasures." MISS BROOKS enters and the children are suddenly quiet and angelic.*

MISS BROOKS:
Good morning, my children.

CHILDREN:
Good morning, Miss Brooks.

MISS BROOKS:
You must have a secret . . .
I know by your looks.

CHILDREN:
We thought of the treasure!

MISS BROOKS:
You did? You don't say.
Well, if you are right
You may put on a play
And ask all the children
In school to attend.

CHILDREN:
And dress up in costume?

MISS BROOKS:
That all will depend.
Now, come, what's the treasure
Too mighty to measure
That gives us all pleasure?
(*A girl dressed like Alice in Wonderland gets up and goes to* MISS BROOKS. *Holds out a thimble*)

ALICE:
I brought you a thimble.
It's only a symbol

Of all kinds of treasure
That give people pleasure.

MISS BROOKS (*Baffled*):

A thimble? That's grand . . .
But I don't understand.
I may appear green,
But *what* does it mean?

(*Two boys representing* TOM SAWYER *and* HUCKLEBERRY
FINN *hurry up with the stuffed cat.*)

TOM:

We've brought a dead cat.

MISS BROOKS (*Horrified*):

W-w-what treasure is th-that?
Oh, take it away
This moment, I say!

(*The* BOYS *quickly hold the cat behind them.* Four GIRLS,
representing MEG, JO, AMY, *and* BETH *of "Little Women"*
come up and hold out a pair of slippers.)

JO:

A new pair of slippers.

MEG:

They haven't got zippers.

AMY:

They may not be stylish.

BETH:

But oh, they're worthwhilish.

MISS BROOKS:

Look, children, I'm baffled.
What treasures are these?
I fear you're in error.
Explain yourselves, please:
This isn't a matter
About which to tease.

MICHAEL BANKS (*Running up*):
   I've brought a fine compass.

HEIDI (*Coming up*):
   Some rolls for your lunch.

ROBIN HOOD:
   A long bow and arrow.

CHRISTOPHER ROBIN:
   A tail that is narrow.

FERDINAND:
   Some flowers in a bunch.

CHILDREN:
   The treasure is endless!

MISS BROOKS:
   But . . . what do you mean?

CHILDREN:
   We'll never be friendless.

MISS BROOKS (*Softly*):
   It's most unforeseen.
   (*Louder*)
   Now, children, I warn you,
   You've gone far enough.
   Just what is the meaning
   Of . . . all of this stuff?

ALICE (*Turning toward class for help*):
   Dodo, Mouse . . . be quick, be nimble.
   Help explain this treasured thimble.
   (DODO *and* MOUSE *stand up from among children in seats.
   The following scene is adapted from "Alice in Wonderland."*)

DODO:
   *Every*body has won, and all must have prizes.

CHILDREN:
   But who is to give the prizes?

DODO (*Pointing to* ALICE):
   Why, *she*, of course.

CHILDREN:

Prizes! Prizes!

(ALICE *searches in her pockets and pulls out a box of candies. She passes them around for prizes. There is just exactly one apiece, but none for* ALICE.)

MOUSE:

But she must have a prize herself, you know.

DODO: Of course. (*To* ALICE) What else have you got in your pocket?

ALICE:

Only a thimble.

DODO:

Hand it over here.

(ALICE *gives* DODO *the thimble, and* DODO *solemnly hands it back.*)

We beg your acceptance of this elegant thimble.

(ALICE *bows, and hands the thimble to* MISS BROOKS.)

MISS BROOKS (*Merrily*):

I think you have guessed, I think you have found
The key to the treasure that lies all around!
This thimble is part of the wealth we collect
From "Alice in Wonderland." Am I correct?

CHILDREN:

That is the answer.

MISS BROOKS (*Looking at the cat, drawing back*):

And now for the cat . . .

TOM:

Wait just a minute, we'll help you with that.

(*The following scene is taken from "Tom Sawyer."*)

Hello, Huckleberry.

HUCK: Hello yourself, and see how you like it.

TOM: What's that you got?

HUCK: Dead cat.

Tom: Lemme see him, Huck. My, he's pretty stiff. Where'd
   you get him?

Huck: Bought him off'n a boy.

Tom: What did you give?

Huck: I give a blue ticket and a bladder that I got at the
   slaughter-house.

Tom: Say—what is dead cats good for, Huck?

Huck: Good for? Cure warts with.

Miss Brooks:
   Splendid. Splendid. That is treasure
   From "Tom Sawyer." (*She eyes the cat.*) Doubtful pleasure!
   Let me make just one more test
   To be sure you've really guessed:
   What about this pair of slippers
   That, you say, do not have zippers?
   (*The following scene is adapted from "Little Women."*)

Jo: Christmas won't be Christmas without presents.

Amy: It's dreadful to be so poor!

Meg: You know the reason Marmee proposed not having
   any presents this Christmas was because it's going to be a
   hard winter for everyone; she thinks we ought not to spend
   money for pleasure, when our men are suffering so in the
   army.

Jo: But I don't think the little we could spend would do any
   good. We've each got a dollar, and the army couldn't be
   much helped by our giving that . . . but I do want to buy
   a book for myself.

Beth: I planned to spend mine on new music.

Amy: I shall get a nice box of Faber's drawing pencils; I really
   need them.

Jo: Let's each buy what we want, and have a little fun; I'm
   sure we grub hard enough to earn it.

Beth: Marmee will be home soon. I've brought her slippers
   to warm.

JO (*Looking sadly at the slippers*): Marmee must have a new
   pair.

BETH: I thought I'd get her some with my dollar.

AMY: No, I shall!

MEG: I'm the oldest . . .

JO: I'm the man of the family now Papa is away, and I shall
   provide the slippers.

BETH: I'll tell you what we'll do. Let's each get her something
   for Christmas, and not get anything for ourselves.

MISS BROOKS:

   That is treasure of the ages
   Out of "Little Women's" pages!
   (*She looks at the other "treasures."*)
   Now, these other things . . . let's see . . .
   Heidi saved these rolls for me.
   (HEIDI *nods and smiles.*)
   And this must be Eeyore's tail—
   (CHRISTOPHER ROBIN *nods.*)
   Let's return it without fail.

   Can this compass be the one
   That gave Michael so much fun
   When Mary Poppins made it run?
   (MICHAEL *nods.*)

   And this long bow must belong
   To Robin Hood . . . or am I wrong?

CHILDREN:

   Right! You're right. And now the flowers.

MISS BROOKS (*Sniffing at them*):

   Hmmmm. They have bewitching powers.
   Let me take them in my hand.
   Were they sniffed by . . . Ferdinand?

CHILDREN:

Yes! You guessed!

MISS BROOKS: And you guessed too.

You guessed the treasure, that is true,
But, tell me, children, how you *knew?*

1ST BOY:

We thought and thought and thought, Miss Brooks.

1ST GIRL:

We looked in all the cracks and nooks,

2ND BOY:

In chests, and drawers, and pocketbooks,

2ND GIRL:

And then, Nathaniel thought of *books!*
He said in books there is a treasure
More than anyone can measure,
Giving everybody pleasure.

MISS BROOKS:

Good! And now what do you say
To putting on a Book Week play
That's based upon some special stunt
Like . . . acting out a treasure hunt,
So boys and girls will ever after
Know the wealth of friends and laughter,
Fun, and joy, and daring deeds
In books that everybody reads.

CHILDREN:

Let's rehearse this very day.
Oh, hooray, hooray, hooray!
(*Children begin to march around the room singing gaily to the*
tune of "Oh, My Darling Clementine.")
Cinderella, Toby Tyler,
Little Women, Ferdinand,
Rip Van Winkle, Thimbelina—
Treasure lies on every hand.

Refrain:
Who can measure all our pleasure
From the treasure that is found
In the pages—wealth of ages—
Of the books we have around!

Mary Poppins, Peter Rabbit,
Mr. Popper, Little Pear,
Polly Pepper, and Aladdin . . .
Treasured friends are everywhere.
(*Repeat refrain*)

Georgie, Winnie, Heidi, Bambi,
And the Cheshire Cat himself,
Uncle Remus, Long John Silver—
Treasure waits on every shelf.
(*Repeat refrain*)

                    THE END

Open Sesame!

BOY: You needn't buy a ticket
         on a bus-line or a train,
GIRL: You needn't ride a rocket
         or a steamer or a plane,
BOY: To go to famous highlands
         and peninsulas and islands
         and to jungle-lands and drylands
         or a cannibal's domain.
GIRL: You needn't pay a penny
         for a long and careful look,
GROUP: You only need,
             you only need,
                 you only need A BOOK.

GIRL: You needn't own a panda
         and you needn't buy a gnu,
BOY: Or an elephant or monkey
         or a jumping kangaroo,
GIRL: To learn about a creature—
         every tooth and claw and feature
         and the tricks that you can teach her
         (or can teach *him*) how to do.
BOY: You needn't peek from bushes
         for a scientific look,

GROUP: You only need,
    you only need,
       you only need A BOOK.

BOY: And so it is with wonders
    in a test-tube and a vat,
GIRL: And astonishing adventures
    of a cowboy or a cat,
GIRL: And the customs and the rations
    of the folks of other nations,
    and their games and occupations,
    and their thoughts, and such as that.
GROUP: You needn't spend a lifetime
    trying to peer in every nook,
    you only need,
       you only need,
          you only need A BOOK!

Modern Magic

Aladdin had a magic ring
and magic lamp, indeed,
a little rub on each would bring
whatever he might need.
    But *I* have something just as grand
    to bring me wealth from every land:
    a card for books to read!

There have been magic bottles too,
which (when the corks are freed)
have sprites inside to make come true
each wish, with magic speed.
    But *I* have something just as fine:
    a card with space on every line
    for magic books to read!

And once there was a magic rug
much faster than a steed
which whisked its rider, nice and snug,
to any place agreed.
    But *I* have something that can swish
    me all the places that I wish:
    a card for books to read!

THANKSGIVING

Mother of Thanksgiving

(A play in radio style)

Note: Since all parts may be read before a mock microphone, lines need not be learned, and this play may be produced with few rehearsals.

Characters

NARRATOR
SOUND EFFECTS BOY
SARAH JOSEPHA HALE
DAVID HALE, *12*
HORATIO HALE, *10*
FRANCES ANN HALE, *8*
JOSEPHA HALE, *7*
WILLIAM HALE, *5*
AUNT HANNAH HALE
A WOMAN
LOUIS GODEY
MRS. LEWIS B. HUNTER, *Frances Ann grown up*
A SOUTHERN LADY
HER HUSBAND
CHARLES HUNTER
ABRAHAM LINCOLN

SETTING: *Since parts are read before a mock microphone, no settings are necessary. Characters should be near the microphone, stepping up when their turns come. At one side is a sound-effects table.*

NARRATOR: This is the story of the mother of Thanksgiving, a woman with vision, fighting a lone battle over the years. She fought with patience and persistence, and she won. And we give thanks to her.

This is the story of a woman who, in a way, became a link between two great presidents: George Washington and Honest Abe.

You've heard it asked a dozen times, no doubt: "But what can one man do to change the world, or even make a pin-prick in its skin? One woman even less! The country's much too big for anyone, working alone, to make a dent in it."

You'd be surprised.

This is the tale of what one woman did over a stretch of years. And we give thanks to her.

Where shall we start?

Well, 1827 seems as good as any time. Our heroine was thirty-nine that year, five years a widow, with five children to support . . . three boys, two girls. They ranged in age from twelve down to five. It wasn't easy in those early days for mothers to support a family. There wasn't much a "lady" found to do, to earn a living. But our Mrs. Hale— Sarah Josepha Hale, that was her name—succeeded some-how. Heaven knows just how.

She tried to sew at first, after her lawyer husband passed away. She wasn't good at it. But all the while her fingers stitched, her mind wove thoughts. She put them down. Some poems she wrote were published in a book. And then she did a long, two-volume tale called *Northwood*. It wasn't published when this play begins . . . but will be soon.

So here we are, in 1827. Mid-November. Days are getting cold, with a New Hampshire wind. The town is Newport, inland from the sea. The time, late afternoon. (SOUND EFFECTS BOY *strikes gong five times*.) Thanksgiving's in the air. And all the Hales are home.

DAVID: Read us what you wrote in your book again, Mother —about the food.

HORATIO: The savory stuffing! The flavory stuffing!

FRANCES ANN: The pumpkin pie. (SOUND EFFECTS BOY *rustles pages of manuscript*.)

MRS. HALE: Again? (*As if reading*) "The roasted turkey took precedence . . . sending forth the rich odor of its savory stuffing . . .

HORATIO: Flavory, savory stuffing!

MRS. HALE: ". . . and pumpkin pie was an indispensable part of a good and true Yankee Thanksgiving."

JOSEPHA *and* WILLIAM: Thanksgiving, Thanksgiving!

DAVID: Will we be having a good and true Yankee Thanksgiving, mother?

MRS. HALE: Not this year, I am afraid, David. But the publishers plan to bring out my book next month, and if *Northwood* sells well . . . if it sells even half as well as they hope, we shall be eating roast turkey and pumpkin pie next November.

HORATIO: And don't forget the stuffing!
        I never get enough-ing
        of savory, flavory stuffing,
        and I am not a-bluffing.

MRS. HALE (*Laughing*): What a poet we have in the family, Horatio.

DAVID: When I grow up I'll always have a good and true Yankee Thanksgiving dinner and invite everybody!

MRS. HALE: Everybody, David?

DAVID: Well, everybody in Newport, New Hampshire. (*Hesitates*) At least, everybody on our street. (*Hesitates*) All the family, anyway. What was it like when father was alive, mother? Was our Thanksgiving good and true and Yankee?

MRS. HALE: Don't you remember? You were six years old, David, that last Thanksgiving we had together.

HORATIO: Then I must have been four.

MRS. HALE: Yes, and Frances Ann was two.

JOSEPHA: How old was I?

MRS. HALE: So little you couldn't even walk. And William wasn't born until months later. Oh, it seems a long time ago—such a long time ago. I remember how your father and I wished that *everyone* could be sitting down to such a festive dinner on the same day, all over the country. What a wonderful thing it would be, having Thanksgiving on the same day, in all the States.

DAVID: It would make a lot of noise, if everyone gave thanks at the same time, out loud!

HORATIO: But doesn't everyone give thanks on Thanksgiving, mother?

MRS. HALE: Yes, of course, Horatio. Only Thanksgiving comes at different times in different places. Just once in all these years has it come on the same day for everyone in the United States. Do you know when that was, David?

DAVID: Yes. In 1789. When President Washington proclaimed the last Thursday in November as Thanksgiving. I know part of his speech—shall I recite it?

HORATIO: If you do I'll make up some more poetry, and I can talk louder than you can.

MRS. HALE: Come, come.

FRANCES ANN: Why *isn't* Thanksgiving on the same day? Isn't it always on Thanksgiving Day?

MRS. HALE: David?

DAVID: It's always on Thanksgiving Day, but Thanksgiving Day is different in some places . . . because of the cows.

FRANCES ANN: What cows?

DAVID: Well, some of the towns want to keep Thanksgiving on the first Thursday . . . is it after, or before, mother?

MRS. HALE: After.

DAVID: On the first Thursday after they drive the cows home from summer pasture. And if it's an early winter that's sooner, and if it's a late winter, it's later.

MRS. HALE: And no one knows just when it will be, late or soon. Your father and I used to wish there could be the same Thanksgiving for everyone. I wrote about it in *Northwood*. (SOUND EFFECTS BOY *turns pages*.) Yes, here it is. (*As if reading*) "We have too few holidays. Thanksgiving like the Fourth of July should be considered a national festival and observed by all our people."

HORATIO: I think so, too. We don't have nearly enough holidays. Holidays . . . loll-idays . . . always capital-idays!

JOSEPHA *and* WILLIAM: Holidays, holidays.

MRS. HALE (*Slowly*): I think . . . I think it would be a good thing to work for. A national Thanksgiving. Everyone giving thanks on the same day. A union of hearts and minds . . . as well as a union of States.

NARRATOR: Two months go by. It's January now, of 1828. A Boston firm brought out the book last month—*Northwood*, by Sarah Josepha Hale. It's selling well. There's even talk of printing it abroad.

This bitter afternoon Aunt Hannah Hale, the author's sister-in-law, has come to call. That's Frances Ann who's skipping to the door. (SOUND EFFECTS BOY *makes sound of skipping*.)

FRANCES ANN: Aunt Hannah, oh, Aunt Hannah. Have you come to see?

AUNT HANNAH: See what, child? (SOUND EFFECTS BOY

makes sound of door closing.) Mercy, but it's cold. When the snow creaks and cracks underfoot so early in the afternoon, you may be sure it's cold. The sun's like a little green persimmon, I do declare. Have I come to see what, Frances Ann?

FRANCES ANN: The letters mother's getting. About the book.

AUNT HANNAH: Already? Oh, I'm glad. Then it's a success, a real success. And a first novel, too. Where is your mother, child?

FRANCES ANN: She's working, at her desk. But I'll tell her you're here. She's expecting you. Oh, Aunt Hannah, there's one letter 'specially . . . that came yesterday.

AUNT HANNAH: 'Specially? What do you mean, Frances Ann?

FRANCES ANN: It's a secret. I heard mother telling David he mustn't breathe a word about it until everything was decided.

AUNT HANNAH: Then I must see your mother at once. I love secrets!

MRS. HALE (*Calling*): Is that you, Hannah?

AUNT HANNAH: Yes, Sarah. I'm coming. Hang up my wraps, will you, Frances Ann? That's a good girl. (SOUND EFFECTS BOY *makes sound of steps, door opening and closing.*)

MRS. HALE: I'm so glad you could come. Did David tell you it was important? Were you able to find someone to tend the shop?

AUNT SARAH: Mrs. Philton could come in for the afternoon. Now, tell me, Sarah, what is it?

MRS. HALE: This letter. From a publishing firm in Boston. Read it.

AUNT HANNAH (*Between pauses*): Hmmmm. Proposing to establish a magazine for *ladies*. Hmmmm. Offering you the editorship. But, Sarah, you don't know anything about being an editor.

MRS. HALE: Not a thing. Only I'm sure I'd be better at it

than I was at millinery. I couldn't be worse! You were very patient with me at the shop, Hannah.

AUNT HANNAH: A lady editor. It's unheard of. And a lady's magazine!

MRS. HALE: There has to be a first for everything, you know. I find the proposal a little frightening, Hannah, but very, *very* appealing. I . . . I think I shall accept, if you are not too strongly opposed. I treasure your good judgment.

AUNT HANNAH: It would mean leaving Newport? Leaving your friends and relatives? Moving to Boston?

MRS. HALE: Yes.

AUNT HANNAH: It would mean being definitely on your own, in a strange place, in a strange new position, with your family to care for?

MRS. HALE: Yes.

AUNT HANNAH: Dear Sarah, I shall miss you and the children. More than I can tell, I shall miss you. But Boston is not too far away . . .

MRS. HALE: Oh, Hannah, then you think I should? A lady editor . . . doesn't it sound exciting! Thank you, thank you. Be assured, Hannah, I shall go to the task with much more confidence and hope of success than . . . than if I were helping you trim hats. (*They laugh.*)

NARRATOR: So Sarah Hale became an editor. *The Ladies' Magazine* was soon in press, was soon a black and white reality. The introduction said:

A WOMAN (*As if reading*): "The work will be national . . . American . . . a miscellany which, although devoted to general literature, is more expressly designed to mark the progress of female improvement . . ."

NARRATOR: For nine successful years the Lady Editor held forth, making *The Ladies' Magazine* a living thing, part of America. She liked her Boston home. But then a better opening came her way from Philadelphia, from Louis Godey, "prince of publishers," proprietor of *Godey's Lady's Book*. He wanted Mrs. Hale as editor. Triumphantly in 1836 he achieved this. These are his words:

LOUIS GODEY: "The present number of the *Lady's Book* closes our career as sole editor. The increasing patronage of the work requires more of our attention to the business department. We are confident our readers will not regret this change, when they learn that Mrs. Sarah Josepha Hale, now editor of the American *Ladies' Magazine*, will superintend the Literary Department of the Book. Mrs. Hale is too well known to the public to need eulogy from us . . ."

NARRATOR: So *Godey's Lady's Book* it was, for Mrs. Hale.

Let's jump ahead across the busy years, to 1845, in Philadelphia, the home of *Godey's Lady's Book* and Mrs. Hale. Thanksgiving time again, on Locust Street—where Frances Ann resides. She's Mrs. Lewis B. Hunter now, a doctor's wife, and married just a year.

Our editor is 57 years—not old, but *young*. She's done a lot for women and their rights, and still has much to do. Thanksgiving, now. That still is on her mind. She must begin in earnest on her plan to make Thanksgiving national. Yes, soon . . . Her daughter Frances interrupts her thoughts:

MRS. HUNTER: I wish the rest of them could be here for Thanksgiving, mother.

MRS. HALE: I wish it too. Some day we may all be together again . . . (*She chokes a little.*) . . . all except David.

MRS. HUNTER: Dear David. I still shudder to think of him being sick so far away from home, and alone. He had so much ahead to live for.

MRS. HALE: My world has been dark and desolate without him.

MRS. HUNTER: I know. But, mother, you have the rest of us . . . such as we are. I wish Josepha could be here today.

Why, oh why, did she have to go way off to Georgia to teach?

MRS. HALE: Because she loves it. Josepha is a born teacher. (*Brightening*) Do you know she writes that she wants to start a school of her own some day, here in Philadelphia?

MRS. HUNTER: Yes. She even has a name for it: Boarding and Day School for Young Ladies. She'll do it, too. (*Pause*) I tried to get Horatio to come for Thanksgiving, mother. But he's so far away, and so engrossed in his Indians.

MRS. HALE: What he is doing is very important, and I'm proud of him. Too little has been recorded about the languages and dialects of our North American Indians.

MRS. HUNTER: Well, for so young a man Horatio has certainly made himself a reputation.

MRS. HALE: He has a natural gift for languages. And I used to think he might be a poet!

MRS. HUNTER: Remember the rhymes he used to make up? That one about the stuffing . . .

MRS. HALE (*Laughing*): "I never get enough-ing
                        of flavory, savory stuffing." (*Sobering*)
Thanksgiving! It's still my hope to see it a national holiday, Frances Ann—one day, the same day, for everyone in the United States. In fact, I am seriously starting a great campaign next year . . . and I shan't give up until I win, no matter how many years it takes.

MRS. HUNTER: What kind of campaign, mother?

MRS. HALE: A campaign of letters. And editorials in *Godey's*. But mostly letters . . . to influential men, to governors, to Presidents. I shall write them myself. Never will there be such a campaign of letters!

MRS. HUNTER: Oh, mother, as if you haven't your hands full already. But don't think about it today! I have a surprise, a Thanksgiving surprise for you. Guess what.

MRS. HALE: I never have been good at guessing.

MRS. HUNTER: William's coming! I couldn't wait another minute to tell you.

MRS. HALE: William? From Virginia . . . just for Thanksgiving?

MRS. HUNTER: It's a sort of celebration for him . . . for passing the bar examination.

MRS. HALE: Oh, I'll be glad to see him. Especially since he talks of going farther south next year. To Texas, of all places! I am afraid when William gets as far away as Texas, we shan't see him again for many Thanksgivings.

MRS. HUNTER: Isn't it good, mother dear, we have such an enthusiastic letter-writer in the family!

NARRATOR: The campaign of letters began, in 1846. Year after year the editor of *Godey's Lady's Book* wrote to the powers-that-be to make Thanksgiving national. A great crusade! One woman all alone!

MRS. HALE (*Slowly, as if writing*): "Let us join in establishing Washington's choice, the last Thursday in November, as a universal holiday." (SOUND EFFECTS BOY *makes sound of sealing and stamping letters.*)

MRS. HALE (*As if writing*): "Thanksgiving Day has a value beyond all expression. It reunites families and friends. It awakens kindly and generous sentiments. It promotes peace and good will among our mixed population. . . . Thanksgiving like the Fourth of July should be considered a national festival."

NARRATOR: Letters, letters, letters. Stacks of them. All neatly penned and sealed. Year after year, year after year again. Letters to congressmen and governors. Letters to presidents—Polk . . . Taylor . . . Fillmore . . . Pierce . . . Buchanan. And finally to Lincoln.

And editorials, too, in *Godey's Lady's Book*. In 1852 she wrote this news:

MRS. HALE: "Last year twenty-nine states and all territories united in the festival. This year we trust that Virginia and Vermont will come into this arrangement and that the Governors of each and all the states will appoint Thursday, the 25th of November, as the Day of Thanksgiving. Twenty-three millions of people sitting down, as it were, together to a feast of joy and thankfulness . . ."

NARRATOR: Year after year, tireless, confident, and firm, she sent the letters out.

In 1859 with war clouds gathering, threatening to crash and break from North to South, she wrote an editorial full of hope. How many women read it (yes, and husbands, too) it's hard to say. A couple of hundred thousand, probably. The words were stirring ones, the editorial's name—"Our Thanksgiving Union."

Wait, here's a southern lady with it now:

SOUTHERN LADY: Tell me what you think of this, George. In *Godey's*, dear. You always know so much about such things, and your poor wife simply never, never can make up her mind without you. Read it, George.

HER HUSBAND: What? Oh, that. "Our Thanksgiving Union." (*Begins to mumble as he reads*) "Seventy years ago . . ." (*Mumble, mumble, mumble.*)

SOUTHERN LADY: Out loud, George. So I can hear . . .

HER HUSBAND (*Clearing his throat, getting oratorical*): "The flag of our country now numbers thirty-two stars on its crown of blue—God save the United States! He has saved, enlarged, blessed and prospered us beyond any people on this globe. If every state would join in Union Thanksgiving on the 24th of this month, would it not be a renewed pledge of love and loyalty to the Constitution of the United States which guarantees peace, prosperity, progress and perpetuity to our great Republic?"

SOUTHERN LADY: Would it not, George?

HER HUSBAND: What?

SOUTHERN LADY: Would it not be as Mrs. Hale says?

HER HUSBAND: Er . . . how's that?

SOUTHERN LADY: Would not Union Thanksgiving be a renewed pledge of love and loyalty to the Constitution of the United States?

HER HUSBAND: Oh, that. Not at all. Not at all! Union Thanksgiving, indeed. What's Thanksgiving got to do with the slavery issue?

SOUTHERN LADY: Quite a great deal, I should think, George.

HER HUSBAND: You should think! Have you not agreed, Millicent, to leave all the thinking to me?

NARRATOR: Letters, letters, letters. Editorials. Pleas. And then came civil war. In 1861 our Lady Editor was urging a Thanksgiving Day of Peace. Lincoln was President. Her Peace Day failed.

She tried again in 1862. A national Thanksgiving! Still no luck. In 1863 she tried again.

Success . . . yet not success!

How's that, you ask?

Let's stop and see. It's summer, 1863, in Philadelphia. A warm July. Our Mrs. Hale is just about three quarters of a century old, but going strong. Still editor of *Godey's*, still alert, still full of eager plans. She's living with her daughter Frances Ann on Locust Street, and there are grandchildren—admiring ones.

After a busy working day, her grandson, Charles, waylays her in the drawing room:

CHARLES (*Eagerly*): You've seen the paper, grandmother?

MRS. HALE: No, not yet. What is it, Charles?

CHARLES: You've probably been expecting it.

MRS. HALE: Expecting what? Come, Charles, don't tease.

CHARLES: Get ready to give us a song and dance, grandmother. Look! And on the front page, too. Only there ought to be a credit line somewhere . . . to Sarah Josepha Hale. (SOUND EFFECTS BOY *rattles newspaper.*)

MRS. HALE: What *are* you talking about, Charles?

CHARLES: Listen to this: "Proclamation for Thanksgiving, July 15, 1863, by the President of the United States of America."

MRS. HALE: At last! And by the President. I've waited years for this, Charles. Ever since 1827, when *Northwood* was published you know. That's . . . goodness me, 36 years ago! At last—a Presidential proclamation for a national Thanksgiving. It hasn't happened since 1789. Washington to Lincoln—a long gap, Charles. I only hope the gap is closed now, forever. What does the proclamation say?

CHARLES: "It has pleased Almighty God to hearken to the supplications and prayers of an afflicted people . . ." Well, it goes on like that for quite a while.

MRS. HALE (*Eagerly*): Skip down to the "Now, therefore," and we'll go back later.

CHARLES (*After some mumbling*): "Now, therefore, be it known that I do set apart Thursday, the 6th day of August next, to be observed as a day for national thanksgiving . . ."

MRS. HALE Wait. Did I hear you correctly? The sixth day of *August?*

CHARLES: That's what it says.

MRS. HALE: Thanksgiving in August! Who ever heard of such a thing? Oh, Charles, after all my work for a national Thanksgiving . . . to have it proclaimed for August. August! It should be November—the last Thursday in November President Washington's choice.

CHARLES: Why, you're right, grandmother. You're not through crusading yet, are you?

MRS. HALE: I shall call on President Lincoln myself. I shall bring a copy of President Washington's proclamation. I

shall plead the case for a national Thanksgiving on the
last Thursday in November.

CHARLES: And you'll win. I'll bet my last penny on that.
You'll win!

NARRATOR: And win she did. The very next year, too.
In 1864, when civil war was like a dripping knife cutting
the States apart, Lincoln, the President, proclaimed Thanksgiving Day. He pointed out that though the war was cruel
within the States, full peace with other nations was pre-
served, order maintained, and federal laws obeyed. And
for these gifts the President gave thanks.

LINCOLN: "They are the gracious gifts of the Most High God.
. . . It has seemed to me fit and proper that they should
be solemnly, reverently, and gratefully acknowledged as
with one heart and one voice by the whole American people.
I do, therefore, invite my fellow citizens . . . to observe
the last Thursday of November next as a day of Thanksgiving and praise."

NARRATOR: The gap was bridged, between two Presidents.
Washington's Thanksgiving was proclaimed again—by
Lincoln, now. And every year since then it has been na-
tional, a holiday in all the many states.
Sarah Josepha Hale, mother of Thanksgiving, could sit
back at last. All those letters, and those worn-out pens!
(SOUND EFFECTS BOY scratches pens on paper.)

NARRATOR: All those stamps, and seals of colored wax!
(SOUND EFFECTS BOY makes sound of stamping letters and
seals.)

NARRATOR· All those words, those earnest paragraphs!
She could sit back . . . but did she? Not at all. She still
was much too young to stop and rest. She checked Thanksgiving off, but there was still a list, a bulging list, of things
to do. And, after all, she wasn't 80 yet!
For many years—she died at 91—she had her good and true

Thanksgiving holiday. She smiled to think that everyone in every single State, on that same day, was giving thanks as well. Thanksgiving in November—everywhere!

ALL: All hail to Mrs. Hale, mother of Thanksgiving.

She fought the long hard fight all by herself, and won.

Who'll say it now, "But what can one man do? One woman even less!"

One vision and one spirit can achieve a miracle.

Mother of Thanksgiving, we lay thanks like oak leaves at your feet . . . like acorns, bittersweet, and purple grapes . . . pumpkins, sheaves of grain, and yellow corn . . . all the symbols of the harvest time. For you have harvested a national Thanksgiving. We give thanks!

THE END

Unexpected Guests

Characters

GOVERNOR BRADFORD
MILES STANDISH
MISTRESS BREWSTER
MISTRESS WINSLOW
PRISCILLA
REMEMBER
MARY
DESIRE
WILLIAM
THREE OTHER BOYS

PROLOGUE

TIME: *Morning of the first Thanksgiving, late fall, 1621.*
SETTING: *In front of the curtain.*
AT RISE: GOVERNOR BRADFORD *and* MILES STANDISH *walk in, talking to each other. They cross slowly in front of the curtain.*

GOV. BRADFORD: We have had our trials in this new land, Captain Standish. Our hardships. Our sorrows. But how much we have to be thankful for!
MILES STANDISH: Aye, Governor Bradford.

GOV. BRADFORD: Nowhere in England could we have grown such a crop of corn on twenty acres.

MILES STANDISH: That is true. And such barley! (*Sniffs the air*) I smell barley loaves baking this very minute. Ah, and pigeon pasty, too, I do believe.

GOV. BRADFORD: 'Tis a busy day today in Plymouth town. Think you Chief Massasoit and some of his braves will heed our invitation to join in the feast of thanksgiving?

MILES STANDISH: Aye, a few will come, I believe, Governor. The Indians have been very friendly.

GOV. BRADFORD: Another thing to be thankful for. Our cup is indeed full. (*As they exit*) Shall we see if the tables are properly set up under the trees, and the meat-spits ready?

* * *

SCENE 1

SETTING: *Kitchen-living room of one of the Pilgrim houses.*

AT RISE: MISTRESS BREWSTER *is working at one of the tables where food for the feast is being prepared. In a moment MISTRESS WINSLOW hurries in, takes off cape, adjusts apron.*

MISTRESS WINSLOW: Good day, Mistress Brewster.

MISTRESS BREWSTER: Good morning to you.
  And, oh, Mistress Winslow,
  There's *still* much to do.
  As sure as I'm living
  This feast of Thanksgiving
  Takes planning and hustling
  And labor . . .

MISTRESS WINSLOW: How true! (*She consults list on wall.*)
  Let's see what is finished.
  The pies are all made,
  Both pumpkin and berry.

The tables are laid? (*Glances out window to see*)
The loaves are a-baking
Next door, no mistaking. (*Sniffs, turns back to list*)
The turkeys need stuffing,
And soon, I'm afraid.

(PRISCILLA, REMEMBER, MARY, *and* DESIRE *hurry in to help.*)

GIRLS: Good morning, good morning.
Thanksgiving is here!

MISTRESS BREWSTER: The busiest morning,
For us, of the year.
Remember and Mary,
Grind corn and don't tarry.
Priscilla, shell beechnuts
For stuffing, my dear.

PRISCILLA: The boys were to help us.
They're always so slow! (*Looks around*)
The woodpile has vanished.
The water is low.
That William—where is he?

(WILLIAM *and three other boys hurry in.*)

BOYS (*Cheerfully*): Good morning.

PRISCILLA: Get busy,
There's company coming
For dinner, you know.

(MISTRESS BREWSTER *gives empty buckets to one boy, indicates the other two should get wood. She puts* WILLIAM *to work helping* PRISCILLA *husk beechnuts.*)

MISTRESS BREWSTER: Desire, start taking
The platters outside—
The fruits we have gathered
And carefully dried,
The grapes and the cherries,
The nuts and the berries . . . (DESIRE *goes in and out.*)

WILLIAM (*Hungrily*): I'm thankful the platters
  Are big ones and wide!

MISTRESS WINSLOW: We all can be thankful
  This bright autumn morn—

PRISCILLA: For Squanto—who taught us
  The way to plant corn.

REMEMBER: For rain and for weather
  And crops . . .

MARY: Being together!

MISTRESS BREWSTER: For finding a homeland
  Where faith is reborn.
  (*They all work busily. Suddenly* WILLIAM, *looking over the
  food supply, gets worried.*)

WILLIAM: I say, Mistress Brewster,
  Would we be prepared
  To feed twenty Indians?

MISTRESS BREWSTER: Our feast may be shared
  With ten or with twenty,
  And there will be plenty.

WILLIAM: But what if there're *thirty?*

MISTRESS BREWSTER: I think we'll be spared.
  Miles Standish thinks maybe
  A dozen might come.

MISTRESS WINSLOW: We Pilgrims are fifty.
  That makes quite a lot. (*Looks over food*)
  But surely there's ample
  For more than a sample
  Of dozens of good things . . . (*Turns to* WILLIAM)
  Just look in the pot.
  (BOYS *come back with wood and water.* MISTRESS BREWSTER
  *puts one in charge of fire, has another stir a bowl of batter,
  sets the third to shucking dry peas.*)

1ST BOY: It keeps us all hopping,
  This having a feast.

2ND BOY (*Hungrily, eyeing goodies*): My mouth starts to water.

3RD BOY: Mine never has ceased! (MILES STANDISH *hurries in, looks around anxiously.*)

MILES STANDISH: These lads—are they needed?
Two boys must be speeded
To gather more clams
From the cove to the east.
(*All the boys are eager to go.*)

MISTRESS BREWSTER: Two lads, Captain Standish?
Well, if it seems fit . . .

MILES STANDISH: Two others should handle
The meat-turning spit
And keep the fires going
So coals will be glowing
For roasting the oysters.

MISTRESS BREWSTER: Grave tasks, I admit. (MISTRESS BREWSTER *nods to boys, dismissing them. They hurry out with* MILES STANDISH. MISTRESS WINSLOW *checks the list again.*)

MISTRESS WINSLOW: The wild geese and turkeys
Are ready to stuff.
The stuffing, Priscilla?

PRISCILLA: Will this be enough?

MISTRESS WINSLOW: Perhaps, but I doubt it.

PRISCILLA: Well, *I'll* go without it.

MISTRESS BREWSTER (*Nervously*): I'm hoping these dumplings won't sink and be tough. (*All work busily. In a few minutes the sound of shouting is heard offstage. The women and girls are startled.*)

GIRLS: What's that? Someone's shouting.

WOMEN: How lusty and loud!

GIRLS: It may be the Indians.
It sounds like a crowd.
(WILLIAM *rushes in excitedly.*)

WILLIAM: Our guests are arriving! (*He keeps looking out the door, turning back to report as more and more Indians arrive.*)
The Indians! I'm striving
To count. At least thirty
Brave warriors and proud . . .
Now forty . . . now fifty . . .
Now *sixty* . . .

MISTRESS BREWSTER (*Unbelieving*): Don't joke!

WILLIAM: Now seventy crowding
There under the oak.
And still they keep coming!

MISTRESS BREWSTER: My poor ears are humming.

MISTRESS WINSLOW: How can we, how *can* we
Feed so many folk?

WILLIAM: Eighty. No, *ninety!*
Chief Massasoit too.

MISTRESS BREWSTER: We figured a dozen . . .
Oh, what shall we do?

MISTRESS WINSLOW: For all our preparing,
The food we'll be sharing
Will scarcely be ample
To last the day through.

DESIRE: And they were invited
To stay for *three days*.

MISTRESS BREWSTER: My head's in a turmoil.

MISTRESS WINSLOW: My mind's in a haze.

GIRLS: We're all in a dither—
From whence and from whither
Shall we get more turkeys,
More meat, and more maize?

WILLIAM (*Excitedly, from post at door*): There's Governor
Bradford. He's coming.

MISTRESS BREWSTER: Poor man,
He's probably worried.

Let's smile . . . if we can.

GOV. BRADFORD (*Hurrying in*):
Dear ladies, I wonder,
Would it be a blunder
To ask you a favor,
A slight change of plan?
The Indians are eager
To help and to share:
They want to bring deer-meat
To add to our fare.
But after your labors
To feed our good neighbors
I felt I should ask you,
Dear friends, if you'd *care?*
They'll handle the roasting.
It might be a treat . . .
Unless you prefer
Our own foodstuffs to eat.

GIRLS (*Gaily*): With deer-meat aplenty
We'll feed eight times twenty!

WOMEN (*Graciously*): Indeed, it will make **our**
Thanksgiving complete.

(GOVERNOR BRADFORD *nods, and goes out.*)

GIRLS (*Amused*): He asked if we minded!
These innocent men . . .

WOMEN (*Amused*): You'd think we had *counted*
On ninety, not ten.

ALL: But now, as we're living,
We'll have a thanksgiving
To speak of with pleasure
Again and again . . .
A feast-day we'll treasure
Again and again!

THE END

Company Coming

MOTHER: Susan, have you put the salt
and pepper on the table?
Peter, find the pickle jar
with "Mustard" on the label.
Linda, is the lettuce washed?
Hurry, if you're able!

LINDA: Oh, what a jolly Thanksgiving Day.
Who cares if the weather outside is gray?
Everyone's busy and everyone's gay . . .
with company, company on the way.

MOTHER: Peter, put the place-cards on.
Don't you go forgetting.
Linda, send your father here—
carving knives need whetting.
Susan, have we finished now
with the table-setting?

SUSAN: The oven is sizzling a merry tune,
and savory tastes fill every spoon.
The clock on the cupboard says half-past noon . . .
with company, company coming soon!

MOTHER: Linda, fill the glasses, dear.
Make the sideboard neater.
Susan, taste the pudding sauce—
shall we make it sweeter?
Would you like to take a peek
at the turkey, Peter?

PETER: Oh, what a wonderful time of year.
The cranberry jelly is firm and clear,
and everyone's busy and full of cheer . . .
with company . . .

MOTHER: Listen. The bell!

ALL: THEY'RE HERE!

Thanksgiving Everywhere

BOY: Oh, the sizzles in the kitchen!
Close your eyes and take a sniff.
Don't they set your nose to twitchin'?
Did you get a proper sniff?

GIRL: And the spices in the dressing!
And the fragrance in the air.

BOY: And the pie! No need for guessing:
it's Thanksgiving, everywhere.

GIRLS: It's Thanksgiving,

BOYS: It's Thanksgiving,

ALL: It's Thanksgiving, everywhere.

GIRL: Oh, the oak leaves in the vases,
and the dishes—Mother's best!

BOY: And the seven extra places,
one for each invited guest.

GIRL: And the acorns down the middle
of the table! I declare
it's a day without a riddle:
it's Thanksgiving, everywhere.

BOYS: It's Thanksgiving,

GIRLS: It's Thanksgiving,

ALL: It's Thanksgiving, **everywhere.**

GIRL: Oh, the merry, merry voices!

BOY: Glad to see you! How you've grown!

GIRL: Here's a day each heart rejoices
with a gladness all its own.

BOY: Out the window it is snowing—
there's November in the air.

GIRL: And indoors each face is glowing
with Thanksgiving, everywhere,

ALL: With Thanksgiving,
With Thanksgiving,
With Thanksgiving . . . everywhere!

A Thankful Heart

Grandma said that turkey,
cranberries, and pie
sometimes have a bitter taste,
and I asked her why.

Grandma said, "A banquet
fitting for a king,
eaten with a thankless heart,
isn't anything.

"And, you know," said Grandma,
"even what-is-least,
eaten with a thankful heart,
can be quite a feast."

Thanksgiving

You do not have
to use your eyes,

There is no "but" or "if":

Turkey roasting,
pumpkin pies—

You only have to SNIFF.

CHRISTMAS

Angel in the Looking-Glass

Characters

MISS PINSTER, *a dressmaker*
LUCY, *a young girl*
JIM YOUNG ⎫ *a married couple*
ALICE YOUNG ⎭
AUNT MARTHA, *a stern old lady*
CHARLES ⎫ *her young nephews*
RALPH ⎭
ZORLOVA, *a dancer*

TIME: *A week before Christmas.*
BEFORE THE CURTAIN: MISS PINSTER *is fitting* LUCY'S *angel costume. There is much pinning and adjusting as the two talk. From time to time* LUCY *looks at herself in a large full-length mirror placed at one end of the stage.*

LUCY: Are you sure I'll look like a real angel when you get my costume finished, Miss Pinster?
MISS PINSTER: Yes, of course. Now hold still while I fix this wing. I had to use cardboard underneath, you know, to stiffen it.
LUCY: Do they look like real wings?
MISS PINSTER: Quite real, I think.

123

LUCY: I wish I could fly with them. I wish I could fly and fly —way up above the town.

MISS PINSTER: Oh, that would be expecting too much. If I could make wings that could fly, I shouldn't have to be a dressmaker, you know.

LUCY: What would you be, Miss Pinster?

MISS PINSTER: Goodness, I have never given it a thought. (*She stands dreamily for a moment with pins and tape measure in hand.*) Oh, I think I should like to have a little shop and sell hand-painted cups and things like that.

LUCY: And red-and-white-striped candy?

MISS PINSTER: Perhaps. Perhaps I could have a little glass case of candy, too. (*She suddenly comes down to earth again.*) But now, my dear, we must see how the halo fits. (MISS PINSTER *picks up the halo.*)

LUCY: Oh, what a beautiful halo! It looks like a real one, all gold and shiny.

MISS PINSTER: I am rather pleased with it myself. I just happened to have some gilt paint on hand, left over from the time I touched-up the radiators. (*She adjusts the halo, stands back and nods.*) You look more and more like an angel, Lucy.

LUCY: Do I? (*Then hesitantly*) But . . . I don't always *feel* like one, Miss Pinster. Do you think it's mean of a person to buy another person a Christmas present and then not want to give it away because it's so nice. I mean . . . I know a girl who saved her money to buy her brother a set of pencils with colored leads—twenty different colors in all—and now . . . she wants to keep them for herself.

MISS PINSTER: Well, I wouldn't say she had much of the Christmas spirit, would you? Now, let's see about the sleeves, Lucy. Are they long enough under the wings?

LUCY: But wouldn't it be all right if she gave her brother

something else . . . that was cheaper? Oh, you can't imagine what beautiful pencils they are.

MISS PINSTER (*Intent on her work*): Yes, I think the sleeves are all right. My, I haven't made an angel costume in years! (*There is a moment or two of silence, as* MISS PINSTER *stands off and looks at the costume.*)

LUCY (*Slowly, thoughtfully*): Do you think if anyone saw me . . . . walking down the hall of this apartment building, maybe . . . they would think I *was* an angel?

MISS PINSTER: They might! The effect is very good, I think.

LUCY: Would it make any difference to them if they *did* take me for an angel, Miss Pinster?

MISS PINSTER: Difference? What do you mean by that?

LUCY: I mean, would it make any difference in the way people acted? I think *I* would act different, if I saw an angel . . . maybe.

MISS PINSTER: Perhaps we all would. But, of course, we shall never really know, shall we? Not on this earth, at least. Now turn to the side a little, Lucy. I don't believe the hem-line is quite straight. No, it isn't.

LUCY: Do many people live in this apartment building, Miss Pinster?

MISS PINSTER: Oh, yes, quite a few. There are twelve apartments in addition to the janitor's. Hold still, now. I must pin up this side a little.

LUCY: Are they nice people?

MISS PINSTER: Yes, I think so—as nice as most people are. I have so little time to talk to them, of course. (*She pins at the hem, then stands back to see if it is straight.*)

LUCY: Are you coming to see our Christmas play, Miss Pinster? It's going to be Friday night, in the school auditorium, and it's free.

MISS PINSTER: Oh, I should like to come. Then I could see how the costume looks from the audience.

LUCY: I'm the only angel who speaks a part. The others just sing. I sing too, part of the time. Would you like me to recite my part for you?

MISS PINSTER: Yes, if you wish. Only you must turn around slowly, slowly, so I can be sure to get the hem right.

LUCY (*Turning very slowly*): Well, you see, the three shepherds are there on the stage, wondering about the star. It's not a *real* star on the stage, you know, but it looks like one. Then we angels come in singing. The shepherds are frightened, and they draw away. You know, they don't expect to see angels in the middle of the night. So then I say to them: "Fear not: for, behold, I bring you tidings of great joy, which shall be to all people. For unto you is born this day in the city of David a Saviour, which is Christ the Lord. And this shall be a sign unto you . . ."

MISS PINSTER (*Softly*): "Ye shall find the babe wrapped in swaddling clothes, lying in the manger."

LUCY: How did you know, Miss Pinster?

MISS PINSTER: Oh, I've known that for a long, long time.

LUCY: Well, then the other angels sing, and then I say: "Glory to God in the highest, and on earth peace, good will toward men." And the shepherds aren't afraid any more.

MISS PINSTER: You do it very nicely, Lucy. Now just a few more pins . . . (*The doorbell rings loudly. She looks at her watch.*) Oh, dear, that must be Mrs. Swishton coming for her fitting. She is a few minutes early, but she is always in *such* a hurry. Would you mind waiting a little while, Lucy? (*Doorbell rings again, loudly.*) I can take care of Mrs. Swishton in the other room.

LUCY: I don't mind, Miss Pinster. (MISS PINSTER *hurries out. For a moment* LUCY *stands still. Then she runs over to the mirror.*) Do you know who I am, looking-glass? I'm an angel. But, of course, you're Miss Pinster's mirror, so you knew it already. I wonder . . . if anyone else would know who *didn't* know already. (*She looks around.*) I could try! I could slip out the door, and go down the hall of the apartment building, couldn't I, looking-glass? It wouldn't take long. I could be back before Miss Pinster would miss me at all. Are my wings all right? Is my halo straight? I don't think anyone will notice the pins in the hem, do you? (*Tiptoes across stage*) Good-bye, looking-glass. Don't tell. (LUCY *exits, and the curtain rises.*)

* * *

SETTING: *The stage is divided into three "apartments": The* YOUNGS' *apartment is on one side,* ZORLOVA'S *on the other, and* AUNT MARTHA'S *in the middle. Each apartment is indicated by a small grouping of furniture. As one family talks, the other two are silent.*

AT RISE: ALICE *and* JIM YOUNG *are talking together in their apartment.*

ALICE: I'm so glad you agree with me at last, Jim. It's much more sensible to save the money for a new car than to go to Mother Young's for Christmas. After all, we've gone every year since we were married. *Four* times.

JIM: But Mother counts on it. It will be hard to tell her we aren't coming.

ALICE: Oh, you can make up some excuse—too busy at the office, or something. Just keep thinking of the new car, and it will be easy.

JIM: Not so easy, Alice.

ALICE: If you write Mother Young today, she'll be all used to the idea by Christmas.

JIM: I wonder.

ALICE: Now don't back down. Let's just think about *ourselves* this year, for a change. Ourselves and the new car. Let's forget about Christmas at Mother Young's.

JIM: I can't help thinking of Mother's face when she gets the letter. I'm afraid I won't have much peace of mind.

ALICE: Nonsense. (LUCY *enters down stage. She stops in front of the* YOUNGS' *apartment, hesitates, and then pretends to knock.*) I wonder who that can be.

JIM: I'll see. (*He goes to front of stage, pretends to open door, then steps back somewhat startled.*) Well . . .

ALICE (*Curious, going to door*): Why . . . who are you?

LUCY: I'm . . . (*Hesitates*) . . . "Behold I bring you tidings of great joy—peace on earth, good will toward men." (*She turns to go, then calls back.*) Merry Christmas! (*Exits*)

JIM: Well, I'll be . . . what do you make of it, Alice?

ALICE: I don't quite know. It's not one of the children from this building, I'm sure of that. Oh, Jim, it gives me the strangest feeling. There must be some reason why it happened just now . . . just when we were going to write the letter.

JIM: Did you hear: "Peace on earth!" Alice, I think that means peace of mind, too.

ALICE: She looked like one of the angels in the art gallery, didn't she? How strange. Jim, perhaps we can't just sit back and forget about Christmas, after all. Write to Mother Young that we're coming.

JIM (*Happily*): Do you mean it?

ALICE: Yes. You see, it came to me, when the angel was standing there: the new car can wait. But Christmas can't! (*They go in and close the door.*) You can't forget about Christmas. (*At* AUNT MARTHA'S *apartment,* CHARLES *and* RALPH *are talking. They seem to be quite unhappy.*)

RALPH: This is going to be the lonesomest Christmas we ever had. Now we've come to live with Aunt Martha I bet we won't ever have a real Christmas again.

CHARLES: She doesn't believe in any of the fun of Christmas, like other people.

RALPH: She says Santa Claus is nonsense, and giving presents is foolish, and a Christmas tree is a *heathen* custom. She thinks you should think about the Christ Child on Christmas . . . and nothing else!

CHARLES: Do you remember the big tinsel star we always had at the top of our Christmas tree? And all the colored balls?

RALPH: And the nice Foxy Grandpa?

CHARLES: Aunt Martha would say he was *heathen*. (*There is a moment's silence.*)

RALPH: We wouldn't dare ask for a Christmas tree, would we?

CHARLES: I should say not. (*Dreamily*) Oh, I wish we could have a great big Christmas tree, full of presents and lights and shining things. And I wish we could have someone for dinner—a big Christmas dinner.

RALPH: Sh! Aunt Martha's coming. (*The boys open books and read.* AUNT MARTHA *comes in with her knitting, and sits down primly. After a moment she looks up over the top of her glasses and speaks to the boys.*)

AUNT MARTHA: I have been meaning to tell you, boys, that I am pleased to see you taking such a sensible attitude toward Christmas. It's just a lot of fiddle-faddle. I am glad that you aren't begging for one of those heathen Christmas trees.

RALPH *and* CHARLES: Yes, Aunt Martha.

CHARLES (*Timidly*): Would it be heathen to want company . . . for Christmas dinner? The janitor's boy says he's never tasted turkey . . . and he's *nine* years old.

AUNT MARTHA: Turkey? Make a fuss over Christmas dinner! Why, Charles! (LUCY *comes on stage, stops before* AUNT MARTHA's *apartment, hesitates, then pretends to knock.*) Christmas is all crusted over with foolishness these days. (*Hears* LUCY's *knock*) What was that? Someone must be at the door. (AUNT MARTHA *goes to the door and pretends to*

open it. The boys come up behind her and peer out too.) Why
. . . why . . . who are you?

LUCY: I'm an . . . (*Hesitates*) . . . "Behold I bring you
tidings of great joy . . . peace on earth, good will toward
men." (*She begins to run off, then turns and calls out, "Merry
Christmas."*)

AUNT MARTHA: Well, of all things.

RALPH: It was an angel!

CHARLES: I never saw an angel before, did you, Aunt Martha?
(AUNT MARTHA *turns back into the room, closes the door,
sinks into her chair. Then she speaks slowly and dreamily,
as the boys sit down.*)

AUNT MARTHA: I was an angel once . . .

CHARLES *and* RALPH: You were!

AUNT MARTHA: I was an angel once . . . in a Christmas play
at the church. It was so long ago I had almost forgotten.
I wore a white costume with wings that had real white
chicken feathers sewn on. And after the play there was a
tall Christmas tree . . .

RALPH (*Surprised*): In the *church!*

AUNT MARTHA: Yes. It almost touched the ceiling. And
everyone got presents . . . and we all sang carols. Oh, it
was a wonderful Christmas.

RALPH (*Thoughtfully*): Aunt Martha, how can it be heathen
to have a Christmas tree, if there was one in church?

AUNT MARTHA (*Giving a start*): What's that? Why . . .
why . . . (*Hurriedly she changes the subject.*) Do you know
the angel's lines were the very ones I had to speak in the
play: "I bring you tidings of great joy . . ." It all comes
back to me now. (*Suddenly*) Boys, there must have been
some reason that angel knocked on our door just now. She
must have come to remind me. I am afraid I had forgotten
all about Christmas. About "good will toward men." (*She*

looks at the boys eagerly.) Shall we have a Christmas tree, after all? A big one that will reach from the floor to the ceiling, with lights and presents on it?

RALPH *and* CHARLES: Oh, Aunt Martha.

AUNT MARTHA: And shall we have company for Christmas dinner? Goodness, I haven't cooked a turkey in years . . . I wonder if I remember how.

RALPH *and* CHARLES: Oh, Aunt Martha! (*At* ZORLOVA'S *apartment,* ZORLOVA *is sitting at her dressing table, primping. She begins to hum. Suddenly she gets up and tries a new dance step. She does it very well, and knows it! The telephone rings and interrupts her dance. She goes to answer.*)

ZORLOVA: Hello. . . . Yes, this is Zorlova, the dancer. (*She does a few steps as she holds the phone.*) Who? Oh, on the Community Christmas Tree committee. (*Her voice falls and she stops dancing.*) Next week—what night? . . . Well, I might be able to do it, but I'm very busy, you know. How much do you pay, by the way? . . . What! Give up the best part of an evening for nothing! Just to entertain the community? . . . Yes, I realize Christmas is coming. And I realize they haven't had much chance to see good dancing. But a person has to live. . . . No, I never attended a Community Christmas Tree program. Really, I am afraid I'm going to be very busy that evening. But if I *should* see my way clear to donating my talent, I'll let you know. Good-bye. (*She shrugs as if to say "What a nuisance." LUCY comes along and pretends to knock on the door. ZORLOVA looks at the door wonderingly. LUCY knocks again. ZORLOVA pretends to open the door.*) Oh! Who are you? How did you happen to come?

LUCY: "Behold, I bring you tidings of great joy which shall be to all people. . . ."

ZORLOVA: To all people. . . .

LUCY: "Peace on earth, good will toward men."

ZORLOVA: Oh! (LUCY *begins to run off, then turns and calls back, "Merry Christmas."* ZORLOVA *speaks softly*.) To all people. . . . (*Slowly* ZORLOVA *goes back into her room. She stands silently for a minute, then grabs the telephone book, looks for a number, and picks up the phone.*) 549, please. (*She does a happy tap dance as she waits.*) Hello. Is this the Chairman of the Community Christmas Tree committee? This is Zorlova, the dancer. Forgive me, but I feel quite different now about dancing at the program. A strange thing has happened. I'll be very happy to do it, really, I will. . . . Yes, there *is* something about Christmas, isn't there? (*The curtain falls.* LUCY *enters and tiptoes across stage.*)

LUCY (*Going to mirror*): I'm back, looking-glass. (*Peers at herself*) Oh, I *do* look like an angel. (*She turns this way and that.*) It makes me feel all different inside, it really does. But the other people I saw just now . . . I couldn't tell if they felt different or not. How can you tell how people feel? You can only see their faces . . . you can't see what goes on inside of them! (MISS PINSTER'S *voice is heard outside.*)

MISS PINSTER: Good-bye, Mrs. Swishton. Remember, tomorrow at three. And I promise not to keep you waiting. Good-bye. (MISS PINSTER *comes on the stage again and sees* LUCY *at the mirror.*) What are you looking at, Lucy?

LUCY: An angel. I don't look like *me* at all, do I?

MISS PINSTER: Well, not exactly. Come now, just a few more pins in the hem and we'll be through for this afternoon. (*She starts to work on the hem again.*)

LUCY: Something happened while you were away, Miss Pinster.

MISS PINSTER: Oh, is that so?

LUCY: Yes. Something about Christmas.

MISS PINSTER: Really? Where?

LUCY: Right here in this apartment building.

MISS PINSTER: You don't say.

LUCY: Yes. You know that girl I told you about . . . the one who bought the beautiful box of color-pencils for her brother?

MISS PINSTER: Yes, I remember. Twenty pencils with different colored leads.

LUCY: Well, she's going to give them to him, after all. She isn't going to keep them for herself.

MISS PINSTER: Why, how nice! That's the real Christmas spirit. But how did it happen, Lucy?

LUCY: Well, you see, Miss Pinster, the girl got to feeling different . . . inside . . . because she saw an angel . . . in the looking-glass!

THE END

•

Time Out for Christmas

Characters

LAST YEAR'S TEDDY BEAR
LAST YEAR'S RAG DOLL
TICK } *who run the clock*
TOCK }
24 DAYS OF DECEMBER

SETTING: *The playroom.*
TIME: *Midnight, November 30.*
AT RISE: LAST YEAR'S TEDDY BEAR *and* LAST YEAR'S RAG
  DOLL *are asleep against chairs, in rather awkward propped-up
  positions. When the clock begins to strike midnight, they wake
  up slowly. By the time the 10th stroke approaches, they are
  fully awake. They jump up and rush to the clock, trying to
  hold back its hands.*

TEDDY BEAR:
  The magic hour of 12 o'clock!
  Listen to us, Tick and Tock.
  We must see you in a hurry!
  Last year's toys are full of worry.
RAG DOLL:
  Listen to us, Tock and Tick—

Stop the clock, and please be quick.
In a second, you remember,
You'll be ticking-in December.
And—boo, hoo!—with Christmas nearing,
We are much in need of cheering!
(TICK *and* TOCK *come from behind the clock. They always
speak in quick, staccato voices, like the sound of a clock ticking.*)

TICK: What
TOCK: is
TICK: all
TOCK: the
TICK: noise
TOCK: and
TICK: clat-
TOCK: ter?
TEDDY BEAR: Something serious is the matter.
RAG DOLL:

Last Year's Teddy Bear and I
Are so worried we could cry.
(*She takes out her handkerchief*)

TICK: Wor-
TOCK: ried,
TICK: Rag
TOCK: Doll?
TICK: Tell
TOCK: us
TICK: why.
RAG DOLL:

Well, it's practically December
(Two more ticks will end November)
And that means that Christmas Day
Isn't very far away,
And—perhaps it may sound dumb
But we wish it wouldn't come!

TICK: Wish
TOCK: it
TICK: would
TOCK: not
TICK: come!
TOCK: How
TICK: so?
TEDDY BEAR:
    Well, it's hard on us, you know:
    Christmas means that girls and boys
    Will be getting brand-new toys—
    Teddy Bears . . .
RAG DOLL: And Rag Dolls, too.
TEDDY BEAR:
    And, since we're no longer new,
    What will we old-timers do?
TICK: What
TOCK: will
TICK: last
TOCK: year's
TICK: old
TOCK: toys
TICK: do?
TEDDY BEAR (*To* TICK *and* TOCK):
    If you'll only help us out,
    We'll be saved—without a doubt.
RAG DOLL:
    Just forget to tick, you two,
    From Christmas Eve, until it's through,
    Then tick again the 26th,
    And all our troubles will be fixed.
TEDDY BEAR:
    If you forget to tick, you see,
    Christmas simply will not *be*.

And, with Christmas blotted over,
Last year's toys will be in clover.

RAG DOLL:

Then, of course, the girls and boys
Will gladly keep their last-year toys.
Oh, how happy we shall be!
(*She dances a wobbly dance just to think of it.*)

TEDDY BEAR: We'll dance the hornpipe merrily. (*He does a funny jig.* TICK *and* TOCK *point at the calendar.*)

TICK: But

TOCK: first

TICK: the

TOCK: days

TICK: must

TOCK: all

TICK: a-

TOCK: gree.

RAG DOLL:

December days should be delighted.
They must feel all snubbed and slighted.
They just tiptoe in . . . and go,
Christmas always steals the show—
It gets all the fame . . .

TICK: That's

TOCK: so.

TEDDY BEAR:

Don't let Christmas tick this year!
Then our standing will be clear—
We will rule the playroom still,
And be bubbling with good will.

RAG DOLL:

No new toys will take our places.
We will have the *gladdest* faces.

TICK: Ask

TOCK: the
TICK: days
TOCK: if
TICK: they
TOCK: are
TICK: will-
TOCK: ing.

RAG DOLL: Oh, their answers will be thrilling! (RAG DOLL
*runs to the calendar, stands before it, and sings to the tune of
"Jolly Old St. Nicholas.")*
Listen, you December days,
Do you think it's right
Christmas captures all the praise,
All the fame in sight?
Don't you think it would be best,
And adventuresome,
If old Christmas took a rest
And just didn't come?

TICK: Ev-
TOCK: 'ry
TICK: day
TOCK: must
TICK: have
TOCK: a
TICK: turn.

TEDDY BEAR: Oh, the secrets we shall learn! (TEDDY BEAR
runs to calendar and sings to tune of "Jolly Old St. Nicholas.")
Christmas captures all the praise.
Christmas stands accused!
Listen, all you other days,
Don't you feel abused?
Step right out and have your say—
Is there any doubt
Christmas is a holiday

We could do without?

DEC. 1 (*Coming from behind calendar*): Do without Christmas? I should say not. I consider it a great honor to be the first day of the month in which Christmas comes. Christmas may be first in some ways, but it can never be the first of December! I'm perfectly satisfied with the part I play. (*Exits behind calendar, as* DEC. 2 *comes out.*)

DEC. 2: You think I'm jealous of Christmas? Why, without me Christmas wouldn't be what it is. Without me . . .

DEC. 3 (*Coming out*): And *me* . . .

DEC. 2 *and* 3: There would be two less days for getting ready for Christmas, for expecting it, and thinking about it, and shopping for it. Why, people *need us*. (*They exit, and* DEC. 4 *comes out.*)

TEDDY BEAR (*Mopping his brow*): It's getting rather warm in here!

RAG DOLL:
At such a season of the year . . .
Something must be wrong, I fear.

DEC. 4: Who said Christmas gets all the praise? In some countries *I'm* the beginning of the holiday season. In France I'm called St. Barbara's Day. That's the day people float grains of wheat on plates of water and put them in a sunny window or near the fire. If the grain sprouts well, there will be a good harvest the coming year. And in Czechoslovakia on December 4, a twig of cherry is put in water. Everyone watches for it to bloom by Christmas Eve. If it does bloom, the girl who took care of it will marry during the coming year. So, you see, how important I am! (*Exits.*)

RAG DOLL (*Subdued*): Perhaps we're rather out of date.

TEDDY BEAR (*Subdued*): We're out of luck, at any rate.

RAG DOLL (*Hopefully*): The rest will side with us, just wait!

TICK: In

TOCK: the
TICK: end
TOCK: we'll
TICK: get
TOCK: this
TICK: straight.

DEC. 5 (*Coming out*): Christmas has nothing on me. On the night of December 5th, which is the same as the Eve of December 6th, St. Nicholas comes to Holland! The children put out their shoes, and next morning. . . . (DEC. 6 *appears*)

DEC. 6: Next morning they find them full of candy and toys and treasures.

TEDDY BEAR (*Amazed*): December 6th! Well, I'll be jiggered.

RAG DOLL: Nothing works the way we "figgered."

DEC. 5 *and* 6: Yes, we're the Festival of St. Nicholas in Holland. We don't envy anyone! (*They exit. Days of* DECEMBER *from 7 through 11 come out separately at intervals, and all five are on the stage at once until after they have sung a carol at the end of their speeches.*)

DEC. 7 (*Skipping out*): I'd be lost without Christmas.

DEC. 8 (*Dancing out*): So would I.

DEC. 7: Along about now every year, school children are learning parts for the Christmas program. . . .

DEC. 8: And speaking pieces. . . .

DEC. 9 (*Coming in with half-finished present*): And making presents . . .

DEC. 10 (*In lilting voice*): And learning Christmas songs . . .

DEC. 11: And selling Christmas seals. . . .

DEC. 7, 8, 9, 10, 11: And singing carols! (*They join together and sing a lively carol, like "Joy to the World." When the song is finished, they exit.*)

TICK: They
TOCK: don't

TICK: en-

TOCK: vy

TICK: Christ-

TOCK: mas

TICK: an-

TOCK: y.

RAG DOLL (*Sighing*): I feel cheaper than a penny.

TEDDY BEAR:

All my fur is getting itchy.

Guess our plan was not so litchy!

DEC. 12 (*Entering*): About this time of year, people are all excited about the community Christmas tree and the community toy shop. It's wonderful! (*Stares at* TEDDY BEAR *and* RAG DOLL) Why, you're perfect, Last Year's Teddy Bear and Last Year's Rag Doll. You're just what they need down at the toy shop. You'd make dandy new presents for someone who wouldn't get much otherwise. That is, if your master and mistress would give you up. Of course, some children are so fond of their last year's toys they'd never give them up.

TEDDY BEAR: Is that true or are you fooling?

RAG DOLL:

Maybe we should have more schooling—

Seems we have some things to learn.

TEDDY BEAR: Seems we acted out of turn.

DEC. 12: Just remember, Christmas has a place for *everyone*, somewhere! An important place. (*Exits*)

DEC. 13 (*Coming in*): I am the day of Santa Lucia in Sweden. On December 13, Santa Lucia, dressed in white, starts going from house to house to tell the Christmas story.

And that's not all. On December 13, twelve days before Christmas, the peasants of France say that they are able to foretell the weather for the next twelve months. I don't feel abused. (*Exits.*)

DEC. 14 (*Hurrying in and out*): Am I having fun! Only nine more shopping days till Christmas!

DEC. 15 (*Hurrying in and out*): You should see the lines of people at the post office. If it weren't for me, I'm sure those Christmas parcels would never arrive in time!

DEC. 16 (*Coming in slowly*): On the night of December 16, the nine-day celebration of the Posadas begins in Mexico.

TEDDY BEAR (*Counting on fingers*):
That will bring us, swift as swift,
Right up to the 25th.

RAG DOLL: Our idea has fallen flat!

TICK: The

TOCK: Po-

TICK: sa-

TOCK: das?

TICK: What

TOCK: is

TICK: that?

DEC. 16: *Posada* means an inn or lodging house in Spanish. For nine days before Christmas, the people of Mexico act out the hardships Mary and Joseph had when they were trying to find an inn in Bethlehem. (DEC. 17, 18, 19, 20, 21, 22, 23, *and* 24 *enter carrying lighted candles. As they come in slowly they sing the Litany of the Virgin, or recite the Rosary; or, if either of these would be too difficult, they might sing an old carol.*)

DEC. 17 (*As if knocking on a door*): Open, please, to a stranger.

DEC. 16 (*As if answering the knock*): Who is it knocks at my door so late at night?

DEC. 17: We are poor pilgrims searching for a place to rest this winter night.

DEC. 18: We have traveled a long way from Nazareth, down the River Jordan.

DEC. 19: The night is cold and windy.

DEC. 20: And we are very tired. We are looking for a place to rest.

DEC. 16: But who are you, asking for shelter so late at night?

DEC. 21: I am a carpenter from Nazareth, Joseph by name.

DEC. 22: And I am Mary, his wife.

DEC. 16: Still, I know you not.

DEC. 23: You should know from the prophecy . . .

DEC. 24: Mary will be the mother of the Son of God!

DEC. 16 (*As if flinging open the door*): Ah, come into my home, then, and welcome. Come in. Come in. (*The* NINE DAYS *join in singing a glad Christmas carol, such as "O Come, All Ye Faithful." Then they exit one by one behind the calendar.*)

RAG DOLL:
Oh, I think our plan was dumb—
Christmas simply *has* to come.

TEDDY BEAR:
There is more to it than caring
How a few old toys are faring!

TICK: Christ-

TOCK: mas

TICK: is

TOCK: a

TICK: time

TOCK: for

TICK: shar-

TOCK: ing.

DEC. 24 (*Appearing again*): I am Christmas Eve. (*To* TEDDY BEAR *and* RAG DOLL) Do you still want Tick and Tock to forget to tick-in Christmas?

TEDDY BEAR: No, No . . .

RAG DOLL: No, No . . .

TEDDY BEAR *and* RAG DOLL:
No, No, No. (*They shake a finger at* TICK *and* TOCK.)
Back into the clock you go!

Don't you skip a single tick
Of December—now, be quick!
Lounging here like this is shocking—
It is time to start tick-tocking!
(TICK *and* TOCK, *laughing merrily, hurry back behind the clock
and begin to "tick-tock" loudly.* TEDDY BEAR *and* RAG DOLL
do a happy wobbly dance, as DEC. 24 *looks on. As they dance
they sing to the tune of* "*Jolly Old St. Nicholas.*")
Jolly old St. Nicholas,
Lend your ear this way—
We have been "ridicolas,"
But forgive us, pray.
Though we acted pretty dumb,
Now we think it's clear
Christmas is for *everyone*
The best day of the year!

THE END

A Christmas Tree for Kitty

Characters

JANNIS
TODD
WILLA
THEIR MOTHER
CAROLERS (*any number of boys and girls*)
MARTHA
MIKE (*non-speaking*)

TIME: *The day before Christmas.*
SETTING: *An attractive living room.*
AT RISE: JANNIS *and* TODD *are decorating a tiny Christmas tree that stands on a table. The ornaments are small-sized, and most of them are hand-made.*

JANNIS: I guess no other kitten in the world will get a tree like this for Christmas. (*Stands off and admires it*) Isn't it *beautiful?* Where did you put the ball of catnip, Todd?
TODD: I haven't put it anywhere yet. (*Looks on table and finds it. Holds it to his nose and sniffs*) I can't figure out what a cat sees in catnip. Where shall we hang it?
JANNIS: Oh, near the top, next to the golden star. Can't you just see Kitty standing on her hind legs, trying to reach it?
TODD: And if she knocks anything off, it won't matter a bit.

(*Fastens catnip ball near the star*) There's not a thing on this tree that can break.

JANNIS: Not a single thing. (WILLA *comes in*)

WILLA: Haven't the carolers come to call for me yet? What are you doing? Oh, what a cute little tree. Who's it for?

JANNIS: We told you, Willa. We're trimming it for Kitty.

WILLA: Oh, yes, I remember. Where's Mother? (*Calls*) Mother!

TODD (*Hurrying to cover the tree with tissue paper*): We don't want Mother to see the tree till it's all finished. (MOTHER *comes in with Christmas ribbons and wrapping.*)

MOTHER: Did you call me, Willa?

WILLA: Do I look all right for a caroler? We're going to sing at the day nursery first, then at the rest home, then at the hospital. (MOTHER *makes a bow of red and green ribbon and pins it to* WILLA'S *coat.*)

MOTHER: I think it's a wonderful idea, to go caroling.

JANNIS: You ought to have Martha sing with you, Willa. She's got such a good voice.

WILLA: Martha? Oh yes, that girl you walk home with sometimes. The one who always wears a blue dress—the same one.

JANNIS: She doesn't have many dresses. But she can *sing!* (*The sound of* CAROLERS *is heard offstage.*)

WILLA: There they are! The carolers.

MOTHER: Do have them come in a minute, Willa. I'd like to hear how you sound together. I'll get some cookies . . . (*She leaves by one exit,* WILLA *by another.*)

WILLA (*Offstage*): Yoo-hoo! Come in a minute! My mother wants to hear how we sound. (WILLA *returns with a group of merry* CAROLERS.) What shall we sing? "O Little Town of Bethlehem"? (*She gives the key, and they begin to sing.* MOTHER *returns with plate of cookies and stands listening. When the song is over,* JANNIS *and* TODD *clap loudly.*)

MOTHER: That was lovely. I am sure you are going to give many people a great deal of joy this afternoon. I almost wish I were your age and could go along! Good luck . . . (WILLA *and* CAROLERS *exit with cookies in their hands. Calls of "Goodbye" and "Thank you."*)

JANNIS: Todd and I have almost finished trimming the little tree for Kitty, Mother.

TODD: But you can't see it till every last thing is on.

MOTHER (*Laughing*): I won't peek, I promise. Call me when you're ready. (*She goes out.* JANNIS *and* TODD *work on the tree again.*)

JANNIS: I wonder what Kitty will like most—next to the catnip.

TODD: The red yarn. She'll get all snarled up in it before you can say "Merry Christmas." That's her idea of fun.

JANNIS: Maybe she'll like the lollipops . . . they're so pretty, all red and green and yellow. (*Cocks her head and looks at tree.*) Or maybe she'll like the paper chains. Or the little cotton lamb.

TODD: I still think we should have used *wool* for the lamb. (*Looks at table*) Well, everything is on the tree now, Jannis.

JANNIS: Let's call Mother then. (*Loudly*) Mother!

TODD: All right, Mother. It's done. Come look! (MOTHER *comes in, looks eagerly at the little tree.*)

MOTHER: Why, it's lovely! I had no idea you were making it so fancy. Such gay colors! Won't Kitty be surprised!

TODD: Do you see our little woolly lamb . . . only it's *cotton.*

JANNIS: And the white-paper angels?

TODD: Not a single thing can break, no matter how rough Kitty is.

MOTHER: It's the prettiest little tree I've ever seen. Quite the prettiest. You ought to move it closer to the window, where it can be seen from the street.

JANNIS: Yes, let's. Kitty can't have it until tomorrow, anyway. Do you think she'll know what it is?

TODD: 'Course not. Cats don't know about Christmas. But that won't matter. (*As* JANNIS *and* TODD *move the table near the window,* JANNIS *suddenly stops and looks out eagerly.*)

JANNIS: Oh, look, there's Martha, coming down the street with her little brother Mike.

TODD: Wherever Martha is, Mike is. Or Johnny, or Freddy, or Millie.

JANNIS: I bet she's never seen a little Christmas tree like this one. They're too poor to have a tree, I guess—even a little one. Mother, will it be all right to have Martha come in and see Kitty's tree?

TODD: Mike will like it, too. But he won't say a thing. He'll just peek around Martha's skirt and never say a word.

JANNIS: Mother?

MOTHER: Why, yes . . . ask them in for a little while, Jannis.

JANNIS (*Running out, calling*): Martha! Martha!

TODD: Martha told Jannis they've got another baby at their house. It's a girl.

MOTHER: Another baby? Dear me, where do they put all the children, in that little house? What have they named it?

TODD: I don't know. Jannis told Martha they ought to call it *Mary*, because it came at Christmastime.

MOTHER: Mary is a nice name.

JANNIS (*Offstage*): Wait till you see, Martha! Wait till you see. You can't guess! Todd and I did it all by ourselves. (JANNIS *comes in with* MARTHA. MIKE, *a small bashful boy, clings to his sister's skirts.*)

MOTHER: Good afternoon, Martha. Is that Michael with you?

MARTHA: Yes, Ma'am. Mike. He's scared. I don't mean really scared, but . . .

MOTHER: Bashful?

MARTHA: Yes, that's it. He's bashful.

MOTHER: I'll go refill the cooky plate. Maybe that will help. (*Exits with plate*)

JANNIS (*Pointing at tree, eagerly*): There it is, Martha. On the table. (*For a moment* MARTHA *stares at the little tree in silence, fascinated.*)

MARTHA: Oh, I never saw such a cute little tree. (*She moves toward it, touching one of the angels reverently.* MIKE *follows, clinging to her.*)

TODD: Jannis and I made most of the ornaments.

MARTHA (*Awed*): Look, Mike. Look at the little woolly lamb. And the *real* little lollipops. (*At that* MIKE *really looks*) And the paper chains and stars and angels. And everything so cute and little.

JANNIS: It *had* to be little. (*Laughs*) You know why? It had to be little . . . because, you see, it's for Kitty.

MARTHA (*Astonished*): For Kitty?

TODD: Sure. For Kitty. That's why we didn't put on anything that could break.

MARTHA (*More astonished than ever*): But how did you *know?* Who told you? We didn't decide ourselves till this noon, at the dinner table. (JANNIS *and* TODD *look at each other, baffled.*)

TODD: What do you mean, you didn't decide?

MARTHA: You said *for Kitty.*

JANNIS: Yes, that's right.

MARTHA: But how did you know? How did you know we named the new baby Kitty? Katherine for real . . . but *Kitty* for short.

JANNIS: Oh, I . . . we . . . well, I guess people know a lot of things at Christmastime. Don't they, Todd? (*She nods at him eagerly, and he nods back.*)

TODD: Sure. At Christmastime!

MARTHA: A Christmas tree for Kitty. Oh, it's wonderful of you. It's like a birthday present and a Christmas present all in one.

TODD: It won't be hard to carry home, Martha, because nothing on it will break.

MARTHA: You even thought of that!

JANNIS: Wait. I'll write a card for it.

TODD (*Hurriedly taking off the catnip ball*): Here, tie the tag in place of this little ball . . . (*In* JANNIS'S *ear*) of catnip! (JANNIS *laughs as she slips the catnip ball in her pocket. She writes the tag.*)

JANNIS (*As she writes*): "A Christmas tree . . . for Kitty . . . from Santa Claus." (*Hangs tag where catnip ball was.*)

MARTHA: Oh, it's so wonderful . . . it makes me feel like singing.

JANNIS *and* TODD: We feel like singing too.

MOTHER (*Coming in with cookies*): Let's all sing! (MARTHA *starts "O Tannenbaum" ("O Christmas Tree") and others join in happily, except* MIKE *who is more interested in peeking at the little tree.*)

THE END

The Spirit of Christmas

Characters

READER
SPIRIT OF CHRISTMAS
1ST WOMAN
1ST GIRL
MILKMAN
GROCERYMAN
2ND WOMAN
2ND GIRL

TIME: *A few days before Christmas.*
SETTING: *No setting is necessary.*
AT RISE: READER *is standing downstage right, where he stays throughout the play.*

READER: The Spirit of Christmas
    Dances down the street,
    With his magic slippers
    On his magic feet.
SPIRIT (*Dancing in merrily, chanting*):
    Closed hands, closed hearts, send me away.
    Open hands, open hearts, make me stay.
READER: The Spirit of Christmas

Sees a yellow house
Slips through the keyhole
Quiet as a mouse,
Tiptoes to the kitchen,
Perches on a shelf
Near the cups and saucers
Talking to himself:
SPIRIT: Closed hands, closed hearts, send me away.
Open hands, open hearts, make me stay.
(1ST WOMAN *and* 1ST GIRL *come in, pantomime as* READER
speaks.)
READER: At the kitchen table
In the yellow house
Stands a frowny woman
In a checkered blouse,
Stands her greedy daughter
Nibbling crumbs and sweets
As they put the frosting
On their Christmas treats—
Cookies cut like circles,
Triangles, and bars,
Cookies shaped like angels,
Little moons, and stars.
(WOMAN *and* GIRL *work in silence for a moment.*)
Then there comes a rattle
On the stoop . . . (*Sound of milk bottles clinking off stage*)
1ST WOMAN: Dear me!
That must be the milkman.
Hope he doesn't see. (*Looks nervously from door to cookies.*)
GIRL: He will want a sample,
He will want a taste,
And we haven't any
Cookies here to waste.
1ST WOMAN: No, we haven't any

Sweets to give away . . .
These are meant for Christmas.
Cover up the tray!
1st Girl (*In loud whisper as she covers tray*):
If we're very quiet
He will never know
We have all these cookies
Cooling in a row.
Reader: The milkman leaves the bottles
At the door, and goes.
The Spirit of Christmas
Wrinkles up his nose.
And mother and daughter
Start to work once more.
(Woman *and* Girl *work in silence for a moment.*)
Then there comes a clatter
At the kitchen door.
1st Girl: That must be the order
From the grocery store.
1st Woman: Hurry, take a tea-towel,
Cover up the treats.
Grocerymen, I fear me,
Have an eye for sweets.
Groceryman (*Off stage*): Order from the market!
1st Woman: Hide away the treats.
Reader: Crack! goes a teacup
On the cupboard shelf.
Zip! go the slippers
Of the Christmas elf.
Whisk! through the keyhole,
(Spirit *hurries to front of stage.*)
Over the mat,
Before the girl and woman
Can say . . .

1ST WOMAN (*Puzzled*): What's that?
(*They look around and then go out*)

SPIRIT: Closed hands, closed hearts, send me away,
   Pity the people on Christmas Day
   Whose hands are closed and whose hearts are small.
   They won't be merry at all, at all, at all.

READER: The Spirit of Christmas
   Sees another house,
   Brushes off his jacket,
   Straightens up his blouse
   Peeks inside the window,
   Squeezes through a crack,
   Perches on a platter
   On the china rack.

SPIRIT: Closed hands, closed hearts, send me away.
   Open hands, open hearts, make me stay.
   (2ND WOMAN *and* 2ND GIRL *come in.*)

READER: At the kitchen table
   In the second house
   Stands a jolly woman
   In a colored blouse,
   Stands her merry daughter
   Smiling at the sweets
   As they spread the frosting
   On their Christmas treats.
   (WOMAN *and* GIRL *work at the cookies, having a good time.*)
   Then there comes a rattle
   On the stoop . . .

2ND WOMAN: I say,
   That must be the milkman. (*Calls out cheerfully*) Do not
      rush away!

2ND GIRL (*Calling*): You must have a sample,
   You must have a bite
   Of our Christmas cookies,

Red, and green, and white.
(2ND WOMAN *and* GIRL *go to door with cookie trays.*)
MILKMAN (*At door*): Thank you. Thank you kindly.
Aren't they pretty, though!
2ND WOMAN: Put one in your pocket,
Munch it as you go.
2ND GIRL: Isn't Christmas jolly?
MILKMAN (*Merrily, munching cookie*): Guess I ought to know!
READER: The milkman goes off whistling,
Merry as a bird.
The elf atop the platter
Doesn't say a word,
But oh, there is a twinkle
Shining in his eye,
And oh, there is a chuckle
As the cooks go by.
(2ND WOMAN *and* GIRL *return to their work.*)
Mother and daughter
Start to work once more . . . (*Slight pause as they work*)
Then there comes a clatter
At the kitchen door.
2ND GIRL: That must be the order
From the grocery store.
2ND WOMAN: Is there any coffee
In the coffeepot?
2ND GIRL: Yes. I'll pour a cup full,
Nice and steaming hot.
2ND WOMAN: And we'll pass the cookies.
My, we've made a stack.
Grocerymen get weary
Rushing forth and back . . .
GROCERYMAN (*Off stage*): Order from the market.
2ND GIRL: Come and have a snack!
(2ND GIRL *and* WOMAN *go to the door with coffee and cookies.*)

READER: Zip! from the platter
　On the cupboard shelf
　Springs a merry fellow,
　Springs the Christmas elf,
　Dancing on his tiptoes,
　Talking to himself:
SPIRIT: Closed hands, closed hearts, send me away.
　Open hands, open hearts. . . . *Here I'll stay!*
　Here I'll stay for Christmas, here I'll dance and jig—
　Blessings on the people when their hearts are big!
　(*He dances a jolly jig.*)

THE END

The Christmas Cake

Characters

NARRATOR
MRS. MCGILLY
MR. MCGILLY
NEIGHBOR BOY

SETTING: *The McGilly kitchen.*
AT RISE: *The* NARRATOR *enters and stands at one side. As the* NARRATOR *speaks, the others pantomime their actions.*

NARRATOR: Mrs. McGilly was very proud,
  A very proud soul was she,
  She knew how to bake a holiday cake
  From a secret recipe. (MRS. MCGILLY *comes bustling in, puts on apron, begins to mix cake.*)
MRS. MCGILLY: Nobody else in the neighborhood
  Can make such a cake as mine:
  The cherries I canned will surely be grand
  To dress up my cake just fine.
NARRATOR: Mr. McGilly was slow and kind,
  As slow as his spouse was fast.
  He fancied to sit and whittle a bit

And dream as the hours went past. (MR. McGILLY *comes in slowly and good-naturedly, and sits down to whittle.* MRS. McGILLY *turns to look at him, her hands on her hips.*)

MRS. McGILLY (*Scolding*):
Get me some kindling and fix the fire.
I'm making a Christmas cake—
It's specially nice with cherries and spice,
And specially hard to bake . . .

Take out the ashes and poke the coals,
Don't dawdle around and halt.
Go rustle some wood . . . if the cake's not good
It surely will be your fault! (MR. McGILLY *puts down his whittling and goes to peer at the stove. He fusses around and pokes the fire.* MRS. McGILLY *keeps one eye on him while trying to follow the recipe with the other.*)
Hurry, I'm almost ready now.
Why isn't that oven hot?
I soon must go down for groceries in town
That *you*, for a change, forgot.

MR. McGILLY (*Shaking head over fire*):
Something's the matter. The fire's no good.
The oven is cold as stone.
If you have to flee, just leave it to me—
I'll tend to that cake alone. (*He puts in more paper and kindling.*)

MRS. McGILLY (*Shaking her finger at him*): See you don't ruin our Christmas cake!
If anything turns out wrong
I'm sure to have fits, so use all your wits.
It's late. I must run along. (*She puts the batter in the pan ready for the oven, then takes off her apron and puts on wraps.* MR. McGILLY *meanwhile continues to fuss with*

the fire. As Mrs. McGilly *exits she turns in the doorway and shakes a warning finger at her husband. Then she goes out.*)

Narrator: Mr. McGilly meant well of course
(In spite of the looks he got),
Intending to bake the holiday cake
As soon as the fire was hot.
But how could he know that a boy would call,
A boy from the neighborhood,
And ask for a lift on a Christmas gift
He was whittling from maple wood? (*There is a knock on the door.* Mr. McGilly *leaves his job at the stove and goes to the door. A* Boy *comes in with a half-finished carving.* Mr. McGilly *examines it, has the* Boy *sit down. Of course he completely forgets about the fire.*)
Mr. McGilly sat down and showed
What grooves in the wood to make,
And, oh, he forgot when the fire was hot
To put in the Christmas cake!

Mr. McGilly (*Helping the* Boy):
Whittle this rounder, and whittle this thin,
And whittle this end away.
The critter will stand on his legs just grand,
All ready for Christmas day.

Boy: Mr. McGilly, I knew you'd help!
There's nothing that you can't do.
(*He looks out of the window, and gives a start.*)
Oh, golly, your wife! She runs for her life . . .
I think I'll be running too! (Mr. McGilly *remembers the cake and rushes to the stove. The* Boy *gathers up his carving and knife and rushes for the door as* Mr. McGilly *rushes for the cake. At the door the* Boy *and* Mrs. McGilly *collide and almost knock each other over.* Boy *hurries out with a frightened glance over his shoulder.*)

MRS. McGILLY (*Frantically*):

Help me to rescue the cherry cake!

Help me to save my skin!

I boasted a lot, and then I forgot

To put any *cherries* in! (*She sees her husband holding pan with the unbaked cake in his hands.*)

Haven't you baked it? You darling man!

The cherries can go on top,

And no one will know my error, and so

My fame as a cook won't stop! (*She sighs with relief, takes the cake pan and puts cherries on top, poking them down in the batter. Then, smiling, she puts the cake in the oven and pats her husband lovingly on the back.*)

NARRATOR: Mrs. McGilly for once was glad

Her husband had dreamy ways.

She urged him to sit and whittle a bit

And showered him with words of praise.

Mr. McGilly looked up and grinned

And said to his spouse . . .

MR. McGILLY: My dear,

Nothing we'll get can compare, I bet,

With our holiday cake this year!

(*They smile happily at each other.*)

THE END

Where Is Christmas?

GIRL: It isn't in the tinsel,
the shining, twining tinsel,
the gleaming, beaming tinsel
that dresses up the tree . . .

BOY: It isn't in the shimmer
of colored lights that glimmer . . .

GROUP: Christmas is . . .
hmmmm, let's see . . .

BOY: It isn't in the presents,
the wrapped-so-brightly presents,
the tapped-so-lightly presents
we stand and wonder at . . .

GIRL: It isn't in the kitchen
where odors are bewitchin' . . .

GROUP: Christmas is
more than that . . .

GIRL: It isn't in the spangles,
the baubles and the bangles . . .

BOY: It's not the jingle-jangles
that set the day apart . . .

GROUP: It isn't in the wrappings,
the showiness and trappings . . .
Christmas is
IN THE HEART!

Christmas!

(BOYS *and* GIRLS *stand toward back of stage holding large cards with letters spelling* CHRISTMAS. *As each one speaks he takes a step forward.*)

C arolers, candles, chimes a-ringing,
H olly wreaths with berries clinging,
R eindeer, fairy-fast and tiny,
I cicles all bright and shiny,
S tars and stockings, shoppers streaming
T hrough the town, and tinsel gleaming,
M istletoe in waxen glory,
A ngels from the Christmas story,
S anta with his sack to carry . . .

That spells CHRISTMAS. Make it merry!

The Christmas Mitten Lady

Once a dear old lady,
when Christmastime was near,
decided that a party
would fill her heart with cheer.
She gave her cat a loving pat
and murmured, "Girls and boys
are fun to see around a tree
with all their jolly noise.

"I truly love a party,"
she said. "I truly do.
I'd love to ask the neighbors—
not merely one or two,
but all the girls with bobs and curls
and pigtails down their backs,
and all the boys in corduroys
and overalls and slacks!"

The cat purred once in treble,
and once he purred in bass,
as if to say, "Sounds dandy."
And then he washed his face,
and in a heap he went to sleep
and dreamed of catnip tea.

While near at hand his mistress planned
her party Christmas tree.

Just then she heard a knocking.
A lad was at the door.
His face was full of freckles
(there wasn't room for more!).
"Hello," he said, and wagged his head,
"we hope you'll help this year.
We have a scheme that's like a dream
for spreading Christmas cheer:

"Our schoolroom plans a party
for Christmas, but, you see,
instead of getting presents
we'll trim a MITTEN TREE . . .
with woolly mitts of proper fits
for kids across the ocean
who haven't much to wear and such.
That's how we got the notion."

The dear old lady twittered:
"With mittens? I declare!
You'll trim a tree with mittens?
I'll gladly knit a pair."
And so she took her pocketbook
and hurried to the shops,
and bought a lot of yarn . . . with what
she'd saved for lollipops!

The mitts she knit were beauties.
The news spread very fast.
"I, too, am hunting mittens,"
said Jerry, coming past.

And Mary Ann, and Hugh, and Dan,
and Phyllis, and Louise—
all spoke of mitts of proper fits
for youngsters overseas.

The lady's party money
bought woolly yarn and gay!
Her dimes for Christmas candy
bought skeins of red and gray!
Till every cent was quickly spent . . .
her party plans were over,
but oh, the Tree, the Mitten Tree,
was certainly in clover.

"I truly love a party,"
the dear old lady said,
"but this year, seems I've chosen
a knitting spree instead!
The girls and boys will have their joys
at school some afternoon,
but I will sit, and knit, and knit,
and sing a mitten tune:

    "Bright mitts, light mitts,
    fit-just-right mitts,

    Blue mitts, new mitts,
    wool-all-through mitts,

    Gray mitts, gay mitts,
    good-for-play mitts,

    Long mitts, strong mitts,
    can't-go-wrong mitts . . .

Oh, how jolly it must be
to dance around a Mitten Tree."

And then an invitation
(all unexpected!) came:
"Dear Christmas Mitten Lady,
we hope you will be game
to dance with glee around our Tree
and join our party fun.
You've helped us more than twenty-four
times twenty folks have done!"

The dear old lady chuckled,
and hurried (with her cat)
to join the Christmas party.
She wore her nicest hat.
And oh, the glee she felt to see
the mitts on every twig,
and hear the joys of girls and boys.
Her heart felt awfully big.

"I truly love a party,"
she said. "I truly do.
I've been to quite a number,
and given quite a few . . .
a Christmas one is always fun,
it makes the heart-bells chime,
but, oh, my dears, I've not in YEARS
had such a lovely time!"

NOTE: This poem could be given as a pantomime for several
children, using a reader or narrator.

With Christmas in the Air

Ours is a house of mystery—
secrets are everywhere:
  Don't go peeking behind the chair!
  Don't look under the cellar stair!
  Close the closet—beware, beware!
Happens each year in history—
with Christmas in the air.

Ours is a house of mystery—
everyone acts so queer:
  Don't look back of the chiffonier,
  or into the basket of fishing gear!
  Don't peek under the chest—you hear?
Happens each year in history—
with Christmas almost here.

At Last It Came

I thought about a little wish
all by myself,
and it wasn't for the cookies
on the pantry shelf,
and it wasn't for an orange
or a candy cane
or permission to draw pictures
on the windowpane,
and it wasn't for a paint box
or a puzzle game . . .
it only was for CHRISTMAS,
and, at last, it came!

NEW YEAR'S DAY

Benjy Makes a Resolution

ALL: The old year was thinning,
the New Year beginning,
when Benjamin's wife made a plan:

WIFE: Some good resolution
might be the solution
of all of our troubles, my man.
Let's take it upon us
to make some good promise.
Let's start the New Year with a bang!

BENJY: I'll start being judicious
and act more ambitious,
if *you* will not scold and harangue.

ALL: So Ben got ambitious!
He helped with the dishes.
Bang! bang! went the platters and pots.
He vacuumed the rug
with such vigor he dug
a hole under each of the spots.
He shook out the pillows
till feathery billows
of down covered dressers and chairs.
Bang! bang! went the vases
in dust-catching places.

169

Bang! bang! went the mop on the stairs.
But the worst came the day
Benjy polished away
at the glass of the old chandelier:
it tore from its socket
and fell like a rocket
on Benjy's bare noddle, poor dear.

WIFE: Such doings! Good gracious,
my plan was fallacious!
Let's give up our promises, Ben.
This pace is terrific.
To be more specific,
please, Benjy, get lazy again!

The Snowman's Resolution

The snowman's hat was crooked
and his nose was out of place
and several of his whiskers
had fallen from his face,

But the snowman didn't notice
for he was trying to think
of a New Year's resolution
that wouldn't melt or shrink.

He thought and planned and pondered
with his little snowball head
till his eyes began to glisten
and his toes began to spread;

At last he said, "I've got it!
I'll make a firm resolve
that no matter WHAT the weather
my smile will not dissolve."

Now the snowman acted wisely
and his resolution won,
for his splinter smile was WOODEN
and it didn't mind the sun!

LINCOLN'S BIRTHDAY

Abe's Winkin' Eye

Characters

ABE LINCOLN, *12*
SALLY, *his sister, 14*
TOM LINCOLN, *his father*
SARAH BUSH LINCOLN, *his stepmother*
MATILDA (*Tilda*), *about 8* ⎱ *his stepsisters*
SARAH ELIZABETH (*Sarah Bets*), *15* ⎰
JOHNNY, *his stepbrother, about 6*
NATTY GRIGSBY, *a friend*

TIME: *Late afternoon on a summer day in 1821.*
SETTING: *The interior of the Lincoln cabin on Little Pigeon Creek in southern Indiana.*
AT RISE: SALLY *is peeling vegetables for the soup kettle.* MRS. LINCOLN *is sewing on a jacket.*

MRS. LINCOLN: Just seems I can't ever get homey-close to your brother, Sally. 'Course I never let on as I'm tryin'. He's real polite and obligin' and all, and he never lies to me, or speaks an unkind word. Still, just seems I can't get close to him somehow. And I'd like to. The good Lord knows I'd like to. Heart close . . . winkin' close . . . if you know what I mean.

SALLY: Abe's queer that-a-way. He's got a mullin'-over streak, Abe has. He can't seem to shake things off, like me. Thinkin' about our mammy, now. Seems he can't get her out of his mind, though it's goin' on three years since we laid her over there in the clearin'. In the path of the deer-run, we laid her. She was always so fond of the deer comin' and goin' on their way to the salt-lick.

MRS. LINCOLN: Poor darlin', takin' the fever, and her still young and all!

SALLY: The week she was ailin', Abe'd just stand and look at her, solemn-like. Just stand a-lookin' at her lyin' under the bearskin in the corner with the fever-light in her eyes. Seems he can't forget that week our mammy was ailin'.

MRS. LINCOLN: Appears he'd rather keep rememberin' her than have me around tryin' to take her place. Not as I'm the kind of stepmother to hold it against him, though. He's got a deep-down feelin' for his mammy, and I say a deep-down feelin's somethin' mighty sacred to have.

SALLY: It was the time of year, too, made it bad. You know how late October is sometimes—with the leaves down, 'ceptin' on the oaks, and a bleak sky showin' through the branches, and gray cold after we'd been a-used to summer. That's the way it was when she took the fever. And nobody knowin' what to do, and the herb doctor thirty miles away.

MRS. LINCOLN: Poor darlin'.

SALLY: Wasn't much sun that week. And wasn't much time for Abe and Pappy and me to get used to the idea of her not up and doin'.

MRS. LINCOLN: I'd like to make it up to you-all for losin' her, I would.

SALLY: Oh, you do, Mammy! We never had things so good before. (*Looks around proudly*) Now we got a board floor and a rag rug, 'stead of just packed-down dirt. And a window! Pappy never got around to cuttin' through a window before. And the bureau-chest you brought, and the feather beds, and the hickory chairs, and the pots and pans, and the books . . . Abe's plumb daffy about the books, though maybe he's never thanked you, out loud, for lettin' him read them.

MRS. LINCOLN: It's real nice the way he tells those Aesop fables to my two young 'uns. Tilda, now, she'd like nothin' better than to follow Abe around like a little yaller dog.

SALLY: He'd rather read or tell stories than eat, Abe would. If only he could have a little more schoolin', Mammy. He'd read real good then, like a preacher. I think Abe's smart, don't you? Though Pappy says he's a lazy one.

MRS. LINCOLN: From the very first day your pappy brought me and mine here from Kentucky, from the very first day I set eyes on your brother, I put him down as a thinkin' boy. Not just ordinary. There's something about Abe that's different, Sally. I can't exactly put my finger on it, but it's there.

SALLY: He never had much chance, but he's real good at learnin' We went to school some when we lived on the Knob Creek farm. That's when Abe was seven. Since we moved here to Pigeon Creek, we only went to school by littles. It was nine miles each way to walk, and then pretty soon the school closed up.

MRS. LINCOLN: I'd like to see Abe get more schoolin', I would for certain sure. He's got somethin' in his head under that mop of black hair. Anyone can tell just watchin' him lookin' off into the distance, thinkin' and thinkin'.

SALLY: *Dreamin'*, Pappy says. He says Abe's got enough education to last his lifetime. He says now he's twelve years old and so big for his age and strong, he can do a man's work.

MRS. LINCOLN: Your pappy gets peculiar ideas sometimes. Only I wouldn't ever tell him, in so many words.

SALLY: Not in so many words. But you got other ways! The window, now. My mammy always hankered for a window, but Pappy said the door was enough. And the floor! He thought a packed earth floor was good enough for anyone . . . before he married you. You got ways!

MRS. LINCOLN: One of 'em is through that cookin' book I brought from Kentucky, Sally. And don't you forget it. Can't any man resist some nice tasty cookin'. (TILDA *and* JOHNNY *come running in.*)

TILDA: When's Abe a-comin' home?

MRS. LINCOLN: Land sakes, you pulled all the weeds out of the bean patch already?

TILDA: When's Abe a-comin'?

MRS. LINCOLN: You'd think you was a little banty hen, Tilda, the way you cluck around after Abe.

SALLY: He'll come as soon as he's through pullin' corn fodder for Jim Gentry. Maybe early, maybe late. Depends on how much there's left to finish up.

JOHNNY: He said he'd read to us.

TILDA: From "Robinson Crusoe."

JOHNNY: Robinson Crusoe, Robinson Crusoe!

MRS. LINCOLN: Then I'm thinkin' you'd better finish weedin' the beans so you'll be ready for him. (*Gets up and goes to cupboard*) Here's a piece o' corn pone if you're hungry.

JOHNNY (*With his mouth full*): Where's Sarah Bets?

MRS. LINCOLN: Don't you remember your sister's helpin' over at Mis' Romaine's today? Ought to be comin' home any minute, though, I should think.

TILDA: She won't play with us . . . now she's so grown up. Now she's got her head all full of Denny Hanks, like to burst.

MRS. LINCOLN: Why, Tilda.

JOHNNY: She won't play with us.

SALLY: Never mind, Tilda. And don't you mind either, Johnny. When your sister and my cousin get themselves married, we-all will be more related than ever.

TILDA: What'll I be to Abe then?

MRS. LINCOLN: Why, let's see—you'll be stepsister and cousin-in-law, I reckon, all at the same time.

TILDA: Is that good?

MRS. LINCOLN: 'Course it's good. Now go 'long with you and finish pullin' those weeds. (TILDA *and* JOHNNY *start out.* JOHNNY *turns back.*)

JOHNNY: Here comes Sarah Bets now.

TILDA: Comin' up the path from the road. Let's go meet her, Johnny. (*They are gone.*)

MRS. LINCOLN: Comin' home out of breath, like as not, so she'll have plenty of time to spruce up for Denny before supper. These young 'uns, how they grow up! Here's Sarah 'Lizbeth more'n fifteen already, and seems just a few years ago she was a babe in arms. She was a pretty baby, Sally. Mr. Johnston and I felt right smart havin' such a pretty baby, for our first one.

SALLY: She's still pretty, I think. Real pretty. Wish I was.

MRS. LINCOLN: Now, there's nothin' wrong with your looks, honey girl. You got your mother's dark complexion, your pappy says. And her gray eyes. And being a girl, you can be glad you didn't come out with a nose like Abe's. 'Course it's all right for a boy, a big nose like that, and a lower lip that likes to want to stick out. I always say looks don' make much difference with a boy. (*Thoughtfully*) There's somethin' about Abe's looks, though . . . somethin' I like . . . even if some folks say he's homely as a mud fence.

SALLY: It's been hard on Abe. That big nose . . . and him growin' so fast he's always a couple sizes too big for his britches. (SARAH BETS *comes in, sputtering.*)

SARAH BETS: That Abe! Couldn't anybody a-done it but Abe.

MRS. LINCOLN: Done what, Sarah Bets?

SALLY: What's Abe a-gone and done now?

SARAH BETS: Wouldn't anybody else a-thought of it just like that. And right along the road too!

SALLY: Along the road?

MRS. LINCOLN: How do you know Abe did it, whatever it is?

SARAH BETS: 'Cause it looks just like one of his pranks, that's why. Fresh cut on a poplar tree. Wasn't any knife but Abe Lincoln's did it, I can see that, easy as lickin' a dish. Initials cut out plain as day and big as life: "S. E. J." . . .

SALLY: S.E.J. That'd be Sarah Elizabeth Johnston, I reckon.

SARAH BETS: And "D.H."

MRS. LINCOLN: Who'd that be now? D. H. Anyone around here with initials of "D.H.," Sally?

SALLY: Couldn't be Dennis Hanks, could it? Couldn't be my cousin Denny?

SARAH BETS: Now you're a-makin' fun of me, you are. It's not that I'm objectin' to havin' my initials and Denny's set together, close-like. It's not that. It's just the way Abe did it, the old smarty.

MRS. LINCOLN: Two hearts linked together, your initials in one and Denny's in the other? That what you mean, Sarah Bets? And what's wrong with that, honey child? It's been done since the beginnin' of time.

SARAH BETS (*Mournfully*): But it's *not* two hearts, Mammy. I wouldn't be objectin' to hearts. Like as you say, that's been done since the beginnin' of time. But that Abe has to think up somethin' different. The smarty!

MRS. LINCOLN (*Teasingly*): Just as I was tellin' Sally a mite ago—Abe's a thinkin' boy, he is.

SALLY: What'd he go think up now, Sarah Bets?

SARAH BETS: If it was hearts, I wouldn't be mindin'. But *eyes!*

SALLY: Eyes?

MRS. LINCOLN: You mean Abe went and carved eyes atop your initials, 'stead of hearts around 'em?

SARAH BETS: Yes, he did. Wouldn't anybody else be so teasin' mean. Two eyes. And one of 'em *winkin'*. That's the worst!

MRS. LINCOLN (*Laughing*): One of 'em winkin'? Well, now, Sarah Bets, I call that real clever, I do. One of 'em winkin'!

SARAH BETS: Well, it's not very funny to *me*. Folks passin' by, seein' that, what'll they think? Oh, Mammy . . .

MRS. LINCOLN: There, there, honey, don't you go feelin' bad. You're not even sure it was Abe did it, though I must say as it sounds like him. He's got a prankin' streak, that's all. Tell you what. When Sally gets through a-peelin' the vegetables, you both go 'long with the parin' knife, and I'm bettin' you can turn those eyes into hearts easy as a cat can lick her paw.

SALLY: 'Course we can, Sarah Bets. (*Giggles*) That'll give Abe somethin' to think about next time he passes by that tree.

SARAH BETS: Wish I could think up some way to get even with him. He's always up to tricks. But it's hard to get even with Abe. He could talk a duck out of its webbed feet!

SALLY: He's got a smooth tongue in his mouth, all right.

SARAH BETS: And a lucky piece in his pocket. Ever since he found that lucky stone, he's been ridin' a high horse. Thinks he can get away with anythin'! If only I could get that lucky stone away from him, maybe he wouldn't act so smart-like.

MRS. LINCOLN: Sarah Elizabeth Johnston, what a way to

talk. Abe sets great store by that lucky piece. You leave him be. (*Goes to cupboard*) Here, have a bit of corn pone and yaller honey, and you'll be feelin' better. (*Chuckles as she gets cornbread*) One of 'em winkin'! (*There is a shrill whistle outside. The women stop to listen. The whistle is repeated.*)

SALLY: Sounds like Natty Grigsby. Come to see if Abe's home, likely.

SARAH BETS (*Looking out the door*): It's Natty, all right. With his fishin' pole. Wonder how he got off work so early.

MRS. LINCOLN: Might be his pappy's hankerin' for a taste of fish for supper. A good change from pork, I say. Have Natty come in and set, Sarah Bets. Till Abe gets home.

SARAH BETS (*Calling*): Abe's not home yet, Natty. Come in and set a minute. (*Pause*) Oh, I reckon he'll be back pretty soon. Come on, we won't take a bite outen you. (*In a minute or two NATTY, a boy of 12, rather small for his age, comes in shyly.*)

NATTY: When'll Abe be home, Mis' Lincoln?

MRS. LINCOLN: Shouldn't be too long now. He figured he might finish up at Gentry's around four.

SARAH BETS: If he didn't get himself mixed up in too much mischief.

SALLY: Or if he didn't get a-hold of a book to read. Did you come along the road, Natty?

NATTY: No, through the woods. Maybe I better not wait. Maybe Abe could meet me at the rapids . . .

MRS. LINCOLN: What's your hurry, Natty? Set still a minute and tell us the news. What's been happenin' over your way?

NATTY: Nothin' much. Aaron's cow had a calf. Twins!

MRS. LINCOLN: Twins! You don't say. That doesn't happen often with cows.

NATTY: They're pretty small, but Aaron thinks they'll be all right.

SALLY: How's Aaron? I haven't seen him for a dog's age.

NATTY: He's all right.

MRS. LINCOLN: And how's your folks?

NATTY: They're all right.

MRS. LINCOLN: And your mammy?

NATTY: She's all right. Only she broke one of her china cups last week and she felt real bad.

SARAH BETS: Well, I should think she would. China cups don't grow on bushes along Little Pigeon Creek. Not that I can see.

SALLY: How's the summer been treatin' you, Natty?

NATTY: All right. You know what? Last week, the day it was Friday the thirteenth, I killed a rattlesnake. Thirteen rattles!

MRS. LINCOLN: What do you think of that? Thirteen! On the thirteenth. And folks let on as Friday the thirteenth is unlucky.

NATTY: Maybe it wasn't unlucky on the thirteenth, but it was afterward.

SALLY: What do you mean, Natty?

NATTY: Come winter, Azel Dorsey's a-goin' to start a school, and Mammy says we've got to go, all us kids. 'Cept maybe Aaron is too old.

MRS. LINCOLN: A school? Is that what you said, Natty?

NATTY: Yes'm. Over at Azel Dorsey's.

MRS. LINCOLN: Where's that?

SALLY: About four miles from here, I think. Abe and I went over once or twice.

NATTY: I wish I was as big as Abe. Then maybe they wouldn't make me go.

MRS. LINCOLN: If Abe was to go, you wouldn't mind it so much, would you, Natty?

NATTY: No'm. It would be fun if Abe went. Do you think Mr. Lincoln would let him?

MRS. LINCOLN: I'd like for Sally to go too, and Tilda and Johnny. I certain sure would. (*She gets up suddenly and puts sewing away.*) Sally, I'm a-goin' to make that special spoon-bread your pappy likes so well. It just came to my mind, all of a sudden. See if the hens have laid any new eggs, will you?

SALLY: The special spoon-bread! (*Smiles at her stepmother*) Oh, Mammy . . . can't any man resist some nice tasty cookin', I've heared tell! (*She runs out.*)

MRS. LINCOLN: A school!

NATTY: Just one of those old blab schools. Everybody talkin' at the same time, learnin' his lessons.

MRS. LINCOLN: Well, I say anybody ought to learn double in a school like that, gettin' educated through his eyes and ears both, at the same time. Sarah Bets, whyn't you go for the winter term yourself?

SARAH BETS: Me? I'm too old, Mammy. Besides . . . (*She picks up the paring knife.*)

MRS. LINCOLN: Besides . . . one of 'em winkin'. (*She chuckles. In a moment* SALLY *comes hurrying back with eggs.*)

SALLY: Here's enough eggs for the best special spoon-bread you ever made, Mammy. Now can Sarah Bets and I go tend to that business with the parin' knife?

MRS. LINCOLN (*Teasing*): I wouldn't have the *heart* to say you couldn't. (SALLY *and* SARAH BETS *go out giggling.* NATTY *looks after them.*)

NATTY: Guess I'd best be goin' too, Mis' Lincoln. Abe can meet me at the crick.

MRS. LINCOLN: I reckon there's a charge for goin' to that school, Natty?

NATTY: Yes'm. I don't know how much, though. And there's books to get. Spellin' book, 'rithmetic book, and singin' book, anyway. You really think Mr. Lincoln will let Abe go?

MRS. LINCOLN: I wouldn't be *too* surprised as he would. But I'm not one to go around countin' chickens till they're well hatched out and walkin'.

NATTY (*Looking out the door*): Holy fishhooks, there comes Mr. Lincoln himself. I'm a-goin'! You tell Abe . . . (*He ducks out the door. MRS. LINCOLN busies herself at the fireplace, poking up the fire, getting out the iron skillet. In a few moments TOM LINCOLN, dressed in backwoods costume, comes in.*)

MR. LINCOLN: 'Evenin', Sairy.

MRS. LINCOLN: 'Evenin', Tom. Come, set right down and rest yourself. Did you have a hard day workin'?

MR. LINCOLN: Hard enough. Trees get tougher every day they get older. Harder to cut.

MRS. LINCOLN: 'Course they do. Just set and get a good rest for your feet before supper.

MR. LINCOLN: Where are the young 'uns?

MRS. LINCOLN: Johnny and Tilda are weedin' in the bean patch. Leastwise they're supposed to be. Sally and Sarah Bets just went for a little walk. Gets stuffy, bein' indoors too long, you know. 'Specially when you're young.

MR. LINCOLN: And Abe?

MRS. LINCOLN: Abe's not home from Gentry's yet.

MR. LINCOLN: I've been wonderin' about Abe.

MRS. LINCOLN: Why for, Tom?

MR. LINCOLN: Big strappin' boy like that—ought to put more work behind him than he does. I'm afeared he's more than a mite lazy, Sairy.

MRS. LINCOLN: He's only twelve. And he's got his thoughts to think about.

MR. LINCOLN: Goin' on big as a man, Abe is. Could almost turn out a man's work if he'd a mind to. Trouble with Abe, he'd rather lie on the woodpile readin' than get down and split a little kindlin', to earn his salt.

MRS. LINCOLN: He's a readin' boy, all right. And he's got a good head on his shoulders. You know, Tom, if he had a little more schoolin' he'd make something out of himself. Preacher, maybe.

MR. LINCOLN: He's got enough education already. Folks in the backwoods don't need any more than to know how to write a little, figure a little, and read a little. Too much education gives a fellow ideas, Sairy. Like as if he's too good for his folks.

MRS. LINCOLN: Abe'd never be like that.

MR. LINCOLN: 'Pears to me you spend a lot of your time standin' up for Abe. I can't see he shines up to you much.

MRS. LINCOLN: I'm just thinkin' what his own mother would be thinkin', Tom. (*Busies herself with mixing bowl*) Had a little extry time this evenin'. Thought I'd mix up some of that special spoon-bread you fancy. That is, if you still fancy it.

MR. LINCOLN (*Pleased*): Can't ever have too much of that spoon-bread. (*In a moment his pleasure turns to a sigh*) Might help me take my mind off Squire Carter.

MRS. LINCOLN: He been after you again?

MR. LINCOLN: Still wantin' me to sell him that little piece of land.

MRS. LINCOLN: I don't trust him, Tom.

MR. LINCOLN: Says he's got everythin' down in black and white. I just got to sign. We could use the money, Sairy.

MRS. LINCOLN: You read what's down in black and white, Tom?

MR. LINCOLN: It's lawyer talk. I can't make much out of it. Lots of big words beatin' around the bush, seems to me.

MRS. LINCOLN: Too bad Abe couldn't a-had more schoolin'. He could of helped you figure it out.

MR. LINCOLN: Hmmm.

MRS. LINCOLN: Maybe he could even be a lawyer himself, if he had more education. Never can tell.

MR. LINCOLN: Oh, Abe'll make out all right. He's big and strong, and can't anyone swing an ax better than he can already.

MRS. LINCOLN: Reckon I'll put in an extry egg. Give it a nice rich yeller color, that-a-way. (*After a pause*) I heard some news this afternoon, Tom.

MR. LINCOLN: Did you?

MRS. LINCOLN: It'll mean more work for me, gettin' the children's clothes in shape and all.

MR. LINCOLN: For what?

MRS. LINCOLN: They'll all be needin' new wool socks for one thing. But I'm glad to do it as a hen settin' on eggs.

MR. LINCOLN: What you talkin' about, Sairy?

MRS. LINCOLN: Natty Grigsby was over this afternoon. Says Azel Dorsey is fixin' to open a school this winter.

MR. LINCOLN: School, eh?

MRS. LINCOLN: Reckon I'll put in a little more shortenin' too, while I'm at it. And sweetenin'. Can't make good spoon-bread unless you put plenty of good things inside. (*She works industriously over the mixing bowl.*) Yes, Azel Dorsey's a-goin' to open a school this winter. Can't think of anythin' could pleasure me more. The young 'uns ought to be in school, all of them. Even Sally. She's not too old—only fourteen. She'll be needin' a new linsey-woolsey dress, I reckon. And Abe'll need a new jacket. His is worn all frazzle-tazzle and out at the elbows.

MR. LINCOLN: Abe?

MRS. LINCOLN: He's just a boy yet, Tom, though he's so strappin' big. And he's got a deep-down hankerin' to larn. He's walked miles just to borrow a book!

MR. LINCOLN: Might spoil him to get more education.

MRS. LINCOLN: Not Abe. I'll make him a homespun jacket, and plenty big . . . so his arms won't go a-danglin' out of the sleeves.

MR. LINCOLN: What you so all-fired concerned over Abe for, Sairy?

MRS. LINCOLN: Could be with a mite more schoolin' Abe could read the fancy words Squire Carter got beatin' around the bush.

MR. LINCOLN: Well . . . could be.

MRS. LINCOLN: 'Pears I never mixed up a better-lookin' spoon-bread batter. And, land sakes, there's so much you'd think I'd a-doubled the receipt! (*Pause*) Wouldn't anythin' pleasure me more, Tom, than if you'd tell Abe he could go to Azel Dorsey's school.

MR. LINCOLN: Well . . .

MRS. LINCOLN: It's only for the winter. There's plenty of time for Abe to work the rest of the year.

MR. LINCOLN: There's the cost.

MRS. LINCOLN: Abe'll be glad to work to pay for it. And he won't be dreamin'-slow about *that* kind of work, I'm a-thinkin'.

MR. LINCOLN: Well . . .

MRS. LINCOLN: You tell him, Tom. Walk out with him for a piece and tell him. Tell Abe when he gets home, this very day . . . (ABE, *a tall, gangling boy of 12, ambles in.*)

ABE: Tell me what, Pappy?

MR. LINCOLN (*Shrugging*): I'm not full minded to tell you anythin' . . . not yet, leastwise.

ABE (*To* MRS. LINCOLN, *with reserved politeness*): 'Evenin', ma'am.

MRS. LINCOLN: 'Evenin' to you, Abe. I hope you didn't go leave your appetite over at Gentry's place. We're a-havin' your pappy's special spoon-bread for supper.

ABE (*Smiling, then becoming reserved again*): Reckon I better tote you some spring water before supper. (*Turns to his*

father as he picks up bucket) I got somethin' I'm full minded
to tell *you*, Pappy.

MR. LINCOLN: Ye have?

ABE: It's about Squire Carter. Happened to mention to Allen
Gentry while we were pullin' fodder that the Squire is
dickerin' to buy a piece of your land. Allen says he heard
his pappy say he'd trust Squire Carter just about as far as
a rattlesnake. Says the Squire is tricky as a red-tailed fox
when it comes to puttin' words down on paper.

MR. LINCOLN (*Standing up*): Reckon I'll walk a ways with
you to the spring, Abe. Got somethin' I'm minded to tell
you, after all. (ABE *and* MR. LINCOLN *exit.* MRS. LINCOLN
*watches them from the door. She smiles as she turns back to
work. In a moment* TILDA *and* JOHNNY *hurry in, look
around.*)

TILDA: Didn't I see Abe a-comin' across the clearin'? Where's
he at?

MRS. LINCOLN: He's gone to the spring for water, Tilda.

TILDA: Come on, Johnny, we'll follow him. (*Eagerly*) We'll
go part way and hide behind the trees like Indians . . .

JOHNNY: Like Indians.

TILDA: And jump out and scare him when he comes back.

JOHNNY (*Jumping*): Like Indians!

MRS. LINCOLN: Not so fast there, Matilda Johnston. You'd
better think of tendin' to your p's and q's. Abe's pappy is
a-walkin' with him on the spring path.

TILDA *and* JOHNNY: Oh!

TILDA: I reckon we won't be Indians and scare Abe then.

MRS. LINCOLN: Sarah Bets and Sally will be comin' home
along the road soon. Why don't you meet them instead?

TILDA (*Always ready for anything*): Come on, Johnny.

JOHNNY (*Suddenly distracted*): Where's my stone? (*He feels
his clothes, looks in pocket of shirt.*)

MRS. LINCOLN: What stone, honey boy?

JOHNNY (*On the verge of tears*): My lucky stone. Like Abe's.

TILDA: It isn't either like Abe's. It's not near as good.

JOHNNY: It is too.

TILDA (*To her mother*): Just a silly little flat stone he found near the crick. Doesn't have a hole in it like Abe's.

JOHNNY (*Whimpering*): I lost my lucky stone.

TILDA: You can find another.

JOHNNY: No, I can't. It was just as flat as Abe's, Mammy.

TILDA: But it's not lucky without a hole, silly.

JOHNNY (*Crying*): It is so.

MRS. LINCOLN: Be a honey-child, Tilda, and go with Johnny back to the bean patch. Like as not he dropped it there.

TILDA (*Pouting as she goes out with* JOHNNY): But it's no good. (MRS. LINCOLN *begins to set the table, humming as she moves around. In a moment* ABE *comes back, with an empty water pail.*)

MRS. LINCOLN (*Surprised*): Why, Abe. You been clear to the spring and back already?

ABE: Pappy told me before we got past the fence. I couldn't tote the water without thankin' you first.

MRS. LINCOLN: Thankin' me? For what, Abe?

ABE: I reckon you heard about the school?

MRS. LINCOLN: Well, yes . . .

ABE: And you brought Pappy 'round to thinkin' I should go.

MRS. LINCOLN: Whatever makes you think that, now?

ABE: I know Pappy. He never took much stock in education. But you. . . . (ABE *hesitates, as if wanting to show affection without quite knowing how.*)

MRS. LINCOLN: I'll be glad as a duck in the rain to make you a new jacket and some wool socks, Abe. And maybe I can do somethin' to lengthen your britches . . . so you'll look right pert to go to Azel Dorsey's school.

ABE (*Much touched*): If I wasn't so ganglin' big, I'd like to cry, I'm that pleased.

MRS. LINCOLN: I'm that pleased myself, Abe.

ABE: It's what I wanted more than anythin', to go to school again.

MRS. LINCOLN: I reckoned you wouldn't be like Natty Grigsby and not want to.

ABE: I can't see how you talked Pappy into it, though.

MRS. LINCOLN (*Chuckling*): As I was tellin' your sister Sally, I brought me some good cookin' receipts from Kentucky.

ABE (*Puzzled*): Can't quite figger that out . . .

MRS. LINCOLN (*Winking*): Your pappy's a great hand for likin' his vittals nice and tasty. I notice it makes a big difference how he feels, what he gets to eat. Maybe that's why I told him about this special spoon-bread for supper tonight . . . after Natty was here tellin' about the school.

ABE (*Grinning*): 'Pears like you got your two eyes open to what goes on around, all right enough.

MRS. LINCOLN: Not two, Abe. Only one open. The other one's a winkin' eye!

ABE (*Taken aback*): A winkin' eye?

MRS. LINCOLN: Above my initials, sort of like.

ABE: Where'd you . . . how'd you . . . ?

MRS. LINCOLN: Anythin' so queer about a winkin' eye, Abe?

ABE: Nothin' queer. Just funny . . . laughin' funny. (*He laughs loudly, and* MRS. LINCOLN *joins in. After a bit he sobers, takes the lucky stone from his pocket, flips it and catches it.*)

ABE: Ever heard tell of a lucky stone?

MRS. LINCOLN: 'Course I have.

ABE: This is a real good one. There's a hole plumb in the middle . . . well, maybe a *little* to one side. (*Holds it out*) I'd be pleasured to give it to you.

MRS. LINCOLN (*Blinking off a tear*): Thank you, Abe. That's real nice of you. It's a heart-close thing for you to do, son. Real heart-close.

THE END

Abraham Lincoln Speaks

BOY: "With malice toward no living soul
          for malice makes man small,
          and what is greater than a heart
          with charity for all?"

GROUP: Abraham Lincoln speaks.

GIRL: "I am not bound to win, succeed,
          but only to be true,
          and so I stand with those who stand
          for what is right to do."

GROUP: Abraham Lincoln speaks.

BOY: "Democracy? A way of life
          to save us from disaster:
          As I would not be made a slave,
          I would not be a master."

GROUP: Abraham Lincoln speaks.

GIRL: "My great concern is not if God
          is on my side. Instead,
          my great concern is: Am I on
          His side, with Him ahead?"

GROUP: Abraham Lincoln speaks.

BOY: "Let us have faith that right makes might
        and, in that faith, to dare
        to do our duty as we see
        our duty—anywhere."
GROUP: Abraham Lincoln speaks.

        Abraham Lincoln speaks to us
        across the bridge of years,
        giving us strength to carry on,
        and faith to still our fears.

        Abraham Lincoln speaks.

Young Abe Lincoln

TOM LINCOLN: "Lazy as all get out, I'm feared,"
his father said, and scratched his beard,
watching his gangling son stand still
with dreamy eyes on a distant hill.
"Lazy . . . yet Abe'll sprint ten miles
after a book, and be all smiles."

SALLY: "Solemn and deep," his sister thought,
"knowin' more sorrow than he ought."
Could he forget his mother lying
humped in the corner, fevered, dying?
"Yet . . .," Sally said beneath her breath,
"yet he can tease me half to death!"

DENNIS HANKS: "Peculiarsome," his cousin said,
watching the black-haired, shaggy head
bend to the fire to catch the light
darting across his book at night.
"Peculiarsome" that Abe should keep
straining his eyes when he might sleep!

SARAH LINCOLN: "Brainy," his second mother saw,
hearing his yarns with pride and awe.

"Abe must go back to school again,
though I'm not knowin' how, or when.
Brainy! And yet he makes me laugh
till I 'most split my sides in half."

ALL:

That was the lad on Pigeon Creek—
wind in his hair, sun on his cheek,
ax in his hand as the round year rolled
winter to warmth, summer to cold.
That was the lad who grew to be
living proof of democracy!

There Was a Lad Who Hungered

There was a lad who hungered,
but it was not for bread.
He hungered for a printed page
he had not six-times read.

There was a lad who thirsted,
but nothing he could drink
could quench his thirst for finding
a page that made him think.

There was a lad whose cupboard
was singularly bare:
not half a loaf, not half a fish,
not half a cup was there.

And yet he feasted, somehow,
with firelight in his eyes,
and patience made him humble
and hardship made him wise.

VALENTINE'S DAY

New Hearts for Old

Characters

WARREN
CAROL
KENNETH
SHARON
MOTHER
FATHER

TIME: *Late afternoon on Valentine's Day.*
SETTING: *A living room.*
AT RISE: WARREN, CAROL *and* KENNETH *are at the living room
table looking over the valentines they received at school.*

WARREN: Here's a beauty.
CAROL: Look at this.
KENNETH: Here is one you shouldn't miss.
  Read the rhyme on this one, Sis.
  (*He hands* CAROL *a valentine and she reads it and smiles.*)
CAROL: Valentines give lots of pleasure,
  Maybe more than we can measure.
  Here is one I surely treasure. (*Hands one around*)
  Oh, I *wish* we could have bought
  That fancy heart for Mom . . .
WARREN: We thought

194

That Dad would help us out. He ought!

CAROL: But we have been afraid to speak.

We had it on our minds all week . . .

KENNETH: But, somehow, Father makes us meek!

CAROL (*Resolutely*): When he comes home we can't delay,

We've got to ask him right away—

A Valentine's good just *today*

And now it's almost dinner time!

WARREN: He won't agree, I bet a dime:

Dad and Valentines don't rhyme!

CAROL: I won't give up until we've tried.

KENNETH (*Dreamily*): That Valentine is deep and wide

And full of chocolate creams inside . . .

Don't you think that Mom would love it?

WARREN: I don't think! I'm *certain* of it.

CAROL: Such a nice red bow above it,

Tied around the big red heart . . . (*Stops suddenly*)

Say, we aren't so very smart—

Let's let Sharon have a part!

WARREN: Sharon? She's too little yet.

KENNETH: Don't forget she's Father's pet.

She could turn the trick, I bet.

CAROL (*Going to kitchen door and calling*): Sharon! Will you
come a minute?

WARREN: Well, perhaps there's something in it.

With her help we'll, maybe, win it. (SHARON *comes hopping
in, singing a nursery rhyme in a singsong voice.*)

SHARON: "Handy Pandy, Jack-a-dandy,

Loves plum cake and sugar candy.

He bought some at a grocer's shop,

And out he came, hop, hop, hop."

CAROL: Sharon, listen, we've a plan

To make Mom happy.

KENNETH   If we can.

CAROL: We'll buy a big red Valentine,
　And you can help with it just fine.
WARREN: A Valentine all full of candy,
　So Mom can feel like Jack-a-dandy.
SHARON: Candy Valentine? That's funny!
WARREN: All we need is just some money.
　The box is waiting at the store.
KENNETH: There's nothing Mom would care for more.
CAROL (*To* SHARON):
　You tell Father when he comes
　Our money is in *little* sums,
　And we just need a paper dollar.
WARREN: I can hear him give a holler!
CAROL: Just a dollar, and we'll hop
　Like Handy Pandy to the shop,
　And buy the Valentine non-stop.
SHARON: Candy Valentine?
CAROL:　　　　　　　　　Yes . . . from
　The four of us, with love to Mom! (SHARON *nods happily,*
　and looks at the valentines on the table.)
WARREN: I bet that Father won't recall
　What day it is today, at all.
　He'll think it's just like any other.
CAROL: I'm sure that's not the case with Mother.
KENNETH: I think a certain heart-shaped gift
　Would really give her quite a lift. (*There is a noise outside,*
　and a door bangs. Children look up.)
WARREN: Guess that must be Father now.
KENNETH: I'm full of butterflies, and how.
CAROL: Sharon, don't forget to ask . . .
WARREN: I'm glad that *I* don't have the task. (FATHER
　comes in briskly with newspaper. He nods at the children.)
FATHER: Good evening, children.
CHILDREN: 'Evening, Father.

FATHER (*Setting himself in his favorite chair*):
Hope you haven't been a bother.
Have you all been good? Where's Mother?
CAROL: Making some dessert or other. (FATHER *begins to read. Children look at each other. Then* CAROL *nudges* SHARON *and nods.* SHARON *hops over to* FATHER, *singing as she goes, to the "Handy Pandy" tune.*)
SHARON: Mom is just like Handy Pandy,
Loves plum cake and sugar candy.
Can't we hurry hop, hop, hop,
And buy it at the candy shop?
FATHER (*Not paying any attention*):
Of course. Of course. And now be quiet.
Father's tired—and won't deny it.
SHARON: You mean you'll let us go and buy it?
FATHER: Buy it? (*Puts down paper*) What?
CHILDREN: You said "of course."
FATHER (*Frowning*):
I'll have to track this to its source:
What's this nonsense anyway?
Buy it . . . ?
CAROL: It's a *special* day.
FATHER: Special? Special? News to me.
There's nothing special *I* can see. (SHARON *runs to living-room table and brings back a pile of valentines.*)
SHARON: Valentines! Just look at these.
FATHER (*Making a face*):
Don't suggest I read them, please.
Valentines are pretty silly.
CAROL: Some are beautiful and frilly.
FATHER: Just a foolish waste of money! (*The children look at each other with foreboding.*)
SHARON: Daddy, now you're talking funny:
You just said of course we could . . .

FATHER (*Impatiently*): Something I misunderstood!

SHARON: You said *of course*, about the candy
    For our special Handy Pandy.

FATHER (*Raising his voice*):
    What's this all about? I say,
    Is everybody daft today?

SHARON: Now we only need the dollar.

FATHER: Dollar!

WARREN (*Aside to* KENNETH): See, I knew he'd holler.

SHARON: Yes, to get Mom's Valentine—
    A candy one that's extra fine.

FATHER (*Almost beside himself*):
    Carol, will you explain this, please?

CAROL: We *could* get Valentines like these, (*Points to valentines*)
    But we wanted Mom's more dandy:
    There's a heart-box full of candy
    Down the street, but we are low
    On cash for *such* a heart, you know.

FATHER: And so you thought that I'd supply it?

SHARON: We'll go hop, hop, hop, and buy it.

FATHER: So. Well, listen—get this straight:
    Valentines don't carry weight
    With a grown-up like your mother.
    One's more foolish than another.
    She knows you love her well enough,
    Without a lot of silly stuff.
    She outgrew that *long* ago.
    As for candy . . . well, I know
    She shouldn't have it. Makes her fat!
    I have to watch a thing like that.
    I have to keep this family sane.

CAROL: But Father . . .

FATHER: Can't I make it plain
    That since I was a ten-year-old

Valentines have left me cold?

Now I'll thank you to keep quiet. (*Goes back to paper*)

SHARON: We can't hop, hop, hop, and buy it? (MOTHER *comes in from the kitchen with her apron on. She is surprised to see* FATHER *home so soon.*)

MOTHER (*To* FATHER):

Good evening, dear.

How nice you're here.

FATHER: I got home good and early. (*Smiles at* MOTHER)

MOTHER: Oh, Valentines! (*Goes to table to look at them*)

How this one shines . . .

SHARON: The edge is cut all curly.

MOTHER: And look at this!

I wouldn't miss

Inspecting all these rhymes. (*She pores over the valentines.*)

FATHER: What's that you say?

MOTHER: How sweet! How gay!

It brings back good old times.

I always thought

That people ought

To send their friends a greeting.

CAROL: And so do I. (*Glances at* FATHER)

FATHER: What nonsense. Why?

I'd rather take a beating.

MOTHER: These new designs

For Valentines

Are different from the old ones:

I have a few

I'll show to you . . .

Some ancient pink-and-gold ones

I found today

All stored away

In mothballs, in the attic.

WARREN: You saved them, Mom?

KENNETH: Whom were they from?

FATHER: Such conduct is erratic!

MOTHER: Just wait for me
And you will see . . . (*She hurries out hall door*)

KENNETH: What did she find, I wonder?

CAROL: She *does* still care.

FATHER: Well, I declare.
I may have made a blunder.

WARREN: Let's decorate
Around Mom's plate
With Valentines, for dinner.

CAROL (*Picking up scissors and red paper*):
Let's cut some darts
And bright red hearts.
Here's one for a beginner.

SHARON: I'll cut some too.

KENNETH: It's hard to do.

SHARON (*Running to* FATHER *with paper and scissors*):
You'll help me, won't you, Father?

FATHER: What's that? Who, me?

SHARON: Just two or three . . .

CAROL: Don't, Sharon, be a bother.
I'll help you cut. (SHARON *hesitates.* FATHER *reaches for scissors and paper.*)

FATHER: A heart? Tut . . . tut . . .
Of course, there's nothing to it. (*Begins to cut*)

SHARON: But, Daddy, look!
You've cut a crook.

FATHER: That's where a dart went through it! (MOTHER *comes back with a cardboard box.* FATHER *quickly gives* SHARON *the scissors and paper and shoos her away. He buries his nose in the paper. The children are curious to see what is in the box.*)

MOTHER: I've saved this, dears,

For twenty years . . . (*Lifts out an old-fashioned valentine*)
It's really quite a treasure.
I still recall
The boy and all . . .
It gave me so much pleasure.
FATHER: What's that you say?
Who was it, pray? (*Clears throat*)
I find this most distressing.
MOTHER: A charming chap.
FATHER: Some silly . . . sap!
MOTHER: Why don't you all start guessing?
CAROL: You mean we *know?*
MOTHER: Oh, yes. Although
He's older now, and fatter,
And quite sedate.
FATHER: At any rate
He's not around to matter.
MOTHER: Your error, dear.
He lives right here!
(*The children look puzzled. Then* CAROL *blurts out.*)
CAROL: You mean that *Father* sent it?
KENNETH (*Reading verse on valentine*):
It says, "Be mine,
Sweet Valentine." (MOTHER *looks at* FATHER *with a mischievous smile.*)
MOTHER: I hope, my dear, you meant it.
FATHER: Of course I did.
A kid's a kid!
MOTHER: You must have been near twenty. (MOTHER *smiles, and the children look at* FATHER *with amusement.*)
FATHER (*Gasping*):
I sent you that!
I'll eat my hat.
WARREN: You must have loved her plenty.

MOTHER (*Holding up a heart-shaped box*):
And next year, this.

KENNETH: Too good to miss!

FATHER: I feel . . . a . . . little harried.

MOTHER: And after a while.
This perfume vial, (*Holds up a little bottle*)
The year before we married.

FATHER (*Weakly*): I've had enough.
You *saved* that stuff?

MOTHER: This box is full of riches.

SHARON: Let's see some more. (*Eagerly the children bend over
MOTHER'S box, looking at the contents. FATHER stealthily
gets up and tiptoes out the hall door.*)

WARREN: What's this thing for—
All full of little stitches? (*MOTHER picks up something that
looks like a little satchet bag and smells it dreamily. She
smiles. Then she passes it to each of the children to smell.*)

MOTHER: Just sniff, and guess.

CAROL (*The last one to take the satchet*): Rose petals?

MOTHER: Yes!
From every gift of roses.
Oh, Valentines
Are treasure-mines
Much more than one supposes.

SHARON (*Looking around*): Where's Daddy?

WARREN: Say,
He's gone away!

MOTHER: He seemed a little harassed.

CAROL: He tiptoed out
Without a doubt
Because he felt embarrassed:
He was so *sure*
You'd not endure
A Valentine. Oh, never!

MOTHER: He's very dear,
   But I've a fear
   He isn't always . . . clever.
KENNETH: If only we
   Could make him see
   That Valentines aren't folly,
   Not dull and dumb
   And wearisome,
   But gay and bright and jolly. (MOTHER *nods, and goes out
   to the kitchen.*)
WARREN: And even yet
   His wife would get
   A lift from such a greeting . . .
CAROL: To know that she
   Is prized, and he
   Does not just think of eating! (*She is silent for a moment,
   then bursts out suddenly.*)
   Let's make a fine
   Big Valentine
   For Father, and surprise him.
KENNETH: He may not know
   We love him, so
   Perhaps we should advise him.
WARREN: And then he may
   Admit this day
   Is really an occasion,
   And next year get
   The best heart yet
   For Mom, without persuasion.
   (*Eagerly the children set to work at the living-room table,
   making* FATHER'S *valentine.*)
CAROL: He'll swell with pride
   To read inside
   This heart, of our affection.

KENNETH: He'll grunt and blush
　And say, "Tush, tush,"
　But make a close inspection.
CAROL: He *can't* be mad.
SHARON: He'll be so glad
　He may give us the money.
WARREN: Then we could get
　The candy yet. (*Sighs*)
　But Father . . . well, he's funny.
　(MOTHER *comes back with a plate of heart-shaped tarts.*)
MOTHER: The King of Hearts
　Shall have some tarts!
　I'll fix them on the table. (MOTHER *works at the dining
　table, her back to the hall door.*)
　I'll trim his plate.
　He'll dine in state.
　I'll please him, if I'm able.
　(FATHER *appears at the hall door with a big red heart-
　shaped candy box. He gestures frantically and comically at
　the children. They are too busy to notice.*)
SHARON (*Proudly, to* MOTHER):
　This Valentine,
　So big and fine,
　We're fixing up for Father. (FATHER *gives a start.* MOTHER
　keeps trimming the table.)
MOTHER: You're fixing, too?
　How nice of you
　To go to all that bother. (FATHER *finally catches* SHARON'S
　eye and beckons to her, signaling her to be quiet. SHARON
　*slips over to him and he gives her the candy box, gesturing
　at the other children. No one else notices.* SHARON *tiptoes
　back to the living-room table with the box and puts it down.
　The other children look at it with their mouths open. Then
　they see* FATHER, *who warns them to keep quiet. He takes*

*a tiny package from his pocket and holds it up for children
to see. They can't figure out what it is.)*
Almost done!
It's always fun
To have a few surprises.
CAROL: Aren't you right! (*She is excited but tries to sound calm.*)
I think tonight
They come in several sizes. (*The children sign a card to
put on the candy box.* FATHER, *still at the door, tries to
make the children understand that he has bought* MOTHER
a little bottle of perfume. He points to MOTHER, *holds up
bottle, sniffs, smiles, sniffs again. He is so funny the
children finally burst out laughing.* MOTHER *turns to look
at them.*)
MOTHER: Why so gay?
CAROL: Because today
Is such a nice invention. (CAROL *jumps up and runs to*
MOTHER, *holding her hands over* MOTHER'S *eyes.*)
CHILDREN: Close your eyes! (SHARON *runs to the dining table
with the candy box and puts it at* MOTHER'S *place.* WARREN
hurries to get the little perfume bottle from FATHER. *He
puts it at* MOTHER'S *place on the table.* KENNETH *quickly
fixes big valentine at* FATHER'S *place.*)
CHILDREN *and* FATHER: Surprise! Surprise! (CAROL *takes
hands from* MOTHER'S *eyes.*)
CAROL: Now, Valentines, attention!
The King of Hearts (*Nods at* FATHER)
Will find his tarts
And message of devotion.
The Queen (*Nods at* MOTHER) will find
Another kind
Of token, we've a notion.
FATHER (*Looking at table*):
What's this I see?

Er . . . er . . . for *me?*

I . . . I feel I'm going to smother.

MOTHER (*Looking at table, picking up candy box and reading card*):

How super-fine!

"A Valentine

From all of us to Mother." (*She picks up the perfume bottle and opens the wrapping.*)

And perfume! Oh, (*Looks lovingly at* FATHER)

How *did* you know?

ALL (*Dancing around*): Today beats any other!

THE END

Hearts, Tarts, and Valentines

Characters

READER
QUEEN
KING
MESSENGER
GUARD
JACK OF HEARTS
A MAN
A WOMAN
A CHILD
TOWNSPEOPLE

TIME: *A day in early February.*
SETTING: *The kingdom of the King and Queen of Hearts.*
The throne is near the back of the stage.
AT RISE: *The* READER *is turning over the pages of a large book*
of fairy tales. He stands or sits on one side of the stage.

READER: Hmmmm. (*Turns over pages*) "Hearts, Tarts, and
Valentines." I never read that before. I wonder what it's
like. (*In a reading tone of voice*) Once upon a time, as everybody knows, the Queen of Hearts made some tarts, all on
a summer day. But as everybody does *not* know, the Queen

of Hearts also made some tarts on a winter day. On a day in February. And someone stole them all away. Now it happened that the King of Hearts (KING *comes in and goes to sit on his throne*) was almost as fond of tarts as he was of his son, the Jack of Hearts. And so, on this February day, the King called for some of his wife's tarts as a special treat. Imagine his surprise and anger when he learned that all the Queen's fresh tarts had just been stolen. (*The* QUEEN *comes rushing in, in a flurry.*)

QUEEN:

My tarts! My tarts have all been taken.
They stole the tarts but left the bacon!

KING (*Rising from his throne and shaking his fist*):

That house of cards across the river
Is back of this, I bet a sliver.
The King of Diamonds and his court
Would do a thing of *just* this sort.
(*Clasps hands loudly*)
Messenger! Messenger! (MESSENGER *runs in.*)
Hurry, my man, and tell all the guards on duty
They must capture the thief who stole the Queen's tarts and return all the booty! (MESSENGER *salutes and runs out.*)

QUEEN (*Almost weeping*):

To make matters worse they were your favorite tarts,
Full of cocoanut and tutti-frutti!

KING (*Holding his hands to his heart*):

Cocoanut and tutti-frutti!
Oh, cocoanut and tutti-frutti.
(*He staggers out with the* QUEEN *holding his arm.*)

READER: The King's Messenger lost no time broadcasting the news of the theft. First he turned his loudspeaker in the direction of the river, where most of the Guards of Hearts were stationed. You see, the river was the boundary between the Hearts and Diamonds, who had been mortal enemies for more than a year. Formerly they had been quite good friends. They belonged to the same clubs. They were alike in calling a spade a spade, and all that. In fact, it had even been rumored on more than one occasion that the two houses might be united in one pack, so to speak. For the Jack of Hearts had lost his head to the Princess of Diamonds. But that was before the unfortunate episode of the lace handkerchief. That changed everything! All the friendship between the Hearts and Diamonds got lost in the shuffle. We will explain about the lace handkerchief in a moment. (*The* MESSENGER *is heard calling offstage, then he comes running in with a megaphone.*)

MESSENGER:

Warning, warning, everyone!
A frightful deed has just been done.
Catch the thief who stole the tarts
Concocted by our Queen of Hearts!

(*A* GUARD *approaches.* MESSENGER *turns to* GUARD.) Have you seen any suspicious-looking Diamonds around? Any Diamonds in the rough? The thief who stole the tarts is undoubtedly a Diamond.

GUARD: Do you think so?

MESSENGER: Of course. Who but a Diamond would stoop so low? Remember the lace handkerchief . . . (MESSENGER *exits.*)

GUARD (*Putting his hand over his heart*): The lace handkerchief! How can I ever forget it? (MESSENGER *is heard calling "Warning, warning" off stage.* GUARD *exits.*)

READER: No one on either side of the river could forget about the lace handkerchief. The Hearts could not forget about it because their King was sure a Diamond stole his lace handkerchief the day of the Tournament of Shuffles. At least, the King rode over the bridge with his handkerchief, and came back without it. The Diamonds could not forget about the lace handkerchief because their feelings were hurt to think the King of Hearts could accuse them of such a deed. You would think that such a trivial thing as a handkerchief could be ironed out without much difficulty. But no. Instead of getting better, dealings between the Hearts and Diamonds got worse with every day that passed. And now, on top of the lace handkerchief, came this matter of the stolen tarts. (*The* JACK OF HEARTS, *carrying a platter covered with a napkin, tiptoes in, looks around stealthily, and prepares to cross the stage. Just then the* GUARD *returns.*)

GUARD: Halt! Who goes there?

JACK (*Putting up his arm to hide his face*): M-m-m-me.

GUARD (*Threateningly*): Who are you and what are you carrying on that plate? (*Looks at* JACK's *face*) Ah, the Jack of Hearts! (*Peeks under the napkin*) You knave! Are those the Queen's tarts?

JACK: Y-y-yes.

GUARD: Well, what have you to say for yourself?

JACK (*Beseechingly*): Have pity on me, Guard. I am in a terrible state. Heart trouble! And of the worst kind. Ever since the episode of the lace handkerchief my parents have forbidden me to see the Princess of Diamonds. And I left my heart in her keeping. (*Clutches his heart*) My poor heart!

GUARD: So? What has that got to do with stealing the Queen's tarts?

JACK: My parents will not even allow me to write to the Princess. And so I thought . . . I hoped . . . if I could bribe a Guard of Diamonds on the other side of the bridge to take these tarts to the Princess . . . she would know I still loved her. You see, these are specially nice tarts— cocoanut and tutti-frutti.

GUARD (*Licking his lips*): Cocoanut and tutti-frutti? (MES-

SENGER *is heard off stage calling: "Warning, warning, every-one," etc.* GUARD *remembers his duty.*)
Sorry, Jack, but it's my bounden duty
To take you to the palace with your booty.
Cocoanut, you say, and tutti-frutti?

JACK (*Looking at the tarts*):
Surely no one can accuse me of wanting to waste them.
If only the Princess of Diamonds were able to taste them,
She'd know that my love wasn't cold or worn down at the heel,
That all would be well if we only could get a fair deal!
But how can my father, the King, see that I want to wed—
At the tiniest mention of Diamonds, my father sees red.

GUARD:
I know. And the culprit's in danger of losing his head.
Which all goes to show that some things are much better unsaid.

(GUARD *puts hand over heart. Then he takes* JACK *out.*)

READER: And so the Guard brought Jack and the platter of tarts back to the palace. As might be expected, the King and Queen were astonished to find it was their own son, and not a Diamond, who had stolen the tarts. There was only one consolation. Not a single tart was missing! Poor Jack. He took his scolding without saying a word. He did not *dare* explain how he planned to send the tarts across the river to the Princess of Diamonds. Ever since the episode of the lace handkerchief, no one in the kingdom had the courage to mention a Diamond in the King's presence. And of course, things were just as bad on the other side of the river. No one dared mention a Heart to the royal house of Diamonds for fear of losing his head. The common people, both Hearts and Diamonds, wondered if it were in the cards for the quarrel ever to be patched up. They thought the whole affair very foolish. Who wanted a lace handkerchief anyway? What use was it? What difference did it make? As punishment for stealing the tarts, Jack was sentenced to guard duty for one week on the river bank. He found himself stationed right next to the guard who had caught him with the tarts. The two struck up a great friendship, and it must be said, they spent much more time talking to each other than guarding the river. Mostly they talked about the foolish quarrel over the lace handkerchief. They wondered what they could do to patch things up. How could they play their cards to turn the trick? (GUARD *and* JACK *enter, and pace slowly back and forth.*)

GUARD:

It's only the high uppy-ups
Who sit with their tarts and their cups
Who argue and stew and make a to-do.
It's only the high uppy-ups.

I've talked to a number of men—
We'd like to be friendly again,
We're tired of fuss—seems foolish to us.
We'd like to be friendly again.

JACK:

But how can you do it, I ask?
It seems an impossible task.
I wish you could trace that small piece of lace . . .
But how can you do it, I ask?

If Diamonds would own to the theft
And send back whatever is left
And say they regret and hope we'll forget,
No cause for a grudge would be left.

GUARD (*Putting his hand over his heart*):

But what if they're innocent, Jack,
And haven't the lace to send back?

It may be a *Heart* picked it up from the start,
All trampled and ragged and black.

And that wouldn't fix things, I fear.
The King would say, "Well, it is clear
They trained a trick horse to do it, of course."
No, that wouldn't fix things, I fear.
(*The* GUARD *takes a rumpled piece of lace from his pocket over his heart and hands it to* JACK.)
JACK (*Amazed, looking at the lace*):
The lace! It's all soiled and abused.
But *Diamonds* cannot be accused
Of having it now. You got it—but how?
I'm certainly very confused. (*They go out.*)
READER: Quickly the Guard explained how it happened. On the day of the Tournament of Shuffles he noticed a piece of lace lying in the dirt on the other side of the river. It was torn and trampled on, for the cavalry of both Hearts and Diamonds had galloped that way. The Guard picked it up, for his mother had taught him always to pick up pins and string and anything that might have the slightest value. He stuffed the bit of lace in his pocket and thought no more of it. The next day he heard the Town Crier reading a proclamation accusing the House of Diamonds of dealing a mean trick. The King of Hearts had gone to the Tournament with his best lace handkerchief. He had come home without it. Proof enough that some Diamond had stolen it from his pocket during the Tournament! Diamonds were not to be trusted! The Guard never once imagined that the trampled bit of lace he found could be the King's best handkerchief. Days passed. The bad feeling between the crowned heads of Hearts and Diamonds grew worse and worse. Finally the Town Crier announced that anyone in the kingdom of Hearts who so much as mentioned a Dia-

mond to the King would lose his head. It was not until two
months after the Tournament, when the Guard was empty-
ing out his coat pockets before sending his uniform to the
cleaner, that he came across the torn bit of lace. Absent-
mindedly he smoothed it out, and then—to his dismay—
he could see it had a border of tiny hearts, with a larger
heart on a coat of arms in the middle. There was no doubt
about it, it was the King's lost handkerchief! The cause
of all the trouble! (*The* GUARD *and* JACK *enter again.*)

GUARD: I didn't want to lose my head
    . . . I didn't want to lose my head. . . .

JACK:
    Oh, something must be done and soon.
    Let's start this very afternoon:
    Let's spread the news—the King won't hear,
    And think of trumps and tricks to clear
    The cold and hostile atmosphere.

GUARD:
    Let's gather up some eager people
    And meet beneath the old church steeple
    And try to figure out a way
    To get both kingdoms feeling gay. (*They go out quickly.*)

READER: And so that very afternoon there was a meeting of
townspeople in the shadow of the steeple of the church.
(*Townspeople begin to come in, some alone, some in groups or
pairs.*) Everyone was anxious to do something to patch up
the quarrel between the two royal houses. The Guard took
charge of the meeting (GUARD *and* JACK *come in*), with
Jack as his trump card. First of all, the Guard explained
that Jack had lost his heart to the Princess of Diamonds,
and she had lost her heart to him. What is more she wore
his diamond. All they needed was a fair deal. Then the
Guard explained that nobody had stolen the lace handkerchief. It was all a mistake. The Diamonds had been un-

justly accused. The King's handkerchief had merely fallen from his pocket and been trampled on by the cavalry of both kingdoms. There was a great chorus of "Ohs" and "Ahs" among the townspeople as the Guard finished his story and held up the bit of lace he had found.

A MAN: Quarrels are mostly just that silly.

GUARD: The King won't listen, willy-nilly.

JACK: Even I could not compel him . . .

A MAN: We dare not risk our necks to tell him.

A WOMAN:
My relatives across the river
Also have to shake and shiver:
They think this quarrel a silly thing
But dare not go and tell their King.

A CHILD: There must be something we can do.

GUARD: Has anyone a plan? A clue?

A WOMAN:
To *write* the rulers might be better—
They can't behead a headless letter!
(*A shout of approval goes up from the crowd.*)
Two days from now is just halfway
In February. On that day
Let's all send letters, not of fear
But love and friendliness and cheer,
Messages of merry sorts
To both the Kings of both the courts.
Let February 14th stand
For kindliness—a special brand.
(*Shouts of approval again*)

A MAN:
We needn't sign our names at all.
The stack of mail will be so tall.
The Kings will *have* to pay attention.

A WOMAN:
I've hit upon a good invention:

Let's deck our notes with doves and darts
And cut them in the shape of hearts.

A CHILD:
And mount them gracefully in place
Upon a piece of paper lace!
(*More shouts from crowd*)

GUARD:
The hearts, of course, will stand for us,
The lace for what provoked the fuss,
With diamonds on the edge . . . and thus
With all united each to each
We'll have this little truth to teach:
United we shall stand and flourish,
Divided we shall fall and perish;
Divided we shall not survive,
United we shall stand and thrive!
(*Applause and shouts from crowd as they exit.*)

READER: And so the news spread among the commoners in both kingdoms that February 14th was to be a day of forgiveness and love. Everyone on both sides of the river, old and young, fat and thin, tall and short, began to write loving messages on bright red hearts mounted on paper lace with diamonds around the edge. Never had the townspeople had more fun. And *never* did the King of Hearts and the King of Diamonds receive as much mail as on that fourteenth day of February. (KING OF HEARTS *comes in with an armload of mail and sits on his throne. He seems to be very happy, as he looks over the messages. In a moment* JACK *comes in with more mail.*)

JACK: These are from across the river.

KING (*Looking at some of the letters* JACK *brings*):
They're so nice they make me quiver.
(KING *reads aloud.*)
Let's be buddies, let's be pards,
Let's dismiss the border guards.

Don't you see, it's in the cards!
(KING *reads another.*)
Friendship never questions whether
It is spring or winter weather—
Hearts and diamonds go together . . . always.
QUEEN (*Coming in with plate of tarts*):
Have another tart, my love.
KING:
What are they concocted of? (*Takes one, looks at it*)
This one surely is a beauty.
QUEEN (*Beaming*):
Cocoanut and tutti-frutti!
READER: At the same moment the same things were happening on the other side of the river in the royal house of Diamonds. The King of Diamonds was enjoying all the lovely messages the mailman kept bringing. And he was munching his Queen's tarts at the same time and feeling very pleased with the world. As might be expected, with such an abundance of love and good nature overflowing the boundaries of both kingdoms, the two royal houses soon got together for a grand reunion. Jack and the Princess of Diamonds fell into each other's arms. The two Kings exchanged tarts and the two Queens exchanged recipes, and everyone had a wonderful time. Needless to say, all hard feelings were quickly forgotten. But just to make sure some silly thing (like a lace handkerchief) would not disrupt the peace and happiness again, the two Kings proclaimed February 14th as a day of forgiveness and love, to be observed each year without fail by all the people of both kingdoms. And from that day to this, everyone has exchanged bright red hearts mounted on paper lace. And without doubt the custom will be continued until doomsday . . . because, as you have seen, it's in the cards!

THE END

What's in a Name?

(BOYS *and* GIRLS *hold bright cards with large letters as they speak their lines*)

GROUP: What do we need for Valentines?
GIRL: A *V* . . . that stands for verses,
some so gay
they're tucked away
in bureau drawers and purses!

GROUP: What do we need for Valentines?
BOY: An *A* . . . that stands for arrows,
for shooting hearts
with paper darts—
instead of shooting sparrows.

GROUP: What do we need for Valentines?
GIRL: An *L* . . . for love a-plenty:
here's love for you,
although it's true
I'm also loving twenty!

GROUP: What do we need for Valentines?
BOY: Some envelopes to hide them.
They start with *E.*

as you can see,
and oh, the fun inside them.

GROUP: What do we need for Valentines?
GIRL: An *N* . . . for novel notions
of how to say
a different way,
"I love you, dear—just oceans."

GROUP: What do we need for Valentines?
BOY: A *T* . . . that stands for target:
a tempting heart
and well-aimed dart
addressed to Ann or Marget.

GROUP: What do we need for Valentines?
GIRL: An *I* . . . for "I-love-you"-ing!
For "I implore"
and "I adore"
and "I am yours for wooing."

GROUP: What do we need for Valentines?
BOY: An *N* . . . for nonsense, maybe:
a funny rhyme
to pass the time
for John or Jane or Abie.

GROUP: What do we need for Valentines?
GIRL: An *E* . . . for emblems showing:
for Cupid's darts
and flowers and hearts
and other signs as knowing.

GROUP: What do we need for Valentines?
BOY: An *S* . . . to stand for sender,
       and secrets, too:
       Is this from you?
       This sentiment so tender!

GROUP: *That's* what we need for Valentines,
       for fancy ones and clever,
       and here's a cheer
       from far and near
       to Valentines . . . forever!

Valentines!

Valentines crimson through and through,
Valentines full of I-Love-You,
frilly ones, shiny,
silly ones, tiny,
middle-sized, big, and please-be-mine-y,
Valentines sweet as sugar and spice,
Valentines, Valentines—aren't you nice!

Valentines winsome as can be,
Valentines gay with love-from-me,
tricky ones, clever,
full of endeavor,
arrows, and Cupids, and love-forever,
Valentines HEARTY—every one,
Valentines, Valentines, aren't you fun!

Valentine's Day

The aspens and the maples now
have lacy frost on every bough,

And through the woods the shadows go,
writing verses on the snow.

The tops of weeds are sealed up tight
in little envelopes of white,

And listen! in the frosty pines
snowbirds twitter Valentines.

WASHINGTON'S BIRTHDAY

Washington Marches On

(*A Living Newspaper*)

Characters

Scene 1: AUGUSTINE WASHINGTON, *Virginia planter*

Scene 2:
{ BETTY WASHINGTON, *13*
GEORGE WASHINGTON, *14*
SAMUEL WASHINGTON, *12*
MARY BALL WASHINGTON, *their mother*

Scene 3:
{ LORD FAIRFAX
LAWRENCE WASHINGTON
GEORGE WASHINGTON, *almost 16*

Scene 4:
{ ANNE FAIRFAX WASHINGTON
GEORGE WASHINGTON, *20*

Scene 5:
{ GENERAL BRADDOCK
GEORGE WASHINGTON, *23*
1ST SOLDIER
2ND SOLDIER
3RD SOLDIER

Scene 6:
{ BETTY WASHINGTON LEWIS, *25*
MARY BALL WASHINGTON

Scene 7:
{ VOICE FROM AUDIENCE
GEORGE WASHINGTON, *43*
JOHN ADAMS

223

Scene 8: $\left\{\begin{array}{l}\text{1ST SENTRY}\\\text{2ND SENTRY}\\\text{MESSENGER}\end{array}\right.$

Scene 9: $\left\{\begin{array}{l}\text{MARTHA WASHINGTON}\\\text{GEORGE WASHINGTON, }46\\\text{ORDERLY}\\\text{MARQUIS DE LAFAYETTE}\end{array}\right.$

Scene 10: $\left\{\begin{array}{l}\text{1ST NEWSBOY}\\\text{2ND NEWSBOY}\end{array}\right.$

Scene 11: $\left\{\begin{array}{l}\text{GEORGE WASHINGTON, }52\\\text{NELLY CUSTIS, }5\end{array}\right.$

Scene 12: $\left\{\begin{array}{l}\text{CHANCELLOR LIVINGSTON}\\\text{GEORGE WASHINGTON, }57\\\text{VOICES FROM AUDIENCE}\end{array}\right.$

Scene 13: SCHOOLMASTER

Scene 14: BOYS *and* GIRLS *with flags.*

CHORUS: *Any number of boys and girls.*

NOTE: *This play may be staged as simply or as elaborately as desired, with or without costumes.* CHORUS *may sit on one side of the stage, or in the audience. If the play is given in front of a classroom, blackboard may be used for dates. Otherwise, large date-cards should be lined up against back wall as play progresses.*

SETTING: *On stage are two chairs and a table holding paper, ink and quill pen. Any scenes requiring furniture take place near these furnishings. All other scenes take place at other parts of the stage.*

CHORUS:

When was he born, George Washington?
What was the place and date?

Solo

(Holding up card or writing on blackboard: Born—1732):

Seventeen hundred thirty-two.
Virginia, the State.

Scene 1

AT RISE: AUGUSTINE WASHINGTON, *a Virginia planter, comes in excitedly, goes to table, takes paper and quill and begins to write.*

AUGUSTINE *(As he writes)*: Wakefield on the Potomac
February 22, 1732
To Lawrence and Augustine Washington
Appleby School. England
My Dear Sons: It is with great pleasure that I inform you that you now have a half-brother, born this very day. The baby and his mother are doing well. We have decided, after some discussion, to name him George. Unfortunately it may be some years before you will be able to make his acquaintance.

I trust you are doing well in your studies and working diligently. I trust also that you are enjoying this acquaintance with our mother country. Enclosed you will find a draft of money for your use, over and above expenses, in celebration of the happy event that has taken place today. Your affectionate father, Augustine Washington.

(He nods with satisfaction, seals letter, hurries out with it.)
CHORUS: Washington marches on!

*   *   *

CHORUS:

How did he grow, George Washington?

Solo:

Strong as a sturdy tree.

Chorus:

Did he have hopes and youthful dreams?

Solo:

(*Holding up card or writing on blackboard: 1746—To Sea?*):

He wanted to go to sea!

Scene 2

At Rise: George, Betty, *and* Samuel *hurry in with packet of mail.*

Betty: *What* will Uncle Joseph's letter say, I wonder . . . about your going to sea, George? I hope he doesn't say you should.

George: When I want to go so badly, Betty?

Betty: But I don't *like* to think of you going so far away. And it's so *dangerous.* That's what Mama says.

Samuel: George isn't afraid of danger. Are you, George?

Betty: I wonder if Uncle Joseph knows how *anxious* we've been waiting to hear from him? (*Takes up letter, tries to look through envelope.*) It certainly takes a long time for a letter to get from London, England, to Fredericksburg, Virginia.

George: Too long. I've had my things packed for weeks. And Lawrence has the promise of a commission in the Navy for me. All I need is for Mother to say *yes.* (*Sighs*) I wish she'd listen to brother Lawrence, instead of asking Uncle Joseph.

Betty: She thinks Lawrence is too young to give advice.

SAMUEL: He's twenty-eight. That's old!

GEORGE: And he's married to Anne Fairfax, and he's been in the Navy fighting in the West Indies, and he's master of Mount Vernon, and . . .

BETTY: Still, Mama thinks Uncle Joseph knows best. You know how she has depended on him, ever since Father died.

GEORGE: Well, there's a good chance he'll say yes, anyway. (*Calls*) Mother! Mother! The letter has come from London. From Uncle Joseph.

MRS. WASHINGTON (*Hurrying in excitedly*): The letter! Did I hear you say the letter has come? At last. (*She takes it, hesitates*) I *trust* your Uncle's judgment is the same as mine. (*Opens letter*) Hmmmm. (*Reads to herself while others watch.*)

BETTY: What does he *say*, Mama?

GEORGE (*Anxiously*): May I go?

MRS. WASHINGTON: Listen to this: "I understand that you have some thoughts of putting your son George to sea. I think he had better be put apprentice to a *tinker*. The common sailor has no liberties . . . they will use him like a dog." (*To* GEORGE) Do you hear, George? It is not only dangerous to go to sea, but they'd use you like a dog! So . . . it is decided. After this excellent advice from your Uncle, assuredly you must not go to sea. What else is there in the post, Betty? (*She and* BETTY *exit one side, looking at mail.* GEORGE *and* SAMUEL *start out other side.*)

GEORGE (*Obviously disappointed*): Want to drive stakes for me, Sammy? I suppose there's nothing to do now but practice with Father's surveying instruments. (*Brightens*) There's something like an ocean . . . an endless sea . . . about the wilderness. If I could be a surveyor in the wilderness, I wouldn't mind not going to sea . . . very much. (*They exit.*)

CHORUS: Washington marches on!

* * *

CHORUS:

When did he help survey the lands
that rich Lord Fairfax had?

SOLO:

(*Holding up card or writing on blackboard: 1748-52—Surveyor*):

Seventeen hundred forty-eight . . .
when he was still a lad.

SCENE 3

AT RISE: LORD FAIRFAX *and* LAWRENCE *enter.* LAWRENCE
takes a paper from his pocket, holds it out.

LAWRENCE: What do you think of this, Lord Fairfax?

LORD FAIRFAX: What is it? (*Peers at paper, takes small magnifying glass from pocket*) A map?

LAWRENCE: Do you recognize it?

LORD FAIRFAX (*Studying paper*): A map of the South Meadow here at Mount Vernon, is it not? Very carefully done. Neat. Accurate, as far as I can judge. Excellent workmanship. Did your young brother George do it? I have seen him with his instruments, again and again.

LAWRENCE: Yes, George did it. Amazing, how serious he is about his maps. For a lad not quite sixteen . . .

LORD FAIRFAX: He has skill. Ambition. Patience. Self-discipline. I have been wondering, Lawrence, about the thousands of acres of wilderness I own west of the Blue Ridge Mountains. Settlers are moving in, taking what land they want, cutting timber, building cabins. I feel I should have my boundaries marked, to establish ownership. Do you think George would care to help?

LAWRENCE: Do I think . . . ! There he comes now, Lord

Fairfax, over the hill. I am sure he can answer your question better than I. (*Calls*) George! Over here, George!

LORD FAIRFAX (*Looking at map again*): A nice piece of work. Very nice indeed. (GEORGE *enters with tripod.*)

GEORGE: Good morning, Lawrence. And Lord Fairfax, sir.

LAWRENCE: Lord Fairfax has a question to ask you, George.

GEORGE: To ask *me?*

LORD FAIRFAX: And not about fox-hunting, either. Or horses. (*Clears throat*) You are interested in surveying, I notice . . .

GEORGE: Yes, sir. Very much, sir.

LORD FAIRFAX: And how far along are you?

GEORGE: I still have a great deal to learn. But I'm not *too* bad, am I, Lawrence?

LORD FAIRFAX: Would you be able to start in three weeks? On March 11, say?

GEORGE: Start what, sir?

LORD FAIRFAX: I am planning to have my wilderness lands surveyed. Would you care to be one of the party? I will pay you well.

GEORGE (*Eagerly*): Would I! Would I, sir! Oh, let me get some of my maps to show you . . . (*He runs out.* LAWRENCE *and* LORD FAIRFAX, *amused, follow.*)

CHORUS: George Washington marches on!

*   *   *

CHORUS:

When did Mount Vernon come to him—
his brother's large estate?

SOLO:

(*Holding up card or writing on blackboard: 1752—Gets Mt. Vernon*):

Seventeen hundred fifty-two,
dropped from the hands of fate.

SCENE 4

AT RISE: ANNE FAIRFAX WASHINGTON *and* GEORGE *enter, talking earnestly.*

ANNE: I need your help, George.

GEORGE: You know I will do anything I can, Anne. But I cannot bring Lawrence back . . . or your little daughter. To think of losing them both, so close together!

ANNE: Within a few weeks of each other. That was July. Now it is November, and the ache is still in my heart. They say that time heals all sorrows. But, oh, how slowly, George.

GEORGE: I know. I miss Lawrence too, more than I can say. He was so much more to me than a half-brother. Had he been full brother and father combined, I could not have loved him more.

ANNE: I am glad you had those months with him in the Bahamas last winter . . . though I missed him terribly at the time.

GEORGE: We were so hopeful the mild air would help him. And for a while it did, you know. But (*Giving gesture of despair*) . . . And so young, only thirty-four.

ANNE (*After a pause*): George, I want your advice—as a brother-in-law, not as one of the executors of the estate. Lawrence left you a large interest in Mount Vernon, and you have always loved the place. Don't you think you should take it over? I have no wish to be burdened with so many acres of farm land. I know nothing about farming.

GEORGE (*Figuring on back of envelope*): No place in the world means more to me than Mount Vernon. But, as Lawrence's wife, you must have a fair return. (*Figures*) How would it be if I paid you eighty thousand pounds of tobacco yearly?

ANNE: Isn't eighty thousand pounds of tobacco a great deal, George?

GEORGE: I would gladly pay it.

ANNE: You are more than fair. You are generous! And it
will be such a load off my mind to know you are here,
carrying on as master of Mount Vernon. You will be very
busy, George . . . with all those acres, and Lawrence's
wish for you to enter the militia . . . and the House of
Burgesses.

GEORGE: Yes, I shall be very busy. But that is exactly what
I like. And now, shall we go check the accounts? (*They
exit*)

CHORUS: Washington marches on!

*   *   *

CHORUS:

When did he fight in what is called
the French and Indian War?

SOLO:

(*Holding up card or writing on blackboard: 1754-8, French
& Indian War*):

Seventeen fifty-four to eight,
with hardships by the score.

SCENE 5

AT RISE: GENERAL BRADDOCK, *brandishing his sword, crosses
stage excitedly.*

BRADDOCK (*Shouting*): Hold ranks! Hold ranks! Take the
fire of the enemy like men. I command you to hold ranks.
(GEORGE WASHINGTON *rushes in to catch up with* GENERAL
BRADDOCK.)

WASHINGTON: General Braddock! General Braddock . . . if
you will order the men to scatter, sir . . . Let them meet

the enemy under cover instead of out in the open. I know how these Indians and French fight, from behind trees . . .

BRADDOCK (*Striding out*): My men will stand in ranks, Washington, as they are bidden, without breach of discipline. (*Exits*)

WASHINGTON: But, sir . . . (*Exits after* BRADDOCK. *Three* SOLDIERS *stagger in.*)

1ST SOLDIER: Let's get out of here, anywhere. Anywhere!

2ND SOLDIER: Where did the shots come from? Did you see the enemy?

3RD SOLDIER: The shots come from all directions. No one sees the enemy.

1ST SOLDIER: We make easy targets in our red coats.

2ND SOLDIER: Did you see Braddock's aide-de-camp, Colonel Washington? He strode among us soldiers, calm as ice, trying to get us to retreat in orderly fashion. His horse was shot out from under him.

1ST SOLDIER: Aye, and he mounted another.

2ND SOLDIER: Men were slaughtered all around him, but he wasn't even wounded.

3RD SOLDIER: I could follow a man like that! Would to heaven he were in charge here. (*They stagger out.*)

CHORUS: Washington marches on!

*   *   *

CHORUS:

When did he marry, settle down
on the land he loved so well?

SOLO:

(*Holding up card or writing on blackboard: 1759-75, Farmer*):

Seventeen hundred fifty-nine,
a happy date to tell.

Scene 6

At Rise: Mary Ball Washington *comes in with sewing, sits and works.* Soon Betty Washington Lewis *hurries in with newspapers. She greets her mother affectionately, and takes off wraps as she talks.*

Betty: Oh, Mama, have you seen the papers—from Fredericksburg and Alexandria? I was afraid you hadn't, so I took the ferry over . . . I couldn't wait to show you.

Mrs. Washington: About George's wedding?

Betty: Yes, look! (*Shows a paper*) A long account, and so glowing, Mama. The charming and beautiful young widow, Martha Custis, and the handsome and gallant young officer, George Washington!

Mrs. Washington (*Looking at paper*): She will be a great help to George in many ways. Perhaps I should not say it out loud . . . but I can't help thinking that her fortune will not come amiss. I hear it is a large one.

Betty (*Sitting down*): And, imagine, a ready-made family for George! Jacky six, and Patsy four. I can imagine how he loves them.

Mrs. Washington (*Reading*): "In the church where the wedding was solemnized there was a bright show of resplendent uniforms with their gold lace and scarlet coats. Later the bridegroom, himself clad in shining blue and silver and scarlet, rode beside the coach that bore his bride homeward . . ." (*Looks up*) George has done well, Betty. I always knew he would.

Betty: And remember how he wanted to go to sea? And how Uncle Joseph agreed with you that he shouldn't?

Mrs. Washington: Indeed I remember. How different his life would have been! Come, let us move closer to the grate. There is a January chill in the air today. (*They exit.*)

CHORUS: Washington marches on!

* * *

CHORUS:

When did the Revolution start—
that placed him in command.

SOLO:

(*Holding up card or writing on blackboard: 1775-83, Commander-in-chief*):

Seventeen seventy-five. In June
he took the task in hand.

SCENE 7

AT RISE: JOHN ADAMS *enters, takes place behind table.*

VOICE FROM AUDIENCE: Sh! John Adams is about to speak. Sh!

ADAMS: Gentlemen of the second Continental Congress,—
We are agreed that we must prepare to defend ourselves
against British tyranny immediately. To my mind the
choice of commander of the continental armies is easy
enough. There is no soldier in America to be compared
with Colonel George Washington of Virginia, either in experience or distinction. He is gallant, straightforward, earnest. (*Looks up*) Did I glimpse the Colonel leaving the
room in confusion just now? Run after him, attendant.
Bring him back! (*Resumes speech.*) I move that Congress,
meeting here in solemn assembly in Philadelphia, put the
gentleman from Virginia in charge of the American army!
(*Cheers, shouts of "Aye, aye" from audience.*) His skill
and experience as an officer, his independent fortune, great
talents, and excellent universal character, would unite the

colonies better than any other person in the union." (*More cheers from audience, calls for "George Washington!" and "Colonel Washington."* WASHINGTON *enters slowly.* JOHN ADAMS *steps up, escorts him to table, then sits down.*)

WASHINGTON: I beg it to be remembered by every gentleman in this room, that I this day declare with the utmost sincerity I do not think myself equal to the command I am honored with. I cannot refuse a call to serve my country. As to pay, I will have none of it. I do not wish to make any profit from the war. I shall keep an accounting of my expenses, and that is all I desire. (*Cheers from audience.* JOHN ADAMS *grasps* WASHINGTON'S *hand, and they exit together.*)

CHORUS: Washington marches on!

* * *

CHORUS:

Month after month the army fought,
and often on the run!
Month after month of toil and trial,
and never a battle won.

SOLO:

(*Holding up card or writing on blackboard: 1776, Crosses Delaware*):

Then on a bitter Christmas night
Washington staged a famous fight.

SCENE 8

AT RISE: *Two* SENTRIES *enter, pace back and forth.*

1ST SENTRY: No morning ever has gone more slowly. (*Slaps arms to keep warm.*) How soon do you think they will send back news?

2ND SENTRY: For the hundredth time, don't expect news till noonday, at the earliest. (*Looks at watch*) Eleven o'clock. Calm down, brother.

1ST SENTRY: If only I could have gone along.

2ND SENTRY: Someone had to stay behind to guard the camp. You and I are as good as the next. (*Stomps feet*) It's blasted cold.

1ST SENTRY: Noonday at the earliest?

2ND SENTRY: Look here. They didn't leave till after midnight. (*He shudders*) And *what* a Christmas midnight! Sleet. Bitter cold. The Delaware choked with cakes of floating ice. Do you think it a quick and easy task to transport 2400 men across the river on such a night? Even with the best planning?

1ST SENTRY: They say General Washington had it all worked out to the smallest detail.

2ND SENTRY: Naturally. Still, after the crossing, they had to march nine miles through snow and cold to Trenton. You think that can be done in a moment?

1ST SENTRY: No . . . ooo.

2ND SENTRY: I say if they arrived at Trenton an hour after sunrise they did well. And *then*. You expect they could march right in and take the town? Against those well-armed German soldiers the British hired to guard it? (*Pounds hands together*) You expect too much.

1ST SENTRY: I am counting on Christmas. I am counting on those Hessians drinking too much, and celebrating too much, last night.

2ND SENTRY: Even so, taking a town is not easy. And have you reason to suppose our luck has changed? Retreat. Retreat. Retreat. That has been our record. Have we won a battle yet—answer me that?

1ST SENTRY (*Grudgingly*): No . . . ooo. But this! We are

all fired with the wish to give General Washington a Christmas present. A victory—at last.

2ND SENTRY: A wish. That's all very well. But wishes don't win battles. Though heaven knows a victory is a Christmas present that would warm all our hearts. (*Bitterly*) They need warming. (*Stomps*) And not only our hearts.

1ST SENTRY: Noonday!

2ND SENTRY: Remember, a messenger would have to get back the nine miles from Trenton, and cross the river again. After the battle.

1ST SENTRY (*Stubbornly*): If the victory were a quick one . . . (*They pace back and forth in silence. In a few moments a* MESSENGER *runs in.*)

SENTRIES (*Challenging him*): Halt! Who goes there?

MESSENGER (*Saluting*): Messenger from General Washington in Trenton.

SENTRIES (*Eagerly*): Speak up, lad. What news?

MESSENGER: We crossed the river on the barges without mishap, in spite of the sleet and bumping ice.

1ST SENTRY: Yes, yes, you crossed the river. But the battle? Do we hold Trenton?

MESSENGER: We marched the nine miles without mishap, arriving after sun-up, deploying to enter by different roads.

2ND SENTRY: Naturally, by different roads. We know the General had it all planned. But the Hessians? Did they put up a good fight?

MESSENGER: There was no place for them to run. They were dazed, drugged from too much celebrating last night. We had no losses to speak of.

SENTRIES: And the Hessians?

MESSENGER: They lost their commander and forty-one others —dead. It was all over in less than an hour. We captured thirty officers and more than a thousand men.

SENTRIES (*Throwing up their hats*): A victory! A victory!

A Christmas present for General Washington! Come, let's tell the others. (*Go out with* MESSENGER) Our first victory in the war . . .
CHORUS: Washington marches on!

*   *   *

CHORUS:

Success was brief. Then more retreat
through countryside and gorge.
What was the time that tried men's souls?

SOLO:

(*Holding up card or writing on blackboard: 1777-8, Valley Forge*):
The winter at Valley Forge.

SCENE 9

AT RISE: MARTHA WASHINGTON *enters with knitting, sits and works busily.* GENERAL WASHINGTON *enters, paces back and forth deep in thought.*

MARTHA: You are worried, George. (*Pause*) Are you angry with me for coming? After you wrote that I would be much more comfortable at Mount Vernon?
WASHINGTON (*Going to her affectionately*): No. No. I am not angry with you, Martha. Assuredly you *would* be more comfortable at Mount Vernon. Valley Forge is not renowned for its comforts! But you have been a cheering note in a bleak landscape ever since you came, my dear. The soldiers feel it. Especially the sick and wounded you so kindly visit.
MARTHA: Oh, I'm glad.
WASHINGTON: And the ones who get the socks you knit think you are an angel from heaven! I wonder if you realize how much a pair of warm socks means in Valley Forge?

MARTHA: I think so, George.

GEORGE (*Bursting out impatiently*): Socks . . . mittens . . . coats . . . shoes . . . uniforms . . . *why* don't we get our supplies? Bread . . . meat . . . ammunition . . . guns . . . we need everything, Martha. Everything! That's why I am worried. Congress is so disorganized and inefficient. Why, these days, we scarcely have what can be called a government.

MARTHA: I suppose the British moving into Philadelphia didn't help matters. You say Congress is in exile at York. It has probably lost heart. (*Hastily*) Though, of course, I understand nothing about politics.

WASHINGTON: Lost heart! Lost head, I should say. (*Paces angrily*) And to think that just twenty miles from here General Howe and his officers are having a gay winter social season in Philadelphia! His men are warm and well-fed. They live in ease and comfort. While my men are starving and freezing! Yet naked as they are, Martha (*There is a catch in his voice*) . . . they show incomparable patience and loyalty. Ah, Thomas Paine is right . . . this is indeed a time that tries men's souls. Mine included.

MARTHA: Is there no way out?

WASHINGTON: None that I can see at the moment, unless Congress can pull itself together. How can we have an army without supplies? And the men have not been paid for months! (ORDERLY *enters, salutes.*)

ORDERLY: The Marquis de Lafayette to see you, sir.

WASHINGTON: Lafayette! Show him in immediately.

MARTHA (*Rising*): Perhaps I should leave . . .

WASHINGTON: Not until you have greeted our young friend, Martha. He, too, is a bright light on a bleak horizon. (LAFAYETTE *enters, salutes. He and* GENERAL WASHINGTON *greet each other affectionately.*) My dear Lafayette!

LAFAYETTE: General Washington!

WASHINGTON: You have met my wife once before. (*She and*

LAFAYETTE *bow*) The soldiers here call her Lady Washington.

MARTHA (*Smiling at* LAFAYETTE *as she exits*) : It is my reward for darning their socks, Marquis!

LAFAYETTE : I could not wait to bring you the news, sir.

WASHINGTON : News?

LAFAYETTE (*Taking letter from inner pocket*) : A secret letter, from friends in France. There is every reason to believe that France will soon declare war on England, and support our cause with money and supplies.

WASHINGTON : Can it be true! Soon, you say?

LAFAYETTE (*Showing letter*) : Very soon. Indeed, I am informed that a handsome sum of money is already on the way.

WASHINGTON (*Much relieved*) : What is it they say . . . that it is always darkest just before the dawn? Come, we must tell Martha. (*They exit.*)

CHORUS : Washington marches on!

* * *

CHORUS :

Year after year the war dragged on,
the verdict still not won.
And then the battle of Yorktown came.

SOLO :

(*Holding up card or writing on blackboard: 1781, Yorktown*) :

Seventeen eighty-one.

SCENE 10

AT RISE : NEWSBOYS *run across stage shouting, waving papers.*

1ST NEWSBOY : Extra! Extra! Cornwallis surrenders after three-week siege. Washington takes 8000 men. Victory! Victory! (*Exits*)

2ND NEWSBOY: The most decisive battle of the war. Washington wins at Yorktown. The war is over! (*Exits*)

CHORUS: Washington marches on!

* * *

CHORUS:

But still a treaty to be signed
before our land was free!

SOLO:

The General had to keep command
till seventeen eighty-three.

CHORUS:

And then, at Christmas, home again!
Mount Vernon. Home, at last.

SOLO:

(*Holding up card or writing on blackboard: 1784-8, Farmer*):

Seventeen eighty-four to eight.
And, oh, the time went fast.

SCENE 11

AT RISE: WASHINGTON *enters, sits at table, begins to write.*

WASHINGTON (*Writing*): To the Marquis de Lafayette, many greetings. At length, my dear Marquis, I am become a private citizen on the banks of the Potomac; and under the shadow of my own vine and my own fig-tree, free from the bustle of a camp and the busy scenes of public life, I am solacing myself with those tranquil enjoyments of which a soldier can have very little conception. I have not only retired from all public employments, but I am retiring within myself . . . (NELLY CUSTIS *comes in a little tentatively.*)

NELLY: Grandfather. Grandfather, you promised to show me the new little colt . . . (WASHINGTON *smiles, puts down quill, and goes out with* NELLY.)

CHORUS: Washington marches on!

* * *

CHORUS:

When was he called to serve again?
Washington, President!

SOLO:

(*Holding up card or writing on blackboard: 1789-97, President*):

Seventeen hundred eighty-nine.
Two terms, eight years, he spent.

SCENE 12

AT RISE: CHANCELLOR LIVINGSTON, *carrying a Bible, and* GEORGE WASHINGTON *enter.*

LIVINGSTON (*Holding out Bible*): Do you solemnly swear that you will faithfully execute the office of President of the United States, and will, to the best of your ability, preserve, protect, and defend the Constitution of the United States?

WASHINGTON: I do solemnly swear that I will faithfully execute the office of President of the United States, and will, to the best of my ability, preserve, protect and defend the Constitution of the United States. (*Bends to kiss Bible. Then, solemnly, with bowed head* . . .) So help me, God.

LIVINGSTON (*To audience*): Long live George Washington, President of the United States!

AUDIENCE (*Cheering*): Long live George Washington. Long

live the father of our country. Hail to the first President of the United States. (WASHINGTON *and* LIVINGSTON *exit.*)

1ST VOICE FROM AUDIENCE: Did you hear? He won't accept a salary as President.

2ND VOICE: Nor did he take a salary all those years he was commander-in-chief.

3RD VOICE: Imagine, he fears he is not good enough for the post!

4TH VOICE: Who *would* be good enough if he isn't?

SEVERAL: No one. No one in our thirteen States.

5TH VOICE: Poor man, we snatch him away from Mount Vernon again. We demand much of him.

SEVERAL: We need him. We need him!

AUDIENCE: Long live George Washington, President of the United States!

CHORUS: Washington marches on!

*   *   *

CHORUS:

When did he die, George Washington?

SOLO:

(*Holding up card or writing on blackboard: 1799—Died*):

Seventeen ninety-nine.

CHORUS:

But he still lives on in our minds and hearts,
and will till the end of time!

SCENE 13

AT RISE: SCHOOLMASTER *enters, with books.*

SCHOOLMASTER: Boys of the Latin School of Fredericksburg, sad news has just reached us from Mount Vernon, this

December day. George Washington is dead! The father of our country is dead.

He was our friend . . . almost our neighbor, when he lived across the river at Ferry Farm years ago. And many of you remember his mother when she lived on Charles Street next door to her daughter and grandchildren.

George Washington is dead. In him were united such qualities of greatness as seldom appear in one man. How long he served our country! How well he served it—as soldier, patriot, statesman, citizen!

Boys, open your copy books and write these words on the title page where you will see them often: "George Washington—first in war, first in peace, and first in the hearts of his countrymen."

Our beloved commander-in-chief, our first President, is dead. But he will never be forgotten. Other heroes, other statesmen, will come and go, but the memory of George Washington is here to stay. (*Nods solemnly, and exits*)

CHORUS: Washington marches on!

* * *

SCENE 14

BEFORE CURTAIN: *A procession of boys and girls of the present generation march across the stage carrying flags, chanting:* "Washington marches on!"

THE END

That Spells Washington

Boys *and* GIRLS *stand toward back of stage holding large cards with letters spelling* WASHINGTON. *As each one speaks he takes a step forward.*

W for wisdom shown
   in war and peacetime, too.
A for the ability
   to act and carry-through.
S for service, year by year,
   with pen as well as sword.
H for a heroic heart
   unheedful of reward.
I for insight, and ideals
   in all his different roles.
N for nobleness of mind
   in times that tried men's souls.
G for gallantry and grit,
   for guidance, soon and late.
T for his untiring toil
   to make our country great.
O for obstacles he met
   and staunchly overcame.
N for nation's need of him
   who never sought for fame.

WASHINGTON'S BIRTHDAY

GROUP: That spells WASHINGTON—the man
who, time and time again,
was *first* in playing many parts
in war, and peace, and in the hearts
of all his countrymen.

George Washington, Farmer

I

1ST BOY: "I think a farmer's life," he wrote,
"the most enjoyable of all.
To watch the wheat and barley sprout
and see the trees grow strong and tall
is best of all pursuits, bar none."
He signed the words:

"G. Washington."

GROUP: And yet this man who loved the farm
was quick to heed the call to arm:
he stayed away four years and more
to fight the French and Indian war.

II

2ND BOY: "The more I learn about the land,"
the better I am pleased," he wrote.
"A farmer's satisfactions grow
like crops . . . I'd happily devote
my life to seeds and soil and sun."
He signed the words:

"G. Washington."

GROUP: And then the Revolution came.
Again his country made its claim.
He drilled the troops and held command—
eight years away from crops and land!

III

3RD BOY: "No sight delights me quite as much,"
he wrote, "as farmland, thriving, neat.
I've added to my coat of arms,
quite suitably, some spears of wheat.
A farmer's work is mostly fun."
He signed the words:
"G. Washington."

GROUP: But, once again, the years were spent
away from home—as President.
Two terms, eight years away again,
handling the strained affairs of men!

IV

4TH BOY: "At last," he wrote, "I can enjoy
the shadow of my fig and vine.
At last I have my heart's delight:
a farmer's life again is mine.
But now my days are almost done . . ."
He signed the words:
"G. Washington."

GROUP: Two final years of "heart's delight"
this Farmer had, who, overnight,
had heeded every beck and call
to do his duty, big or small . . .
though he loved farming best of all!

Washington at Valley Forge

(December, 1777)

ALL: A wooded valley and a frozen creek,
the hills surrounding, high and cold and bleak;
a little forge for melting metal down,
a valley forge—the kernel of a town,
a dreary place with Christmastime so near . . .

1ST BOY: The General called a halt: "We're camping here.
We'll need some huts as shelter from the cold.
Work quickly, men, the year is growing old."

ALL: The General watched his soldiers chop and saw.
Their feet were bleeding and their hands were raw.
They lacked supplies and clothes and shoes and
food,
but, like their leader, they had fortitude.

2ND BOY: The General stood upon a rise of ground.
His heart was heavy as he looked around:
"My unpaid men are weary, hungry, cold,
while twenty miles away the Redcoats hold
fair Philadelphia and live in state,
and sit in comfort near a blazing grate!

The snow at Valley Forge is stained with red.
My soldiers dream of boots and gloves and bread."

ALL: The General thought of home—Mount Vernon's
        charm.
        His soldiers wintered, what would be the harm
        in going home? The cold had months to run!
        He turned and looked into the puny sun,
        and chose the hardship—as he'd always done—
        the General by the name of Washington.

At Mount Vernon

(1798)

General Washington? He's around—
down by the grove he may be found,
or riding beyond that rise of ground,
with a hickory switch in a hand that's browned.

What is he wearing? Something plain,
with an umbrella, sir, for rain,
hung from his saddle like a cane.
He'll have his eyes on grass and grain.

What is he like? He's sixty-six,
thinking of bushels, bales, and bricks,
glad to be through with politics,
glad to be home with barns to fix.

Look for a man who stops to chat
of crops and trees and such as that,
pointing out sights to marvel at.
Look for a broad-brimmed, old, white hat.

Look for a man with his battles won,
weathered by time and trial and sun,
thinking a farmer's life is fun—
that, sir, is . . . General Washington.

ST. PATRICK'S DAY

St. Patrick and the Serpent

I

NARRATOR: St. Patrick drove the serpents out
of Ireland (so 'tis said),
from here and there and roundabout,
from Cork to Malin Head
he banished all the snakes there were . . .
A GIRL: Except for one that wouldn't stir!
A BOY: Except for one that wouldn't leave!
GROUP: And, sure, it made St. Patrick grieve.

II

NARRATOR: St. Patrick drove the serpents out
of Ireland (so they claim).
From here and there and roundabout
it brought St. Patrick fame.
He cast the serpents in the sea . . .
A BOY: Except for one that wouldn't flee!
A GIRL: Except for one that wouldn't drown!
GROUP: And, sure, it made St. Patrick frown.

III

NARRATOR: St. Patrick was a canny man,
a prudent man (they state),

and so he conjured up a plan—
he built a box-like crate,
and sweetly asked the serpent in.

A GIRL: The serpent stroked its satin skin,
and wouldn't try the box at all.
But said,

SERPENT: For me, it's much too small.

IV

NARRATOR: St. Patrick was a learnéd man
and subtle (so they tell).
He coaxed the serpent:

ST. PATRICK: Faith, you can
fit very, very well.
I'm sure you can, with room to spare.

SERPENT: I can't, you know I can't, so there.

ST. PATRICK: You can.

SERPENT: I can't.

ST. PATRICK: I know I'm right.

SERPENT: You're wrong.

NARRATOR: They argued day and night.

V

NARRATOR: St. Patrick had a mighty voice,
persuasive (so they state)—
it made the Emerald Isle rejoice
to hear the great debate:

ST. PATRICK: You'll fit the box.

SERPENT: I won't at all.

ST. PATRICK: It's plenty big.

SERPENT: It's pinchy small.

ST. PATRICK: Unless you prove it, I am right.

SERPENT: I'll show you, then. The box is tight!

VI

NARRATOR: St. Patrick watched the serpent glide
into the box ('tis told),
and when it mostly was inside
the canny Saint made bold
to close the lid, and tie it tight,
and throw the box with all his might
upon the waves that rolled away.

GROUP: And, sure, it made St. Patrick gay.

VII

NARRATOR: St. Patrick drove the serpents out
of Ireland (so 'tis said),
he scoured the country roundabout
from Cork to Malin Head,
and banished all the snakes there were . . .

A GIRL: Including one that wouldn't stir.

A BOY: Including one that left the isle
all boxed and tied, in state and style!

GROUP: And, sure, it made St. Patrick smile.

Sure, Don't You Know?

GIRL: Oh, what's the smile for, Paddy boy,
   that goes from ear to ear?
PADDY: Sure, don't you know what day it is?
   St. Patrick's Day is here!

BOY: And what's the green for, Paddy boy,
   the wearing of the green?
PADDY: It's tokening the Emerald Isle—
   the greenest place you've seen.

GIRL: And what's the shamrock, Paddy boy,
   with leaves that come in three?
PADDY: And don't you know that illustrates
   the Holy Trinity?

BOY: And what's the song for, Paddy boy,
   that sets the day apart?
PADDY: 'Tis just the Irish joy in me
   a-bursting from my heart.

Wearing of the Green

It ought to come in April,
or, better yet, in May
when everything is green as green—
I mean St. Patrick's Day.

With still a week of winter
this wearing of the green
seems rather out of season—
it's rushing things, I mean.

But maybe March *is* better
when all is done and said:
St. Patrick brings a promise,
a four-leaf-clover promise,
a green-all-over promise
of springtime just ahead!

Easter Morn

GROUP: Now everything is born again
all up and down the earth,
for it is Easter morn again—
the morning of rebirth.

BOY: The grass is turning green again,
with frosty winter over.

GIRL: And dandelions are seen again,
and daffodils, and clover.

BOY: And all the roots and all the shoots
and all the seeds are stirring.

GIRL: And in the trees, the willow trees,
sit pussywillows, purring!

GROUP: Now everything is new again
all up and down the land,
for Easter has come true again
and hillsides understand.

BOY: The wind is bright and warm again
in all the open places.

GIRL: The meadow larks perform again.
And daisies show their faces.

BOY: And all the leaves on all the trees
are starting to unfold.

GIRL:　While, on the run, the Easter sun
　　　　shakes out its living gold.

GROUP:　Now everything is bright again
　　　　all up and down the world.
　　　　The tendrils that were tight, again
　　　　are magically uncurled.
BOY:　And voices start to sing again.
GIRL:　And eyes begin to see
　　　　the worth of everything again,
　　　　as Easter turns the key.
BOY:　And mankind feels the pull again
　　　　of Something from above.
GIRL:　And everyone is full again
　　　　of faith, and hope, and love.

GROUP:　And everyone is full again
　　　　of faith, and hope, and love.

Easter's All Dressed Up Today

BOYS: Easter's all dressed up today!
   I wonder if she'll see
   the puddle in the pasture
   near the weeping-willow tree.

GIRLS: She doesn't! Oh, she stumbles,
   and skids and slips and tumbles,
   and, getting splashed, she mumbles:
   "Now *would* you look at me!"
ALL: Easter frowns beneath her bonnet:
   "Oh! My dress has splashes on it.'

BOYS: The sun says, "What a sorry sight."
   The clouds say, "Goodness, yes."
   The rain says, "Come, let's rescue her,
   this maiden in distress."

GIRLS: So, with some silver tinkles,
   the clouds send cleaning sprinkles,
   and sun irons out the wrinklᵣ
   that rumpled Easter's dress.
ALL: And Easter smiles beneath her bonnet:
   "Look! My dress has sunshine on it."

Easter Tulip

I planted a tulip,
put it in a pot,
put it in the shadow
where the sun was not,
watched it, watered it,
never once forgot.

The tulip was a slow-poke.
It wasn't to be seen.
But up popped a pale weed,
thin, and yellow-green,
looking like the periscope
of a submarine.

The periscope took bearings:
"Pretty nice, I'd say."
Reported to the tulip:
"Hurry, don't delay."
And so the tulip hurried . . .
and bloomed for Easter Day.

EARTH DAY

What Now, Planet Earth?

Characters

JANE
DON, *Jane's husband*
JANE'S MOTHER
TWO BOYS
ED, *a concerned citizen*
BILL, *his friend*
CHRIS, *young boy*
PAM, *his friend*
MRS. PHILLIPS
MRS. NEVIN
MODERATOR
SCIENTIST
LIBRARIAN
HISTORIAN
REPORTER
GEORGE PERKINS MARSH
CHARLES SCRIBNER
SADIE, *young girl*
FATHER }
MOTHER } *her parents*
JOHN MUIR
ROBERT UNDERWOOD JOHNSON
FRED

RUTH
BILLY
RACHEL CARSON
MRS. CARSON, *her mother*

BEFORE RISE: *Stage apron is bare, except for a crumpled tin can, lying near center.* DON, JANE, *and* JANE'S MOTHER *enter in front of curtain. They do not notice can.*

JANE: Of course you'll understand the program, Mother. (*To* DON) Won't she, Don? There's nothing mysterious about conservation of natural resources.

JANE'S MOTHER: But what does it *mean*—natural resources?

DON: Why, soil, water, air, timber, minerals, wildlife . . .

JANE'S MOTHER: Even scenery, I suppose.

JANE: That's right. Conservation is just another word for saving our resources, Mother.

JANE'S MOTHER: Like putting our resources in a bank?

DON: That's an idea. The United States Natural Bank! (*Laughs as they go down steps to sit in audience.* TWO BOYS *run onstage.* 1ST BOY *sees tin can and grabs it eagerly.*)

1ST BOY: That's eighty-three cans for me this week and twenty-seven bottles.

2ND BOY: If you're not careful, you'll catch up with Lisa! (*Shakes head*) Where she finds all that stuff is beyond me. She's way ahead of anyone else.

1ST BOY: Queen of the Recyclers, Unlimited! (*They go down into audience as two men,* BILL *and* ED, *enter.*)

BILL: What do you make of this gas shortage, Ed?

ED: I think it's the real thing.

BILL: Some people say it's a trick to crowd out the independents and raise prices.

ED: No. We're just plain driving too many cars and using too much gas compared to what we produce. And it's going to get worse instead of better, unless someone comes up with a different kind of car.

BILL: Do you really think so?

ED: No question. I read that by the end of this century—and that's not many years away—the earth will be out of oil and natural gas. Not just running short, but *out*.

BILL: What are we going to *do*?

ED: That's the question—"What Now, Planet Earth?" And that's the name of the program tonight. Maybe they'll have a solution. (*They go down to sit in audience. Two children,* PAM *and* CHRIS, *come in.* CHRIS *lags*.)

PAM: Hurry up! We'll be late for the program.

CHRIS: I don't feel so good, Pam.

PAM: You didn't swallow any of that water, did you, Chris, when you fell into the creek this afternoon?

CHRIS: Maybe I did, a little.

PAM: Everyone knows that creek isn't fit to swim in, let alone swallow. It's full of germs and stuff.

CHRIS: I couldn't help it. I slipped. (*Bends over*) I feel terrible. (MRS. PHILLIPS *enters, hurries by, stops to look at* CHRIS.)

MRS. PHILLIPS (*Concerned*): Are you all right, child?

PAM: He says he doesn't feel good.

MRS. PHILLIPS: He doesn't look good. You'd better send him home. Where do you live?

PAM: Not far. Come on, Chris. (*She takes* CHRIS *by arm and leads him off.* MRS. PHILLIPS *starts across stage again.*)

MRS. NEVIN (*Calling from offstage*): Oh, Mrs. Phillips! Wait for me. (MRS. PHILLIPS *stops as* MRS. NEVIN *enters and hurries to catch up.*) I had to rush to finish the dishes.

MRS. PHILLIPS: I thought you had a dishwasher put in when you remodeled the kitchen.

MRS. NEVIN: I did. But I'm disciplining myself not to use it. There's so much talk about the energy crisis, it seems the least I can do.

Mrs. Phillips: It's going to take more than one idle dishwasher to solve the energy crisis. (*As they go down steps to audience,* Pam *re-enters, runs across stage, and follows them. Sound of recorded or live music to "This Land Is Your Land" or "America the Beautiful" is heard from offstage. Curtains open.*)

* * *

Setting: *Stage is furnished for a panel discussion. At left there is a table with five chairs behind it and name plates before each place reading:* Moderator, Scientist, Librarian, Historian, Reporter. *At right are three chairs and a desk.*

At Rise: *Music grows louder.* Moderator *enters, carrying papers and books, followed by* Scientist, Librarian, Historian, *and* Reporter, *who also carry papers. They take appropriate seats at table, facing audience. Music fades out.*

Moderator (*Rising*): Three hundred years ago, America was a horn of plenty, rich in forests and wild game and grass waving in the wind . . . a country beautiful to look upon, although man, the newcomer, had little time for beauty. He wanted to clear a field, plant a crop, fill a granary. . . . There seemed to be no end to the bounty of the country.

Scientist: The philosophy of the early settlers was simple: Clear the land, wear it out, and move on. Why worry about the future in a country as boundless as America? The word "conservation"—saving resources for the future—was not in the Colonial vocabulary.

Historian: With a few exceptions.

Moderator: Can you give us an example?

Historian: William Penn made it a rule in his Pennsylvania colony that a settler should leave at least one acre of forest for every five acres he cleared.

Librarian: But the rule was hard to enforce. People came to the new world to be free, not to be told how to manage their farms. (*Music grows louder, becomes softer for a few moments, then fades out.*)

MODERATOR: Soon the demand for lumber, both from abroad and from townspeople along the Atlantic seaboard, initiated the age of tree-cutting on a large scale. The era of the lumberjack began. Crews moved in with their steel axes and sawmills whined and screeched along the fast-moving streams. The tall white pines and the young immature pines crashed and fell.

SCIENTIST: Forests were "leveled clean."

MODERATOR: By the end of the Revolutionary War, most of the land between the Atlantic coast and the Appalachians was cleared of its timber. Hills lay exposed to drenching rains that tore at the soil. Rivers swelled with the runoff and turned brown with silt. People were changing the country without worrying about the after-effects. As trees came down, wildlife had to flee or feel the sting of the newcomers' guns or the snap of their traps. People were making money by taking more from the country than they were putting back.

REPORTER: The lumber barons followed the forests of white pine from Maine to New York.

HISTORIAN: From New York to Pennsylvania.

SCIENTIST: From Pennsylvania to Michigan.

LIBRARIAN: From Michigan to Wisconsin and Minnesota.

MODERATOR: And when the white pine was gone, the lumber barons went after yellow pine in the South, and Douglas fir in the Northwest. They thought in terms of their own lifetimes, not in terms of generations to come. But by the time of the Civil War the principles of conservation were in the mind of at least one man.

LIBRARIAN: One man . . . a scholar-lawyer-diplomat named George Perkins Marsh. He saw the changes taking place in America, and he became alarmed enough to write a book about man and nature. It was actually a first book of ecology, although "ecology" did not become a household word for another century. (GEORGE PERKINS MARSH *and* CHARLES SCRIBNER *enter and sit at desk.* MARSH *carries manuscript.*) Let's go back to a day in the late fall of 1863, in the office of Charles Scribner, a New York publisher. (*Spotlight comes up on desk, right.*)

MARSH: I am greatly concerned, Mr. Scribner, about our country's fate if present practices continue. As a diplomat whose travels have carried me to all parts of the world, I have been struck over and over again by the results of man's interference with nature.

SCRIBNER: Just what do you mean, sir?

MARSH: I mean that man's negligence and lack of foresight have brought about the ruin of many civilizations. It could happen here. Have you ever wondered what became of the so-called "cradle of civilization" in the fertile valley of the Tigris and Euphrates rivers in Asia Minor?

SCRIBNER: Yes, I have often wondered.

MARSH: To put it simply, when the forests at the head of the valley were cut down, the fertile soil that fed and clothed that ancient civilization washed away. We cannot disturb the balance of nature without suffering for it.

SCRIBNER: But I don't understand . . . why did the soil wash away?

MARSH: In every forest the ground is covered with a matting of fallen leaves and debris. The force of a heavy rain is checked by tree branches, so water has time to soak into this thick matting instead of running off. When the forest is cut, the great reservoir of moisture trapped in the vegetable mold evaporates. Pounding rain disintegrates the matting, which is washed away. Then the soil beneath is also washed away—and eventually clogs streams and rivers with silt. (*Shrugs*) The fertile valley is no more. We can no longer go on mistreating the earth without considering the cost.

SCRIBNER (*Pointing to manuscript*): And is that what your book is about?

MARSH: My book is about the relationship of man to nature—perhaps I should say the interrelationship of all living things to each other. People must be convinced that the strength of our nation is based upon the wise and careful perpetuation of its natural resources. (SCRIBNER *rises, offering hand to* MARSH, *who also stands.*)

SCRIBNER (*Shaking hands with* MARSH): That is a book I shall be proud to publish, Mr. Marsh. (*Spotlight goes out.* MARSH, *carrying manuscript, exits with* SCRIBNER.)

LIBRARIAN: Charles Scribner did publish Mr. Marsh's *Man and Nature,* the fountainhead of the conservation movement. The book had a certain amount of influence here and abroad, but more in intellectual circles than in practical application. Ten years later Scribner's put out a revised edition under the title *The Earth as Modified by Human Action.* Unfortunately Mr. Marsh's warnings about forest clearance, overgrazing and overplowing of prairie land did not often reach receptive ears.

SCIENTIST: Not until much later did his policy of planting shelter belts of trees to blunt the force of destructive winds become common practice.

HISTORIAN: And many economists still agree with his rule-of-thumb that a healthy landscape must have about one-fourth of its land planted in vegetation that first flourished there.

MODERATOR: Twenty years after Mr. Marsh's book was published, most of our original forests were gone; the face of America had been completely altered. Millions of acres of charred and ugly stump land told the sad story.

HISTORIAN: Depletion of resources.

SCIENTIST: Soil erosion.

LIBRARIAN: Disruption of watersheds.

REPORTER: Threatened wildlife.

MODERATOR: But in Nebraska, in the spring of 1872, another

strong voice was speaking out for trees, living trees. (SADIE, FATHER *and* MOTHER *enter right.* SADIE *carries shovel. Spotlight comes up on them.*)

SADIE (*Raising shovel*): But, Papa, I *have* to take a shovel to school today. Mr. Morton said so . . . he's on the Board of Agriculture.

FATHER: What kind of nonsense is this? (*Scornfully*) Bring a shovel to school!

MOTHER: What did this Mr. Morton say, Sadie?

SADIE: He said that today—Wednesday, the 10th of April, 1872—is specially set aside for tree planting in Nebraska. It's called Arbor Day. We're going to plant some trees around the schoolyard.

FATHER: Arbor Day—that's right. I remember when the resolution was passed in the state Congress early this year. It struck me as rather strange at the time.

MOTHER: Why strange, Henry?

FATHER: The forests of America, what's left of them, are still being cut, right and left, and here's Mr. Morton talking about planting trees.

MOTHER: Probably *because* the forests are being cut, Henry.

SADIE: Mr. Morton thinks trees will make a prairie state like Nebraska more beautiful. He wants us to have an Arbor Day every year. (*Excitedly*) He'd like to see people plant a *million* trees today.

FATHER (*Skeptically*): A million trees! Does he know how many that is? It's a thousand times a thousand. Why, there aren't enough people in Nebraska to plant all those trees, Sadie. (*Spotlight goes out.* SADIE, FATHER *and* MOTHER *exit.*)

MODERATOR: But there were! *More* than a million trees were planted on that first Arbor Day. Julius Sterling Morton's idea spread across the country, and in the next twenty years more than 600 million trees were planted, and a hundred thousand acres of waste land were turned into forests. Yes, a few farsighted citizens were beginning to think about the future. John Muir, lover of trees and mountains, fought valiantly to save the redwoods of California. He made speeches whenever he had a chance. One of his most enthusiastic supporters was Robert Underwood Johnson, Editor of *Century Magazine*.

HISTORIAN: In the year 1889, John Muir took Mr. Johnson on a camping trip to Yosemite Valley, California. Sitting around their campfire one evening, after hiking through the Tuolumne* watershed, the two men reviewed their day. (MUIR *and* JOHNSON *enter right and sit as if around campfire. Spotlight comes up on them.*)

JOHNSON: I'll never forget our hike today, John. I hope you'll write an article about the watershed that readers of *Century Magazine* won't be able to forget!

MUIR: I'll try. (*Pauses, musing*) The only thing I regret is that we had a day without a trace of wind. You would have enjoyed seeing the trees blow in the wind.

JOHNSON: I thought it was a beautiful day.

MUIR: But nothing is more exhilarating than to climb a great tree and travel with it in the wind. (*Shakes his head*) I'm afraid I had you looking more at the ground today than at treetops, Rob.

JOHNSON: But we had to look at the ground for the evidence you wanted to show me. Until today I never realized how damaging grazing sheep can be to the countryside.

MUIR (*Angrily*): Locusts with hoofs! That's what hordes of sheep are like . . . hoofed locusts!

JOHNSON: Sheep are much harder on land than cattle, aren't they? Nibbling down the young seedlings, and cutting the sod to shreds with those sharp hoofs.

MUIR: Overgrazing by cattle can be devastating, too. This beautiful country must be saved from such scourges. Why, as

---

* Too-ol'-uh-me

long as thirteen years ago I proposed that a national commission be appointed to take measures for saving the trees. (*Sadly*) Am I a voice crying in the wilderness?

JOHNSON (*Warmly*): You are a voice being heard, John. (MUIR *rises and walks right.*)

MUIR (*Looking up*): The greatest dream of my life is to see a national park established here, including the best of the Sequoia groves, so the future of the king of trees will be assured.

JOHNSON (*Jumping up; eagerly*): Let's make your dream a reality, John! Let's work together to initiate a campaign to establish such a national park! I'm confident that public-spirited citizens all over will rally to the cause. You do the writing and *Century Magazine* will do the publishing . . . and *now* is the time to start! (MUIR *and* JOHNSON *exit.*)

MODERATOR: And so around a campfire began one of the greatest conservation eras in our country's history. Spurred on by the Muir-Johnson movement, Congress passed the Yosemite National Park bill the very next year. The year after, in 1891, Congress passed an act empowering the President to create forest reserves. John Muir's dream was on its way to fulfillment. Another milestone marked the year 1892, when Muir helped found the Sierra Club, dedicated to the task of preserving America's wild beauty. He became the Club's first president.

HISTORIAN: The conservation wheels were really beginning to turn. One after another, leaders appeared to set the course. (REPORTER *rises.*)

REPORTER (*Reading*): "No man is entitled to call himself a decent citizen if he does not try to do his part toward seeing that our national policies are shaped for the advantage of our children and our children's children." (*Looks up*) Those are the words of Theodore Roosevelt, President of the United States from 1901 to 1909. (*Sits*)

MODERATOR: Roosevelt and his good friend Gifford Pinchot, Chief Forester of the United States from 1898 to 1910, were two of our greatest conservationists. Pinchot believed that instead of allowing our natural resources to be wastefully exploited, we should learn to use our wildlife, forests, grazing ranges, and water power scientifically and not faster than they could be reproduced. In that way they would last forever. President Roosevelt and Mr. Pinchot, working together, were responsible for saving millions of acres of public land for forest preserves for the use and benefit of all Americans. (*Music grows louder, then becomes softer, fading out.*)

HISTORIAN: Yet in spite of the conservation milestones there were setbacks. The early 1930s were tragic years for the nation. Not only was the entire country suffering from the Great Depression, but the prairie states thirsted for rain. A long drought gripped the land. (FRED, RUTH, *and* BILLY *enter right, sit at chairs around desk.*) People learned what it was like to live in a dust bowl. (*Spotlight comes up on desk.*)

FRED: The ground's plowed, the wheat's planted, but there's no rain. The ground is as dry as can be, and the wind is whipping up the dust more than ever.

RUTH: I'm afraid the wind's going to uncover all the new seed, Fred.

BILLY: I'd like to be able to play outside without getting dust in my eyes and throat.

RUTH (*Thoughtfully*): That speaker at the church meeting the other day said some things I can't get out of my mind. He said that long before man set eyes on these prairies, they belonged to the buffalo. The buffalo herds moved back and forth, cropping the grass as they went, hardly leaving a footprint or a sign they'd passed. Then the buffalo were all killed off, and the prairies became the cattlemen's. They fenced the land and let too many cows graze inside the fences. Some of the grass

roots died, and the ground showed bare in places. Then the
farmers took over the prairies.

FRED (*Nodding*): And we plow them up mile after mile and plant
wheat. . . .

RUTH: The speaker said that's the trouble. There's no grass to
hold the earth together anymore, as there was in the beginning, when the wind could blow without bringing a dust storm
with it.

FRED: So what does this speaker think we should do?

RUTH: He thinks some of the land should be planted back to
grass . . . and fewer cows be put out to graze in the pastures.
He thinks we should plant windbreaks to blunt the force of
the wind. (*They all jump, as if startled.*) Just listen to that
wind! It's making the whole house shake! (BILLY *rises.*)

BILLY: I wonder if it blew away the chicken coop. (*Peers offstage*) No, it's still there. But, Mom! Sand is piling up all over
the lilac bush Grandma brought us last summer.

FRED (*Gloomily*): At the rate western Kansas is blowing away,
some of it will probably land on your grandma's lilacs in
lower Michigan! (*Spotlight goes out.* FRED, RUTH, *and* BILLY
exit.)

MODERATOR: The long drought and terrible dust storms came
during the years when President Franklin Delano Roosevelt
was trying to conquer the Depression and get the country on
its feet again. An ardent conservationist, like President
Theodore Roosevelt before him, FDR set about to solve the
problems that shook the country from one end to the other.
Through work relief programs in forestation and flood and
erosion control, and through Civilian Conservation Corps
camps for young men, he helped millions of our citizens survive the Depression and improve our country at the same
time.

REPORTER: His greatest and most controversial experiment was
in the depressed area of the Tennessee River valley, where the

cash income of most families was about $100 a year. Their poverty was aggravated by periodic floods. They lived on run-down farms without electricity or running water . . . or hope. President Roosevelt created the Tennessee Valley Authority—TVA it was called—in 1933, chiefly to supply farmers and industry with cheap electric power.

SCIENTIST: But also to check erosion.

LIBRARIAN: To improve navigation on the river.

HISTORIAN: To control floods.

LIBRARIAN: To reforest cut-over land.

SCIENTIST: To encourage scientific farming.

HISTORIAN: To give the people hope again.

REPORTER: In spite of severe opposition, the TVA program went through. The experiment was a success—the Tennessee Valley was upgraded, and hope and prosperity came to a renewed land. (*Music is heard for a few moments, then fades out.*)

MODERATOR: But what about the problems of our own day? We face problems which could not have been imagined by George Perkins Marsh, or John Muir, or Theodore Roosevelt and Gifford Pinchot. What about the problems created by the gasoline motor and the age of technology?

SCIENTIST: Air pollution.

LIBRARIAN: Water pollution.

HISTORIAN: Soil pollution.

REPORTER: The energy crisis.

MODERATOR: As everyone knows, the chief villains in the air pollution drama are power plants, factories, and automobiles.

SCIENTIST: In spite of the installation of smoke-reduction devices for factories and emission controls on cars, polluted air is still very much with us, often in dangerous proportions.

REPORTER: America is on the alert about air pollution . . . and recognizing the danger is half the battle.

LIBRARIAN: In the past few years the quality of air in most American cities has improved.

SCIENTIST: Engineers say that air in most urban areas will meet health standards by the late 1980s.

MODERATOR: We've made some progress with water pollution, too—cleaning up streams, rivers, lakes. But then again in some instances we've made progress backwards. (*Takes clipping from table*) Here is a recent clipping which states that at least 665,000 square miles of the Atlantic Ocean from Cape Cod to the Caribbean are heavily polluted, with floating tar, plastic debris, and oil spills from the tankers that cruise the waters. (REPORTER *picks up clipping*.)

REPORTER: But here's a brighter note! (*Reads*) "Lake Erie, once considered 'dead,' is showing marked improvement."

HISTORIAN (*Picking up clipping*): And another. (*Reads*) Officials of the Environmental Protection Agency say that by 1983, most U.S. rivers will be relatively clean.

MODERATOR: We are alerted and we are acting. All it takes is a leader, someone like John Muir or FDR to show us the way. Sometimes the voice of only one man can wake up the whole world . . .

LIBRARIAN (*Sharply*): One man! Why does it always have to be a man?

MODERATOR: It doesn't. But up to now most of our leaders in the conservation movement have been men.

REPORTER: What about Rachel Carson? She sounded the alarm for this generation about the dangers of destroying the balance of nature. (RACHEL CARSON, *carrying a stack of mail, enters right with* MRS. CARSON. RACHEL *puts mail on desk and helps her mother to a chair*.)

MODERATOR: You're right. She was one of those dedicated souls who appeared in the right place at the right time.

REPORTER: The place is Rachel Carson's home near Washington, D.C., and the time is January 1958 . . . (*Spotlight comes up on desk*.)

MRS. CARSON: You always have so many letters to answer, Rachel, on top of your other work. I only wish I could help you, the way I used to before this arthritis took over.

RACHEL (*Affectionately*): Where would I have been without you, Mother? Think of all the books you typed for me! (*Dreamily*) *Under the Sea Wind . . . The Sea Around Us . . . The Edge of the Sea.*

MRS. CARSON: Three best sellers in a row! I'm so proud of you, Rachel. I don't see how you did it . . . working at the Government Fish and Wildlife office all day, and then coming home and writing at night.

RACHEL: You were a great help. (*Picks up letter, opens it, scans it*) Another invitation to be guest speaker at a women's club. (*Puts it aside, picks up another*) This is from a young housewife on a Colorado farm, thanking me for bringing the sea to her. She's never had a chance to walk on a beach or listen to the surf. (*Looks at* MRS. CARSON) And neither did I until I graduated from college. (*Picks up another letter*) Why, here's one from my old friend Olga Owens Huckins.

MRS. CARSON: I remember her. (RACHEL *takes clipping from envelope.*)

RACHEL: She's enclosed a clipping from the *Baltimore Herald*, a letter she wrote to the editor. (*Scans it unhappily.*) Oh, how dreadful! (*Looks up*) Olga and her husband own a small place in Massachusetts, just north of Cape Cod. They made it into a bird sanctuary. Recently the state sprayed the area from the air to control mosquitoes. But the poison didn't stop with mosquitoes . . . it killed harmless insects, too, and fish in the pond, and birds.

MRS. CARSON (*Distressed*): That's terrible!

RACHEL: Oh, I'm sure the state didn't realize what it was doing. (*Angrily*) But anyone should know that spraying from the air might be dangerous. Olga wonders if I can get in touch with some officials in Washington who would put a stop to this sort of thing.

MRS. CARSON: After working all those years in Washington, Rachel, you must know the right people to contact.

RACHEL: I'll get some letters off this afternoon. Spraying like that could have tragic consequences. (*Spotlight goes off* RACHEL *and her mother and up on* MODERATOR.)

MODERATOR: Although Rachel Carson was hard at work on another book, she took time to write to men of authority in Washington who might stop indiscriminate spraying. She also began to read up on DDT and other chemicals. Discovering that some naturalists were already up in arms about spraying, she wondered why more action had not been taken. (*Spotlight comes up on* RACHEL *and* MRS. CARSON, *who are reading letters.*)

RACHEL: So many replies to my inquiries are coming in! The more I learn about pesticides, the more appalled I become. (*Angrily*) Why, Mother, we're slowly poisoning our good earth and many of the creatures that live on it.

MRS. CARSON: Somebody should write a book about it.

RACHEL: That's what many of my correspondents say. What's more, they suggest that *I* am the one to do it.

MRS. CARSON (*Surprised*): You? But it isn't your field, Rachel. Pesticides haven't much to do with the sea, have they? Pesticides are sprayed on the land.

RACHEL: But some of them get washed into the sea, of course. People must be told what's happening . . . before it's too late!

MRS. CARSON: Rachel, this pesticide problem is controversial. You'd make a lot of enemies.

RACHEL: No doubt.

MRS. CARSON: You've worked so hard for so long. You should take a rest. (*Sighs, looks at* RACHEL *thoughtfully*) Still . . . how could we live in a world without birds to sing?

RACHEL: That's just it . . . we couldn't, Mother. A silent spring is impossible to imagine. (*Suddenly determined*) I am aghast at our country's heedless tampering with nature. I must put my other work aside and find out all I can about pesticides. It will take a long time to gather the material, organize it, and make it readable. But I'll do it!

MRS. CARSON (*Warmly*): I'll do all I can to help, Rachel. (*Spotlight goes out. RACHEL and MRS. CARSON exit.*)

REPORTER: And so Rachel Carson began her monumental task, to show the effect of DDT and other pesticides on growing things. Her mother, always eager to help and encourage her, died in December of that year, 1958. Rachel carried on alone.

MODERATOR: Four years later, in 1962, *Silent Spring* was published. (LIBRARIAN *picks up book and stands.*)

LIBRARIAN (*Reading from "Silent Spring"*): "The most alarming of all man's assaults upon the environment is the contamination of air, earth, rivers, and sea with dangerous and even lethal materials . . . that have the power to kill every insect, the 'good' and the 'bad,' to still the song of birds . . . and to linger on in the soil." (*Sits*)

REPORTER: *Silent Spring* created a sensation. It was, of course, bitterly attacked by the makers of pesticides and other vested interests. But the facts were there for all to see, and the reading public was impressed . . . and grateful. *Silent Spring* quickly became a best seller.

MODERATOR: Thanks to Rachel Carson, the use of DDT and several other pesticides is now either banned or restricted, and scientists are re-studying the whole problem. (*There is stir in audience. 1ST BOY begins to come forward, followed by 2ND BOY and PAM. At same time CHRIS enters right, crosses stage to join others.*)

1ST BOY (*Going up steps*): Sir . . . (2ND BOY *and* PAM *climb steps.*)

2ND BOY (*To* MODERATOR): May we say something, sir? (*All four meet at* MODERATOR's *table.*)

MODERATOR (*Pleased*): Why, of course. We always appreciate audience participation in a program like this.

1ST BOY: You've been talking about what happened in the past . . . and what's happening now. What we want to know about is the future!

PAM: Yes. We're the ones who're going to have to run things in the future. What about a few years from now, when it's the end of the century? What will it be like when we're adults?

2ND BOY: How many of those natural resources you've been talking about will be left?

HISTORIAN: Well, timber is a replaceable resource. Trees will grow again, fortunately. New methods of tree-planting and tree-cutting are keeping us pretty well in balance. So we hope you won't have to worry much about being out of lumber and paper.

CHRIS: What about minerals? Like copper . . .

PAM: Tin.

1ST BOY: Iron.

2ND BOY: Zinc.

CHRIS: Uranium.

SCIENTIST: I'm sorry to say they're *not* replaceable resources. Once dug up and used, they're gone forever. It took a billion years and more for those ores to be laid down in the earth's crust. It's taken only one hundred years, more or less, for most of them to be used.

TWO BOYS, PAM, *and* CHRIS (*Together*): *Gone!*

SCIENTIST: Some lower-grade ores will be left, but it will cost a great deal to extract them.

CHRIS: Then what are we going to *do*? (SCIENTIST *and* HISTORIAN *look at each other, shrug.*)

SCIENTIST: That's a question we can't answer yet. There is only one thing I can say. We have used our resources wastefully over the past hundred years. If we turn about right now, and become savers instead of wasters, the ores that are left will last on into the next century . . . until, let us hope, substitutes are invented.

CHRIS: And what about gasoline for cars, and oil and natural gas for heating houses? How long will they last?

REPORTER: Not long, at the rate we're using them. They're in short supply right now. By the time you're adults, they will probably all be gone from the crust of the earth and burned.

PAM: So how will we drive our cars?

REPORTER: That's another million-dollar question. As you know from the headlines, fuel to run a gasoline engine is getting more scarce and expensive all the time. There's enough coal left in the ground to last for several hundred years, and it could be converted into liquid fuel, but the cost would be high, very high.

PAM (*Annoyed*): I don't think those people who used up all the resources were very fair to us.

LIBRARIAN: I don't, either. But now that Americans know the danger they're in, perhaps they'll change. As I said before, being aware of a problem is half the battle of solving it. We can speed up programs we have already started, to save our resources. . . .

SCIENTIST: Recycle more paper. Most towns have a pick-up service for newspapers and magazines.

LIBRARIAN: Don't throw away your metal cans! Americans discard billions of cans a year. Only a small proportion are now recycled.

REPORTER: The same applies to glass bottles. In fact, many states, in spite of opposition from large manufacturing companies, have passed legislation requiring deposits on bottles. These "bottle bills" mean that bottles can be washed, sterilized, and reused—rather than thrown away in the trash, or worse still, left as litter on streets and sidewalks!

HISTORIAN: We can also conserve by burning more trash in city plants for fuel . . .

SCIENTIST: And by reclaiming metals from scrap piles.

LIBRARIAN: Save more gas. Walk instead of ride, or use a bike.

REPORTER: Take the bus, the subway or train, or join a car pool.

HISTORIAN: Drive smaller cars that use less gas.

SCIENTIST: Save electricity.

LIBRARIAN: Save heat.

REPORTER: Save food.

ALL (*Enthusiastically*): Save everything!

MODERATOR: As newcomers to this planet, we have had a lot to learn. And we are still learning. We have made many mistakes. But fortunately we are flexible, we have intelligence, we can correct our mistakes and, at least in some measure, repair the damage we have done. Two hundred million Americans can accomplish great things in a short time, if they set their minds to it. And when they realize that they have been unfair to future generations, I am sure they will join together to help save and recondition this beautiful planet we call earth. (*Music to "This Land Is Your Land" or "America the Beautiful" is heard, growing louder. All may sing, if desired, as curtains slowly close.*)

THE END

Trouble in the Air

Characters

MASTER OF CEREMONIES
CHORUS
MRS. WILLIAMS
ANNA
PEGGY
ERNIE
RADIO VOICE
THREE NURSERYMEN
TWO WOMEN
YOUNG WOMAN WITH BRIEFCASE
CHILDREN
TOWNSPEOPLE
OFFICIAL
SECRETARY
MAILMAN
WOMAN IN AUDIENCE
METEOROLOGIST
BUSINESSMAN
THREE CLUBWOMEN
TWO BUILDING INSPECTORS
TWO BOYS
ALAN
SHEILA

SETTING: *A sparsely-furnished stage. There is a lectern for the Master of Ceremonies. Behind lectern are chairs for Chorus. At left is a park bench, and at right, a small table and chairs.*

AT RISE: MASTER OF CEREMONIES *and* CHORUS *are on stage.* M.C. *has script.*

M.C.: What we done, America?

What have we done to our broad and spacious land?

We have cut down our hillside forests and let the soil wash away.

We have plowed prairies that should have been left in sod, and let the wind blow away the good earth.

We have allowed our estuaries to become clogged with silt, and our gullies to cut ugly scars across the land.

What have we done, America, to clear streams and rivers that once sparkled on their way to the sea?

We have plowed our slopes so that silver water turns brown with every rain that falls.

We have polluted rivers and lakes with our wastes until they are no longer fit for fish to swim in or for man to drink.

But most startling of all, America, what have we done to the clear expansive skies that once formed a dome of blue over our great country? What have we done to the air we breathe, America? What have we done?

CHORUS (*Chanting*):

> Trouble in the air. . . .
> Azure once was there . . .
> Now a sea of murky smog
> Is anything but rare.

M.C.: Back in the days of our innocence, we thought belching smokestacks and puffing motors a blessing, a sign of prosperity. We thought factories giving work to hundreds and thousands of people were a symbol of progress.

Was not America the horn of plenty?

Were not our resources of land, water, and air inexhaustible?

We refused to look at our desecrations. We assumed that the blue sky would be with us forever, that we would be assured of a continual supply of pure air. But in 1948 something happened in Donora, Pennsylvania, that gave us pause to reconsider.

CHORUS: Trouble in the air . . . trouble in the air.

M.C.: Donora, a little steel town in Pennsylvania, lies in a bowl-like valley of the Monongahela River, about thirty miles south of Pittsburgh. In the old days, residents could sit on their porches and see the mountaintops twenty or thirty miles away. But as the town became more and more industrialized with steel mills, and zinc and sulfuric acid plants, distances hazed over, and finally disappeared from sight.

Residents of Donora became used to the grimy air of an industrial town. And so they thought little of it when they awoke on the morning of October 26, 1948, to find their town engulfed in a sooty fog. The air hung heavy and still, filled with the stench of sulfur. As the morning wore on, the murkiness increased. Streetlights were unable to make a dent in the darkness. By noon, doctors' telephones were ringing constantly. Residents who were very old and very young were having difficulty breathing. Others suffered from nausea, sore throat, or smarting eyes.

CHORUS:

> Trouble in the air . . .
> Fumes and smog to spare!
> How to get a wholesome breath
> of unpolluted air?

M.C.: The fog did not lift. A lid of warm air, like a huge cover over a bowl, trapped the poison-laden fog in the valley. That was on a Tuesday. Wednesday came. Smoke kept pouring from chimneys and smokestacks, mingling with the fog. The thick sulfurous murk was worse than ever. By Thursday, scarcely a household in Donora was free from suffering. On Friday, the poisonous air, thicker, darker, and more lethal than ever before in the valley, still hung over the little town. Saturday dawned, dark as night. Residents of Donora were desperate. They could scarcely breathe. Early in the afternoon at the Williams home near the edge of town, Mrs. Williams and Anna sit at the dining room table, miserable, desperate. (MRS. WILLIAMS *and* ANNA *enter and take their places at the table.* MRS. WILLIAMS *coughs periodically.* ANNA *sits with head in hands.*) They both think the same thoughts. How much longer can it go on? How much longer can they stand the sickening smell of sulfur, seeping in through every crack and crevice?

MRS. WILLIAMS (*Calling offstage, coughing*): Peggy! Did you take Grandma her dinner as I asked you to?

PEGGY (*Entering right*): She can't eat, Ma. She can hardly breathe. She just keeps on gasping. Makes me scared, Ma.

MRS. WILLIAMS: Put Grandma's plate in the warming oven, then. (*Coughs*) Maybe she'll feel more like it later. (PEGGY *goes out. There is silence for a few moments, punctuated by sound of coughing. Then* ERNIE *comes in, looking heartbroken.*)

ERNIE: Ma . . . Rover's dead. (*Goes near her*) Just couldn't get his breath anymore . . .

ANNA (*Getting up suddenly*): Well, neither can I! Neither can *I.* (*Starts out, then turns*) I feel as if we're in a tomb, and can't get out. Yesterday, Grandma's canary died. Today, Rover. Tomorrow . . . I shudder to think. (*With a frightened cry, she hurries out.*)

MRS. WILLIAMS: If it doesn't rain soon . . . if the fog doesn't lift, I don't know what's going to happen to us. (*Coughs; counts on fingers*) Tuesday . . . Wednesday . . . Thursday . . . Friday . . . Saturday. Today's the fifth day that black fog and sulfur have been filling our lungs. It's never been so long before.

ERNIE: Rover never even opened his eyes to take a last look at me, Ma.

MRS. WILLIAMS: We can't go on like this—

ERNIE: He couldn't eat. His breakfast's still in his pan.

MRS. WILLIAMS: I wish your father would get another job, in a cleaner town . . . even if it wouldn't pay so much, even if we'd have a harder time getting along.

ERNIE: But he tried to lick my hand a little.

PEGGY (*Running in; excitedly*): I heard something on the roof.

ERNIE: Soot falling, that's what you heard. Cinders.

PEGGY: No, listen! It sounds like drops.

MRS. WILLIAMS (*Lifting her face expectantly*): Can it be *rain*, Peggy? (*Pauses, as if listening*) Yes. Yes! It *is* rain! Rain to wash the air clean again. We must go tell Grandma! (*They hurry out.*)

M.C.: Yes, on Saturday afternoon, October 30, 1948, rain began to fall on Donora, breaking the five-day siege of sulfurous pollution. When it was all over and the figures were tallied, here is how the score stood.

RADIO VOICE (*From offstage, through microphone or loudspeaker*): Latest reports show twenty people dead from the smog. Almost 6,000 people—forty-three percent of the population of Donora—suffering from acute poisoning. An undetermined number of animals dead—mostly cats, dogs, and canaries.

M.C.: But the figures tell only part of the story. They fail to show how many people, seriously affected by the smog, will have less resistance hereafter. They fail to show how many will get sick more often and die sooner than they otherwise would.

What have we done, America?

What have we done, planet Earth?

The same year as the Donora disaster, three hundred residents of London died during an air-pollution episode, when fumes of burning soft coal, mixed with fog, were trapped over the city. Four years later, *four thousand* died in a similar London episode, and another thousand in 1956. Still another smog disaster in 1962 caused the death of seven hundred and fifty more Londoners.

CHORUS:

> Trouble in the air . . .
> Striking here and there.
> Poisons trapped above a town
> Are more than folks can bear.

M.C.: What have we done?

What have we done to California, famous for its sunny skies and mild climate? To Los Angeles, the city of angels?

Clarity of the air was one of the reasons the motion picture industry decided to make its headquarters in Los Angeles. For a few decades all was well. But gradually distances became hazy. Residents tried to ignore the trouble, tried to think of it as a temporary condition caused by the weather. But soon the haze could be ignored no longer. During the Second World War real trouble struck.

CHORUS:

> Trouble in the air . . .
> Nothing now so rare
> As the blue unsullied sky
> That once was shining there.

M.C.: Residents began to worry. Tourists began to ask questions. Gardeners and nurserymen began to wonder out loud what was wrong. (THREE NURSERYMEN *enter right, and cross stage slowly while talking.*)

1ST MAN: It's my orchids I'm concerned about. My orchids!

2ND MAN: What's wrong with them?

1ST MAN: I can't figure it out. Haven't changed a thing . . . temperature, humidity, water, care. I do just what I did last year and the year before. But my orchids don't thrive. Worse still, most of them refuse to grow at all . . . and they're a big part of my business.

2ND MAN: It's spinach I'm having trouble with. Seems I just can't raise spinach here anymore. And it always was such a good money crop. What's gone wrong with Los Angeles, anyway?

3RD MAN: With me, it's citrus. Trees start dropping their leaves too early and the fruit's too small. I don't understand—I'm giving my grove the same care I always have. Something must be wrong with the air. Too many people . . . too many industries . . . too much smoke or something. (*They exit.*)

M.C.: Something *was* wrong with the air over Los Angeles . . . but what? Everyone could see that the sky was getting hazier . . . but why? Consternation mounted. Strange things happened. (Two WOMEN *come in left, and walk across stage.*)

1ST WOMAN: Did you hear about the nylon stockings?

2ND WOMAN: No. What happened?

1ST WOMAN: Vera told me someone's nylon stockings went to shreds. Right on the street. From the smog or something.

2ND WOMAN: To shreds? (*Looks down at her stockings*) Mine still seem to be all right, thank goodness. But the smog's getting worse and worse, isn't it? If that's true about the stockings, we women ought to do something about it. Where's it going to stop? Might be our *dresses* going to pieces next.

1ST WOMAN: *Somebody* ought to do something about it, that's for sure. (*They exit right.*)

M.C.: At first people blamed a government-financed synthetic rubber plant for the smoke and fumes that muddied the sky. But after the war, the plant closed down, and smog conditions in Los Angeles were no better. Then the oil refineries were blamed. Then industrial expansion, with increased smoke from plants and factories. Then back-yard incinerators. For some years Los Angeles tried through trial and error to pinpoint the major source of the smog. The air pollution control board eliminated one possible source after another. Ordinances forbade the use of soft coal, the home-burning of trash, the amount of fumes emitted from smoke-stacks. But the smog persisted.

CHORUS:

>Trouble in the air . . .
>Quandary to share:
>The sky is dark with smudgy smog
>But what has put it there?

M.C.: For the time being the question remained unanswered. Meanwhile other towns and cities across our fair land were having troubles, too. But the cause of hazy skies and evil-smelling fumes was not always as mysterious as in Los Angeles. (YOUNG WOMAN WITH BRIEFCASE *enters, sits on bench to listen and take notes.*) Up in Oregon, in the little town of Springfield, residents knew well enough what the trouble was. In August, 1949, the Weyerhaeuser Company had opened a mill in Springfield for the making of kraft paper. The stench from the mill was terrible. (CHILDREN *and* TOWNSPEOPLE *cross stage making faces, holding noses.*)

People began to protest, quietly at first. Then clubwomen brought up the matter at their meetings. Letters to the Editor appeared in the paper. But the stench continued. Finally in February, 1950, someone had a brilliant idea, and spread the news around the town. Men, women, and children smiled hopefully and went to work with paper and paste and pen and purpose. On the morning of February 14, a mailman staggered into the Weyerhaeuser office with an overflowing mail pouch. He overturned it on the desk of one of the officials, who was dictating to his secretary. (OFFICIAL *and* SECRETARY *come in and take places at table.* MAILMAN *enters with pouch full of mail, overturns it on table.*)

MAILMAN: Sorry. There's no room in the mailbox.

SECRETARY: You mean all this mail is for us? The whole pouchful?

OFFICIAL: Is this April Fool's Day or something?

MAILMAN: Not April Fool. Valentine's Day. And this isn't all. Valentines are still coming in by the dozen. I'll be back! (*Goes out*)

OFFICIAL: Valentines! (*Nods to* SECRETARY) Open a few. It looks as if the worthy citizens of Springfield are grateful for the jobs we're giving them.

SECRETARY (*Scanning letter*): I'm not so sure. Listen to this. (*Reads*)

> Roses are red,
> Violets are blue,
> Nobody smells
> As strong as you.

OFFICIAL (*Taking another letter, opening it, reading*):

> Hickory, dickory, deal,
> You wonder how we feel?
> Instead of being gay
> On Valentine's Day,
> Your odors make us *reel*.

SECRETARY (*Opening big envelope*): Here's a big, red heart.

OFFICIAL: What does it say?

SECRETARY (*Reading*):

> A hen's a fowl,
> A duck's a fowl,
> A cock's a fowl, it's true,
> But nothing,
> Horrid paper mill,
> Is quite as foul as you!

OFFICIAL: Hm-m-m. Looks as if we haven't made such a hit in this town, after all. (*Opens another letter*) Here's another card that has only two words. *You stink.* (*He sniffs the air, then gets up and walks around, sniffing.*) Maybe they've got something there. Come on, let's show the boss. (*He and* SECRETARY *gather letters and exit.*)

M.C.: Weyerhaeuser officials took the Valentine barrage very seriously. They began at once to find a solution to the stench. Purchasing a war surplus barrage balloon, they rigged it up to collect the smelly gases and feed them back to a special furnace where they could be eliminated. Later they refined the system even further, with the result that Springfield residents no longer had cause to object to odors from the mill. (YOUNG WOMAN *gets up from bench and steps forward.*)

YOUNG WOMAN: It all goes to show that when the cause of air pollution is known, something *can* be done about it.

M.C.: True—there are many shining examples of the way businesses do cooperate. And lack of cooperation doesn't come only from business. Much of it comes from ordinary people who don't want to be inconvenienced by being told how to stoke their furnaces or dispose of their trash and garbage. What happened in Pittsburgh, though, shows what can be done when people get together with a common ideal.

YOUNG WOMAN: Pittsburgh—the Smoky City?

M.C. (*Nodding*): For years it had the reputation of being the dirtiest, grimiest, smokiest, smudgiest, murkiest city in the United States. Every day tons of soot and cinders, smoke and fumes poured from steel mills and factories, railroad yards and foundries. (*Thumbs pages of script, looks around on floor, behind chairs and table, checks script again*) Something seems to have happened to Pittsburgh. There's a page missing. (*Looks some more*)

WOMAN IN AUDIENCE: Mr. Chairman . . .

M.C.: Yes?

WOMAN: I know something about Pittsburgh. I lived there in 1948, at the time the reform movement started.

M.C.: Good. And can you tell us something about it, before and after? (WOMAN *comes to stage*.)

WOMAN (*Shuddering*): Before I don't know how we ever stood the constant soot and grime, the dirty buildings, the greasy dark windowpanes, the constant pall of smoke over the city. Sometimes streetlights and car lights burning in the middle of the day could hardly penetrate the murk.

M.C.: And then?

WOMAN: Civic leaders and businessmen and city officials got together to try to find a solution. They prevailed upon the railroads to replace coal-burning locomotives with diesel engines. We homeowners were required by law to use smokeless coal in our furnaces, or change to gas or oil. Mills, factories, and foundries had to install smoke-control devices or pay a heavy fine. Coal-burning tugboats on the rivers had to change to diesel power. In four years, Pittsburgh had its face completely lifted. The dirtiest city in the United States became one of the cleanest.

M.C.: And has it stayed that way?

WOMAN: Yes, it has. I moved away during the cleanup, but I was back on a visit not long ago. Of course, controls on industries haven't been a hundred percent effective, and the sky isn't always a bright and shining blue, but the change is dramatic . . . almost miraculous. (YOUNG WOMAN *sits on bench, takes notes silently*.)

M.C.: Thank you, my friend. Thank you for filling in the missing page. (*Turns back to script*) Not long after Pittsburgh's transformation, New York City had its first ordeal by smog. For ten days, in November, 1953, a temperature inversion trapped polluted air over our country's biggest city.

CHORUS:

>Trouble in the air . . .
>Poisons trapped, beware!
>Smarting eyes and burning lungs
>Make citizens despair.

M.C.: Temperature inversion, coupled with pollution, the cause of four thousand deaths in London the year before, now threatened New York City with disaster. Under the lid of warm air holding down the fumes, New Yorkers faced the ordeal of smarting eyes and burning lungs . . . until rain came or wind began to blow away the polluted air. (METEOROLO-GIST, *holding a book, enters, reading as he slowly crosses stage*.) "Blow, wind, blow!" was the prayer on everybody's lips, for wind is a city's savior during an episode of smog.

METEOROLOGIST (*Looking up*): Pardon me, sir. I'm just a passerby. But I happen to be a meteorologist. Are you saying that wind is always a cure-all for air pollution?

M.C.: It is, isn't it?

METEOROLOGIST: Usually, yes. But then again, it may not be entirely helpful. It may rescue one city, only to threaten another. A strong wind has been known to blow pollutants hundreds of miles away, causing no end of damage and suffering.

M.C.: I hadn't thought of that.

METEOROLOGIST: Sadly, air pollutants contribute significantly to the death rate in urban areas. According to a study done several years ago, if we could reduce by half the amount of air pollution in our cities, we would cause the death rate to be lowered by nearly five percent.

M.C. (*Softly*): No city is safe these days.

METEOROLOGIST: And it's not only the cities that are troubled by pollutants. For instance, some years ago, the government selected a site in the Rocky Mountains close to the Continental Divide for a solar observatory. Climax, Colorado, was chosen because of isolation and clear air. Now, even there, so much haze moves in from the West that the new 16-inch corona-graph is no more effective than an 8-inch one was twenty-five years ago. But don't let me interrupt your story. I'm just putting in a word as I passed by. (*Exits, reading his book*)

BUSINESSMAN (*Coming forward*): I object to all this talk about smokestacks polluting the air. I've been talking it over with some of my friends, leading business executives. We can't see that there's anything to get excited about. People have to put up with a little smoke as a price of progress. They ought to be glad to see factories running full blast; it means business is booming. It costs a lot of money to install devices to control the smoke and fumes from industrial wastes. Prices would have to go up to absorb the cost, and people are kicking about high prices as it is. I think all this talk about air pollution is just a lot of ballyhoo. (*He starts to go.*)

YOUNG WOMAN (*Jumping up from bench*): Just a minute, sir. I've a little present for you.

BUSINESSMAN: For *me*?

YOUNG WOMAN: Yes, blinders aren't enough. You might as well get used to wearing one of these . . . because if you have your way, *everyone* will soon have to wear them. (*Takes small package from briefcase, hands it to him.*)

BUSINESSMAN: What is it?

YOUNG WOMAN: Open it and see. It won't bite you.

BUSINESSMAN (*Unwrapping contraption with goggles and tube*): I still don't get it.

M.C.: A gas mask!

BUSINESSMAN (*Dropping it quickly, drawing back*): I've no use for that, young lady.

YOUNG WOMAN: Oh, yes, you have. Anyone who believes as you do—

BUSINESSMAN (*Striding out angrily*): Nonsense!

YOUNG WOMAN (*To M.C.*): That's one of the big difficulties in controlling air pollution. Many people haven't seen the light yet. Of course, it costs to install smoke-control devices.

M.C.: *Not* to install them costs in other ways. In life and health. In graciousness and beauty. We are ruining, almost beyond repair, the clear skies that have been our heritage these many years.

YOUNG WOMAN: Emphysema, lung cancer, bronchitis . . . even the common cold are linked to air pollution. Why, experts say in the future our big cities may become uninhabitable . . . unless drastic steps are soon taken.

M.C.: What have we done, America?

CHORUS:

> Trouble in the air . . .
> City folk, prepare
> To solve the problem speedily
> Or buy a mask to wear.

YOUNG WOMAN (*Putting mask back in briefcase*): Doesn't it strike you as strange that we have let this pollution problem get such a head start? That we just sort of stand helplessly by? We are smart enough to put men on the moon, to concoct wonder drugs, to invent computers, to solve the most intricate problems. Yet we don't seem to be able to conquer this problem of poisoned air that is slowly killing us. It doesn't make sense, does it?

M.C.: If air pollution were a sudden and spectacular killer like a flood, or a fire, or a plague, or an earthquake, we'd meet the crisis speedily enough. But, except for a few dramatic episodes, it's a slow-moving, continuous kind of affliction. It doesn't rouse the average citizens to action . . . the way it did the residents of Springfield, Oregon, and Pittsburgh, Pennsylvania. But I think it's safe to say that more people are becoming interested and taking action. Let's go back to Los Angeles and see what happened there. That gas mask of yours makes me think of it.

YOUNG WOMAN: It does?

M.C. (*Nodding*): In the early days of the Los Angeles smog, a few housewives banded together in an organization called SOS—Stamp Out Smog. They proposed to do something about the thickening smudge that hung over the city. Armed with facts, and sometimes with gas masks, they appeared at public meetings. They talked to factory managers. They roused their neighbors and friends. Before long, membership in SOS was soaring.

YOUNG WOMAN: The idea spread all over the country. The last I heard, there were thousands of organizations in the United States made up of citizens fighting pollution. That means formidable voting strength! I must find out if there is a local group here. (*Makes a note*)

M.C.: It was largely through pressure from the women that smog-control measures were put into effect by the Los Angeles pollution control board. Officials of 40,000 offending plants were hauled into court, and most of them were convicted for polluting the air. But the women were not always satisfied with the size of the fines. When one large California oil company was convicted of pollution and fined only five hundred dollars, the women were up in arms. At a hastily-called meeting everyone wanted to talk at once . . . (THREE CLUBWOMEN *enter left, all talking*.)

1ST WOMAN: What's five hundred dollars to a corporation earning millions a year?

2ND WOMAN: They're probably laughing up their sleeves.

3RD WOMAN: They'll pay the piddling fine and keep right on polluting the air!

1ST WOMAN: Let's think of a penalty that will really dig into their profits. That's a penalty they can understand. And let's strike fast. Oh. I've thought of just the thing! (*Calls out off left*) Madam Chairman! Madam Chairman! (*Gavel sounds off right*.) I move that every one of us turn in our family gasoline credit cards. (*Cheers*) Turn in our credit cards and tell others to do the same . . . and others . . . and others! (CLUBWOMEN *exit, talking excitedly.*)

M.C.: The next day the management of the oil company was astounded to find that fifteen hundred gasoline credit cards had been mailed back to the office.

YOUNG WOMAN: I'll bet they hurried to correct the trouble.

M.C.: They did. But the smog persisted. Controls on smoke-producers in the Los Angeles area helped, of course, to diminish the brownish smudge that hung over the city. (BUSI-NESSMAN *appears at wings again, listening.*) But by the 1950s, smokestacks and industrial fumes had been ruled out as the main culprit in Los Angeles.

BUSINESSMAN: There! Didn't I tell you?

YOUNG WOMAN (*To* BUSINESSMAN): Remember, sir, we are talking only of the city of Los Angeles. Places differ. Air pollution isn't always caused by the same thing. Look at Pittsburgh. The main trouble there was smoke and fumes from foundries, steel mills, railroad yards and tugboats.

M.C.: As the young lady has pointed out, air pollution isn't always caused by the same thing.

YOUNG WOMAN: I have the figures here somewhere. (*Thumbs through papers*) Estimates by the U.S. Public Health Service. (*Finds paper*) Here we are. The country over, industry contaminates the air with harmful sulfur dioxide and other gases. It is outranked nationally only by the culprit they uncovered in Los Angeles.

YOUNG WOMAN *and* M.C. (*Together*): Motor vehicles!

M.C.: At the end of the long trial-and-error path in Los Angeles, officials found that carbon monoxide and other gases from cars, millions of cars, were the main cause of the air pollution. Recent figures show that motor vehicles contribute 60 percent of the carbon monoxide found in the atmosphere.

CHORUS:

> Trouble in the air . . .
> Autos everywhere . . .
> Car exhaust on every street
> And busy thoroughfare!

BUSINESSMAN (*Entering*): O.K. O.K. So pollution is caused by smokestacks and burning garbage dumps and car exhaust and what-not. So a few days out of the year streetlights go on in the middle of the day. A few people have trouble breathing and a few others' eyes begin to smart. But it's only temporary. Things soon get back to normal. Where's there any permanent damage, I'd like to know? What's all the fuss about?

YOUNG WOMAN: Our Chairman has already pointed out that it's hard to assess permanent damage when an affliction is slow-moving and more or less continuous.

M.C.: Would you say, sir, that something powerful enough to corrode stone might be powerful enough to cause permanent injury to a sensitive breathing apparatus?

BUSINESSMAN (*Cagily*): What kind of stone?

M.C.: Marble . . . limestone . . .

BUSINESSMAN: What kind of corrosion?

M.C.: Enough to weaken a building, let's say.

BUSINESSMAN: What kind of building?

M.C.: The City Hall in New York, for example.

BUSINESSMAN (*Sure of himself*): Yes, I'd say that anything powerful enough to damage the City Hall of New York might be considered dangerous.

M.C.: Have a seat, sir, and I'll tell you what happened to City Hall in New York. (BUSINESSMAN *and* YOUNG WOMAN *sit on opposite ends of the bench.*) A few years ago the problem of what to do about City Hall was brought home to the tax-payers of New York. Because of corrosion caused by air pollution, extensive repairs seemed to be in order. (TWO BUILD-

ING INSPECTORS *enter, carrying blueprints, which they spread on table. Both sit.*) At a table cluttered with papers and blueprints in the office of the Building Inspector, two men earnestly talk over the problem.

1ST INSPECTOR: As I told you, I wanted an independent estimate before submitting my report to the Mayor. Have you checked the building carefully?

2ND INSPECTOR: Yes, and with some concern, I might add. I'm shocked by the amount of corrosion in the stone during the past decade.

1ST INSPECTOR (*Nodding*): You have to see it to believe it, all right.

2ND INSPECTOR: Without any doubt, the oxidizing agents in the air are causing it. Sulfur dioxide mostly. It eats into limestone and marble, to say nothing of mortar.

1ST INSPECTOR: I sometimes wonder if it isn't eating into *us*.

2ND INSPECTOR: I was talking to a sculptor the other day. He's upset about what's happening to our statuary around the city. You know that stone obelisk of Thutmose III in the Park? He says that eighty years of New York's air have caused more damage to the stone than three thousand, five hundred years of weathering in the Sahara.

1ST INSPECTOR: And that's the air we breathe!

2ND INSPECTOR: He blames the sulfates. Says they dissolve in the rain and cause pitting in the stone. According to him the only safe place for works of art these days is *indoors*.

1ST INSPECTOR: I believe it. (*Picks up papers*) But we can't put the City Hall indoors! What's your overall comment on its condition?

2ND INSPECTOR: I'd say it has been dangerously weakened by corrosion and needs extensive repairs. I have the details here. (*Takes papers from pocket and hands them over*)

1ST INSPECTOR (*Looking at sheets*): And the cost?

2ND INSPECTOR: Conservatively, two and a half million dollars.

1ST INSPECTOR: That's roughly what our office estimated. And all because of our polluted air! (*They go out, talking together.*)

M.C.: Actually, because of corrosion of the stone, it cost New York City three million dollars to repair City Hall.

BUSINESSMAN (*Getting up from bench and stalking out*): How do they know it wasn't *termites*?

YOUNG WOMAN (*To* M.C.): I've gathered a lot of figures. Do you think it would help to call him back?

M.C.: You might try.

YOUNG WOMAN (*Running after* BUSINESSMAN): Yoo-hoo, sir.

CHORUS:

> Trouble in the air . . .
> Now we're well aware
> Buildings age from gas and fumes
> More quickly than from wear.

(YOUNG WOMAN *comes back with* BUSINESSMAN.)

YOUNG WOMAN: You know perfectly well that termites don't tunnel in stone. But I have on hand a few other facts that you should be interested in as well. Do you have any idea of the estimated annual health costs brought about by air pollution in the United States each year?

BUSINESSMAN: No, I don't.

YOUNG WOMAN (*Looking at paper*): Air pollution was responsible for 10 billion dollars in health expenses nationwide. That takes into account the money spent to treat respiratory ailments, such as asthma, and other diseases and health problems as well.

BUSINESSMAN: Ridiculous. (*Begins to stalk out.* YOUNG WOMAN *follows, reading aloud as he exits.*)

YOUNG WOMAN: Every day the burning of coal sends 48,000 *tons* of sulfur dioxide into the air. Every day the country's ninety million motor vehicles release 250,000 *tons* of carbon monoxide, to say nothing of tons and tons of hydrocarbons and nitrogen oxides. (*She turns back, slumps into chair at table.*)

M.C.: Briefly, my friends, motor vehicles are responsible for more than half of the poisons in the air.

CHORUS:

Trouble in the air . . .
Motorists, beware!
Stop the fumes your cars release
Or fold your hands in prayer.

YOUNG WOMAN (*Perking up*): Car manufacturers knew about the danger of automobile fumes long ago. Why didn't they do something about it? I suppose we're all partly to blame because we fall for glamorous interiors, push-button windows, and labor-saving gadgets. We didn't have enough sense to demand that the big auto companies do something to keep cars from pouring poisons into the air. But we're waking up. (*Jumps up and hurries out*)

M.C.: We're waking up, America! After the Los Angeles experience, California led the country in passing laws requiring exhaust-control devices for cars. Later, the federal government made control devices mandatory on all new cars, beginning with the 1968 models. Today, about seventy-five percent of the cars on the road have catalytic controls. We're waking up! (TWO BOYS *enter and cross stage.*)

1ST BOY: My dad says that even those new devices on cars don't cut out all the exhaust. They only take care of about two-thirds of the fumes, so one-third still goes into the air.

2ND BOY: Well, that's two-thirds better than it used to be.

1ST BOY: Yeah. But only the new cars have to have the devices. Most cars are still running around without any exhaust control. My dad says only one car in ten is new.

2ND BOY: So they haven't got it licked *yet*. (*They exit.* SHEILA *and* ALAN, *high school students, enter, and cross stage, talking.*)

ALAN: When you come right down to it, Sheila, the main trouble is people.

SHEILA: Do you mean because they do the polluting?

ALAN (*Nodding*): Yes, because there are so many of them . . . all wanting cars. And there just aren't any foolproof devices for catching all the fumes before they get into the air—from the tailpipe, the crankcase, the carburetor, the gas tank. Not yet, there aren't.

SHEILA: You know all about motors, Alan. Why don't you figure out a safer kind of engine?

ALAN (*Laughing*): Lots of smarter people than I are working on it.

SHEILA: But I still think it would be great if a senior in high school came up with just the right solution.

ALAN (*Amused*): So do I! (*They exit as* BUSINESSMAN *and* YOUNG WOMAN *come in talking together.*)

YOUNG WOMAN: All right, then. If you know so much about cars, why do we have to put up with the internal combustion engine, as you call it? If we can't absolutely control it, why don't we change to some other kind of car? Why don't we use nuclear energy or something?

BUSINESSMAN: Much too expensive.

YOUNG WOMAN: My brother keeps talking about new types of engines—the Wankel engine, for instance, and diesel engines. Since diesel engines burn oil instead of gas, he says you don't get any of those gasoline vapor pollutants . . . none of that tetraethyl lead. And lead poisoning is serious business. I read somewhere that crops grown near a highway, where they get car exhaust, contain more than twice as much lead as plants grown five hundred to a thousand feet from the highway. They wouldn't get *any* lead from diesels.

BUSINESSMAN: But what about the smoke and smell of a diesel? No, thank you!

M.C.: Some people favor a gas turbine adapted for cars.

BUSINESSMAN: The turbine car wouldn't pollute much, that's

true enough. But it wouldn't accelerate fast either. That engine is still full of bugs. And who'd want to pay a thousand dollars more for a turbine car? I wouldn't.

YOUNG WOMAN (*Making a note*): A thousand dollars more . . .

M.C.: Which brings us to the electric—the car without noise, without fumes, without much that can go wrong. Electric cars also promise to be less expensive than some gasoline-powered.

YOUNG WOMAN: That sounds like the car for me.

BUSINESSMAN: Who wants to cart around all those heavy batteries and get recharged every sixty miles? Besides, you can't make any speed in an electric car.

M.C.: I hear there's an experimental model that can go fifty-five miles an hour over a short distance.

BUSINESSMAN: Over a short distance!

M.C.: An electric car isn't suggested for cross-country driving.

YOUNG WOMAN: It sounds ideal to me for a town or country car. Easy to stop and start . . . and *no* exhaust. No fumes engulfing you when you wait behind a car at a red light.

BUSINESSMAN: As near as I can find out, it will be years before a moderately-priced electric car will be produced in volume. And fumes or no fumes, there's going to be a lot of opposition to making such a change. Think of the investment car manufacturers have in internal combustion engines! Think of all the oil companies selling gasoline! Think of all the service stations geared to serving gasoline-motored cars! (*Shakes head*)

M.C.: Think of the murky haze where mountains used to gleam against the sky.
    Think of the towns and cities buried under a pall of smog.
    Think of what we have done to the pure air of America.

YOUNG WOMAN (*To* BUSINESSMAN): The fight against pollution has started in earnest, and you businessmen might just as well make the best of it. California and a number of other states now operate pollution-control programs. Since Congress passed its first clean-air program in 1955, it has been broadening the front every year.

BUSINESSMAN (*Going out*): I still say the problem is exaggerated. Tommy-rot!

YOUNG WOMAN (*Calling after him*): Don't forget your gas mask!

M.C.: We can be glad people like that are in the minority. They bury their heritage under the sign of the almighty dollar and the delusion that our resources will last forever. They close their eyes to our desperate need to solve the biggest air pollution problem in the world.

YOUNG WOMAN: I think they'll come around eventually, if only to get on the bandwagon.

M.C.: But eventually is too far away. The need is now. *Now.*

YOUNG WOMAN: Most of us are alert to the problem . . . now, sir. The celebration each year of Earth Day reminds us of the importance of preserving our environment against pollution. That's the first big step. Once we know more about the causes of pollution, we can see that we, as individuals, don't add to it. That's the second big step. And the third big step is to stop the major causes of pollution at the source. We can help there by joining our fellow citizens to raise our voices in organized group protest.

M.C. (*Hopefully*): We are waking up, America! (*Voices singing "America, the Beautiful" are heard offstage.* CHORUS *takes up song. During the following speech, the cast, except for* BUSINESSMAN, *begins to crowd in from wings, singing first stanza.*)

What we have done, America, we are beginning to undo.

What we have done, we vow never to do again.

Working together, we will reclaim our birthright of pure air and spacious skies, and shining distances.

We are on the move, America. We are on the move! (*As all finish singing last stanza of "America, the Beautiful," the curtains close.*)

THE END

We Wanted a Hill

1ST GIRL: We wanted a hill,
             a hill so high
             we could stick our heads
             right up in the sky.

1ST BOY: We wanted a hill
             to run down fast,
             to ski on, to slide on
             as winter passed.

GROUP: But we lived in a place
             where all the land
             was flat as a plate,
             as flat as a hand,
             with hardly a knoll
             where we could stand.

2ND GIRL: Then somebody said,
             "I've thought of a plan" . . .

2ND BOY: And talk about getting
             a hill began,
             with its feet down flat
             and its head in the sun.

GROUP: We all pitched in
and we all had fun.
We picked up litter
for miles around,
and piled it high
in a hill-like mound:

3RD GIRL: Sticks and plastic
and worn-out sandals,

3RD BOY: Pans and buckets
with broken handles,

1ST GIRL: Cans and bottles
and stubs of candles,

1ST BOY: Foil and boxes
and trash and rubble,

2ND GIRL: Papers caught
in the shrubs and stubble.

GROUP: We piled it all
at the edge of town
where men with tractors
packed it down.

And the more we worked
with vim and vigor
the taller our hill
became, and bigger.

2ND GIRL: The council voted
to cover it well
with earth scooped out
for a new hotel.

2ND BOY: But we needed more earth—
our hill kept growing
and tops of bottles
and cans kept showing.

3RD GIRL: "Let's dig out a place
that a pond can fill,
and get enough earth
to cover our hill."

1ST BOY: Our hill was broad
and our hill was high.

1ST GIRL: It showed in the pond
with a hat of sky.

2ND BOY: But our hill was bare
and earth-color brown,
and somebody said
with a telltale frown:

2ND GIRL: "What if the wind
blows up a gale?
Away the soil
of our hill will sail."

3RD BOY: "And what if it rains?
What will we have
for all our pains?
Our hill will certainly
wash away
with nothing growing
to make it stay."

GROUP: We needed some roots
to interlace

and hold the soil
of our hill in place.
We needed some green
to cover the brown . . .
a carpet of grass
to hold it down.

3RD GIRL: So . . . up and away!
We planted clover
and hardy grasses
the whole hill over.

1ST BOY: Young folks planted,

1ST GIRL: And old folks, too,

GROUP: And, oh, what a sight
when our work was through
and a warm rain fell
and the hill turned green!
The brown was hidden,
the grass was clean,
and a prettier hill
was never seen.

2ND BOY: A hill to run on,

2ND GIRL: A hill to sun on,

3RD BOY: A hill to slide on,

3RD GIRL: A hill to stride on,

1ST BOY: A hill . . . with a friend
to-sit-beside on!

GROUP: "Now," we shouted,
"our hill will stay.

It never, no, never
will wash away.
Our pond will shine
like a mirror of gold,
a skating rink
when the year turns cold."

1ST BOY AND GIRL: Then we laughed
and climbed
where the hill was high,
and looked from the top
with a shout and cry,
and stuck our heads
RIGHT UP IN THE SKY.

Wake-Up Time

Wake up, seeds
of flowers and weeds!
You slept the winter through.
Put down roots
and send up shoots . . .
there's such a lot to do.

Wake up, trees!
You took your ease
while winter stormed and blew.
Now that spring
is on the wing,
there's such a lot to do.

Wake up, roots,
beneath the sod!
You slept all winter, too.
The calendar
says "Time to stir.
There's such a lot to do."

Wake up, world!
The sky is blue,
the cold is gone,
the sun is new,
and there's SUCH A LOT to do.

Trees

Firs and spruces like to point
their fingers at the sky,

Elm trees sweep the very clouds
with branches swirling high,

Weeping willows make a cave
beneath them, green and dry,

Aspens always talk to us
when we go walking by.

On Strike

Characters

OWL
SQUIRREL
ROBIN
WOODCHUCK
BAT
MOLE
SKUNK
RABBIT

SCENE 1

TIME: *A summer day.*
SETTING: *A clearing in the woods.*
AT RISE: *All except* RABBIT *are gathered together at a meeting place under a tree. The* OWL, *looking very wise in his glasses, is chairman of the meeting. He has a book under one arm.*

OWL (*Rapping on the tree for order*): The meeting will come to order. Is everyone here? Squirrel?
SQUIRREL (*Standing up quickly*): Here. (*Salutes*) At your service.
OWL: Robin?
ROBIN (*Chirping*): Here.

OWL: Woodchuck, otherwise known as Groundhog?

WOODCHUCK (*Puffing because he is so fat*): P—p—present.

OWL: Bat? (*There is no answer. In a moment, louder*) Bat!

BAT (*Very sleepily*): Y-e-s . . . your Honor. (*Yawns*)

OWL: Are you awake?

BAT (*Yawning*): Oh, yes . . . your Honor.

OWL: Mole?

MOLE (*In a small voice*): Here.

OWL: Skunk?

SKUNK (*Standing up and strutting, showing off beautiful coat*): Here.

OWL: Rabbit? (*No answer*) Rabbit!

RABBIT (*Timidly peeking from behind a bush, looking around cautiously, then speaking in a hushed voice*): Here.

OWL: Come on, Rabbit, show yourself. I think we are quite safe here at the edge of the woods, out of sight of the farm-house.

RABBIT (*Looking around*): I never harm anyone . . . but someone is always trying to hurt me. (*Sighs, then timidly comes from behind the bush*)

OWL: Now that we are all here, we can proceed with the business in hand. (*Clears throat*) Ladies and gentlemen of the Grievance Committee, we are gathered here today to decide on ways and means of combating the great conspiracy against us.

SKUNK (*Indignantly*): Farmer Dullard's conspiracy. The old dullard!

OWL (*Rapping for order*): No interruptions from the floor, please. As I was saying, we are meeting today to air our grievances against Farmer Dullard, and to decide what can be done. For countless generations our families have lived here on the farm now owned by Farmer Dullard. For count-less generations we have lived in comparative peace with the human race.

RABBIT (*Timidly*): We have always had to be . . . (*Looks around*) very cautious . . . though.

OWL: Of course, we have had to use our wits. But until Farmer Dullard moved here last year, our lives went along quite smoothly. Am I right. Yea or nay?

ALL (*Except* BAT): Yea. Yea.

BAT (*Coming in sleepily at the end*): Yea.

OWL: Farmer Dullard is making life unbearable. The time has come for the Grievance Committee to decide on a course of action. Our homes are being destroyed. Our food is being taken from us. Our lives are constantly in danger. Evidence is mounting that Farmer Dullard is deliberately trying to get rid of us. Robin, will you please state your case.

ROBIN (*Standing, tipping back and forth in birdlike fashion*): I live in the orchard, as my family has for more years than I can count. It has been a wonderful place to live until . . . until lately . . . (*Chokes up*)

OWL: Please control yourself, Robin. We realize this is a painful matter for you to discuss, but the Committee must know the facts. What has happened?

ROBIN: Ever since Farmer Dullard moved in, the orchard hasn't been the same. We robins are in constant danger. Maybe we *do* eat a few of his cherries now and then, but is that any reason . . . (*Gets out handkerchief and wipes eyes*)

OWL: Any reason for what, Robin?

ROBIN: For . . . for hiding behind the grape arbor and shooting at us. Yesterday my Aunt Elizabeth and Cousin Charley got hit. I'll never see them again. (*Sits down and buries face in handkerchief*)

OWL (*Consulting his book*): "Insect pests do untold damage to fruit crops every year. Birds are the greatest insect destroyers. Without birds, farmers would have to go out of the fruit business." (*Looks up*) I guess this is one book Farmer Dullard never has read. (*Reads again*) "Scientists have found as many as 250 tent caterpillars in the stomach of one bird."

ROBIN: And what about weed seeds?

OWL: Hmmm. (*Turns pages*) Oh yes, here we are: "Birds eat not only insects, but they eat quantities of weed seeds. Scientists discovered that a bobwhite ate 1,700 weed seeds at one meal, and that a snowbird ate 1,500 pigweed seeds." (*Turns pages*) Robins . . . robins . . . (*Reads*) "The robin as an insect destroyer more than makes up for any injury he does to fruit crops."

ROBIN: There now!

SKUNK: If Farmer Dullard weren't such a dullard, he'd know that himself.

SQUIRREL: I shudder to think what his orchard would look like without robins.

OWL: Does anyone wish to make a motion?

MOLE (*Squeakily*): I do. I move . . . that the Committee move . . . that every move of Farmer Dullard against the robins . . . is . . . is . . .

OWL: Wicked, cruel, and unreasonable. Excellent! All in favor say "Aye."

ALL (*Except* BAT): Aye.

BAT (*Coming in at end again*): Aye.

OWL: Now, Skunk, do you wish to state your case?

SKUNK: I certainly do. And the facts don't smell very sweet, I can tell you. Farmer Dullard is after me and my family. Not only with a gun, but with traps. And he is cutting out the brush along the creek where we have lived for generations. Maybe we *do* take an occasional egg from his hen-house, but is that any reason . . .

OWL: No reason at all, considering how many rats and mice you skunks eat around the barns.

SKUNK (*Smacking lips*): Ummmm, rats and mice! We like them much better than eggs, if Farmer Dullard only knew it. To say nothing of liking grasshoppers and beetles. He just doesn't realize how much good we do around the place. I accuse him of . . .

OWL: Of cruel, wicked, and unreasonable conduct! All in favor . . .

ALL (*Except* BAT, *interrupting*): Aye.

BAT (*Yawning*): Aye.

OWL: Woodchuck, can you think of any good you woodchucks do around the farm?

WOODCHUCK: G . . . g . . . good? Well, I should s . . . s . . . say. Don't we go after the J . . . J . . . June beetles? Don't we eat them by the h . . . h . . . hundreds?

OWL: And how does Farmer Dullard treat you, may I ask?

WOODCHUCK: Like c . . . c . . . criminals. That's how. He is always sicking his d . . . d . . . dogs after us, or hiding near our b . . . b . . . burrow with a gun, or trying to d . . . d . . . dig us out. He makes life m . . . m . . . miserable for us. Maybe we d . . . d . . . *do* eat a few things from his g . . . g . . . garden once in a while, but . . .

OWL: But his action is uncalled for and unwarranted. Is everyone agreed?

ALL (*Except* BAT): Agreed.

BAT (*Sleepily*): Me too.

OWL: All right, Bat. Better late than never. Just where do *you* stand, by the way? (BAT *has fallen asleep again.* MOLE *nudges him.*)

BAT: Huh?

OWL: I said where do you stand? (*Shakes* BAT *gently, and stands him on his feet*)

BAT (*Still sleepy*): Stand? I don't, you know. I always hang when I sleep. (*Gets a thought that rouses him*) Oh, and that's the trouble. I'm in danger of losing my den tree!

MOLE: Your *what?*

BAT: My den tree. The tree where I live. The tree with the nice hollow in it where I hang with my family and sleep . . . (*The thought makes him sleepy again*) . . . all day long. (*Yawns*) Oh, it's a wonderful tree. But Farmer Dullard is clearing out the woods, and he marked our tree to cut down. Our wonderful tree! It's been in the family for years. (*Wipes eyes, yawns*)

OWL: I know just how you feel. My hollow tree is in danger, too.

SQUIRREL: And so is mine. Of course, in summer I live in a nest of sticks and bark high up in the branches. But for winter I *do* like a hollow tree. Farmer Dullard just doesn't understand about forestry and trees. Why, his woods will be overrun with insects if he cuts down our den trees and drives us all out.

BAT: Mosquitoes . . . (*Rouses himself*) Ummmm, mosquitoes!

OWL: What are you talking about?

BAT: We bats dote on mosquitoes. If Farmer Dullard cuts down our tree, I move . . . (*Yawns*) that mosquitoes . . . (*Yawns*) sting him all to *pieces.*

WOODCHUCK: I s . . . s . . . second the motion.

OWL (*Rapping on tree for emphasis*): The motion about mosquitoes is carried . . . unanimously. Now, Mole, what is your grievance against Farmer Dullard?

MOLE: Oh dear, life has never been so hard. We moles don't know which way to tunnel! Farmer Dullard is always trying to dig us out and block our doorways. Maybe we *do* hump up his lawn a little, but is that any reason . . .

OWL: Decidedly not. (*Thumbs through book.*) Moles . . . moles. Here we are. "Although moles disturb lawns with their tunnels and eat earthworms which are beneficial to the soil, more than half their diet . . ." (OWL *looks up*) take note of this, my friends . . . "more than half their diet consists of harmful insects like cutworms which cut off little cabbages and corn plants at the ground and kill them."

MOLE: Ummm, cutworms! (*Smacks his lips*)

OWL: Farmer Dullard is outvoted . . . (*Quickly counts noses*) eight to one!

ALL (*Except* BAT): Yea.

BAT (*Yawning*): Yea.

OWL: Now, Rabbit, do you think you could step up before the Committee and tell how you have been treated? Nobody's going to bite you.

RABBIT (*Coming out timidly*): Yes, sir. (*Keeps looking around cautiously*)

OWL: First, explain your service to humanity.

RABBIT: I don't understand, please.

OWL: In other words, what good do you do in the world?

RABBIT (*Sighing*): I'm afraid not very much, sir. I don't (*Looks at* BAT) eat mosquitoes. I can't say (*Looks at* WOOD-CHUCK) I like June bugs. I haven't the right kind of teeth (*Looks at* SKUNK) for eating rats and mice and grasshoppers. I can't (*Looks at* ROBIN) sit up in the cherry and apple trees and eat pests. I have no taste for (*Looks at* MOLE) cut-worms or grubs. (*Sighs humbly*) I guess I'm not much good for anything.

SQUIRREL: Why, you are too! You're awfully nice to look at!

OWL: I must say everyone admires the way you can jump.

MOLE: And your ears—they're most unusual, you know.

BAT (*Dreamily*): Mosquitoes . . .

RABBIT: My fur is of some value, I understand. But, without my fur, I'd never be here to tell the tale . . .

OWL: I think we are all agreed that rabbits have a definite . . . shall we say *artistic* . . . value for mankind.

RABBIT: Farmer Dullard doesn't seem to think so. He is always after us, he and his dogs. And he is cutting away the briar patch where we have lived for generations. Maybe

we *do* eat some of his clover and alfalfa, but is that any
reason . . .

OWL: Emphatically not.

SKUNK (*Strutting*): Emphatically *not*.

OWL: Motion carried. And now, friends, I too have a case.
We owls like mice and insects quite as much as skunks do.
But Farmer Dullard does not seem to realize it. (*Looks
around*) It is obvious from the evidence that we are all
victims of a conspiracy. Innocent victims of a cruel conspiracy. Now the question before us today is—what shall
we do about it?

RABBIT (*Timidly*): All I know is . . . I can't go on like this.
I'm a nervous wreck.

SKUNK: We can't any of us go on like this. It isn't *dignified*.

ROBIN: It isn't just.

MOLE: Or intelligent.

WOODCHUCK: Or h . . . h . . . healthy.

OWL: Ladies and gentlemen of the Grievance Committee, as
Chairman, I say there is one thing for us to do.

ALL (*Except* BAT): What? What?

BAT: Where?

OWL: The only thing for us to do is to beat Farmer Dullard
at his own game. Since Farmer Dullard insists on taking
unfair advantage of us, we must strike for our rights—all of
us, all at the same time.

ALL (*Except* BAT): Strike?

BAT (*Yawning*): I second the motion.

OWL: Farmer Dullard has been making life miserable for us.
All right then, we strike. We pack up and move out on
him, in a body. Let the rats overrun his granary! Let the
mice overrun his hay mow! Let beetles and cutworms and
grasshoppers and other pests take over his garden and
orchard. Let mosquitoes . . .

BAT (*Waking up*): Mosquitoes! (*Smacks his lips*)

OWL: Let mosquitoes sting Farmer Dullard right and left!

ALL (*Except* RABBIT): When do we strike?

OWL: The sooner, the quicker.

RABBIT (*Fearful*): But . . . to move to a strange place . . . think of the danger. I am so fond of my briar patch.

OWL: I have an idea we won't have to strike very long. We'll need a picket, though. Someone who can keep an eye on things and report to us while we're off the job. Who will volunteer for picket duty?

SQUIRREL (*Quickly*): I will. I'll stay here and keep you posted on everything that happens. I can hide in the treetops and see without being seen.

OWL: Providing you can remember to scold to yourself and not out loud!

SQUIRREL: Who, me?

SKUNK: I second the motion. I think Squirrel will make a very good picket.

WOODCHUCK: P . . . p . . . peach of a p . . . p . . . picket.

OWL: We'll set up strike headquarters out of sight of the farm, and whenever there is news, Squirrel can make a report. Everyone in favor say "Aye."

ALL (*Except* BAT): Aye.

BAT (*Rousing*): . . . my, mine, me, we, our, ours, us.

MOLE (*Nudging* BAT): Wake up, you're dreaming again.

OWL: All right, then. It's agreed. We strike. We move out immediately and set up strike headquarters nearby, with a picket on duty. And in six weeks, to a minute, (*Consults watch*) we'll meet here again, under this same tree, to decide what to do next.

RABBIT (*Jumping up excitedly*): I hear dogs! Way off in the distance, I hear dogs. Farmer Dullard must be coming. Run . . . run for your lives.

Owl (*Calling out as all scatter in different directions*): In six weeks. Remember! Six weeks, to the minute.

CURTAIN

* * *

Scene 2

Time: *Later.* (*A curtain does not have to be used at the end of the first scene, since the passage of time is indicated in the speeches. This scene should start slowly and speed up gradually.*)
Setting: *Same as Scene 1.*
At Rise: Owl *is sitting on a stump as* Skunk *saunters in.*

Skunk: Hoo, hoo, Owl. Are you there?
Owl: Hoo, hoo.
Skunk: We've been on strike four weeks today, brother Owl. I wonder what Squirrel will report when he comes again. He's been a pretty good picket, hasn't he?
Owl: Excellent. Hoot! There he comes now.
Squirrel (*Coming in importantly*): Hear ye, hear ye. Farmer Dullard is in a dither. He can't begin to catch all the rats in the barn. He can't begin to catch all the mice in the hay mow. (*Exits, calling "Hear ye, hear ye."*)
Owl: Did you hear that Skunk?
Skunk: Did I? Mice in the hay and rats in the barn. It looks as if we're winning the strike.
Owl: Hoot and ahoy. All we need is patience. Everything comes to him who waits. (*Yawns, ducks back behind foliage.* Skunk *goes back behind stump. In a minute* Squirrel *comes in again a little faster than before.*)
Squirrel: Bulletin! Bulletin! The cutworms are cutting off

the cabbages. The cutworms are cutting off the corn. The
June beetles are eating the garden. A million new grubs
have been born. (*Exits calling "Bulletin," etc.*)

WOODCHUCK (*Crawling out of burrow, behind bush*): M . . .
m . . . mole. Mole!

MOLE (*Sticking head out*): Woodchuck. Woodchuck!

WOODCHUCK: D . . . d . . . did you hear the news?

MOLE: I did indeed. The cutworms! The grubs!

WOODCHUCK: The J . . . J . . . June beetles. (*Chuckles*)
W . . . w . . . wonder what Farmer Dullard thinks now.
(*Goes back to burrow*)

MOLE (*Backing behind bush*): Plenty, brother. You can be
sure of that. (SQUIRREL *comes in again, a little faster.*)

SQUIRREL: Extra! Extra! Insects are swarming over the orchard, eating the leaves, eating the fruit. Mosquitoes are
driving Farmer Dullard frantic. Zooommmm, zzzzzz.
(*Exits, calling "Extra!" etc.*)

ROBIN (*Hopping in*): Bat, Bat. Where are you? (*No answer*)
Bat! (*There is a feeble, sleepy answer from behind a tree.*)
Bat!

BAT (*Sticking head out*): Oh, it's you, Robin. What's up? Or
down?

ROBIN: Did you hear the news? Insects are swarming over
the orchard. Mosquitoes are driving Farmer Dullard frantic.

BAT (*Smacking lips*): Mosquitoes—ummmm. Aren't they
wonderful? (*Yawns*) Wonder . . . ful. (*Retires to sleep
again.* ROBIN *hops out. From here on* SQUIRREL *comes in
faster and faster, to show passage of time. Heads of other
animals bob back and forth.*)

SQUIRREL: Farmer Dullard can do nothing to stop the invasion
of rats and mice. They are eating all his hay and grain.
They are even chewing up the harness. (*Exits and soon
returns*) Farmer Dullard can do nothing to stop the invasion
of cutworms and June beetles, to say nothing of grass-

hoppers and other insects. His garden will soon be in ruins. (*Exits and returns quickly*) Farmer Dullard is in despair over his orchard, which is swarming with pests. He can't do a thing . . . except scratch his mosquito bites. (*Exits, re-enters almost at once*) Extra special! Extra special! Farmer Dullard admits his mistake! He regrets he drove us out on strike. He is willing to call off the whole conspiracy. He sees now that it hurts him more than it hurts us. Extra special! (*Exits*)

OWL: What did I tell you, folks? Tomorrow the six weeks are up. The Grievance Committee will meet at the meeting place.

CURTAIN

*   *   *

SCENE 3

TIME: *The next day.*

SETTING: *The same.*

AT RISE: OWL *is again in charge of the meeting, which is already in progress.*

OWL: Everyone seems to be here except Rabbit. Rabbit! (*Calls out*) Rabbit!

RABBIT (*Hopping in excitedly*): Pardon me for being late. But I'm so excited. (*Looks around*) Is it safe to talk?

OWL: Quite safe.

RABBIT: I was so lonesome for my old briar patch this morning I slipped back at dawn to take a look. And what do you think?

SQUIRREL: I could have told you. Instead of cutting down the last of the briars, Farmer Dullard is letting them grow again. He's discovered that rabbits are worth looking at. That's one of the things I had to report. (*Holds up list*)

RABBIT: It's wonderful. My nice safe briar patch. Now I'm sure I won't get a nervous breakdown.

OWL (*Rapping for order*): Fellow strikers, we are all assembled . . .

ROBIN (*Eagerly*): May I say a word?

OWL: Robin has the floor.

ROBIN: I was feeling very lonely for the old orchard this morning. And so I flew back, at dawn, to have a look. And what do you think. That old grapevine is so eaten up with insects Farmer Dullard can't hide behind it with his gun any more.

SQUIRREL: I was going to report that too. And something you couldn't see, Robin! Farmer Dullard *hasn't* a gun any more. He sold it to the junk man.

ROBIN, WOODCHUCK, SKUNK *and* RABBIT: No gun! No gun! (*They do a joyful dance.*)

SQUIRREL: He sold his traps too.

WOODCHUCK *and* SKUNK: Whee! (*They dance together*)

OWL (*Rapping for order*): Order! Order! Dancing is out of order. Squirrel, we couldn't have picked a better picket. Have you anything else to report?

SQUIRREL: Since Farmer Dullard came to his senses, things have been happening thick and fast. (*Looks through his notes*) He wants to make things pleasant for us, so we'll call off the strike. Now he won't cut down all our den trees in the woods.

MOLE (*Nudging* BAT): Bat, did you hear that?

BAT (*Sleepily*): Gnat? (*Smacks lips*) Gnat!

MOLE: No, den tree.

BAT (*Waking up*): Den tree? My den tree—where I used to hang and sleep?

SQUIRREL: It's still there, Bat. Waiting for you. And swarms of mosquitoes too.

BAT (*Dreamily*): Ah . . . isn't life wonderful?

OWL: And is my tree all right too?

SQUIRREL: Your tree is still there, Owl. Unfortunately mine got cut down before Farmer Dullard saw the light. But I'm not worried. I can find another, before winter.

WOODCHUCK: What about my b . . . b . . . burrow?

SQUIRREL: It's there waiting for you. Farmer Dullard decided it was better to have you and your family eat a little of his garden than have the June beetles and their relatives eat *all* of it.

WOODCHUCK: Ah . . . June b . . . b . . . beetles. (*Sighs with happiness*)

SKUNK: And what about me?

SQUIRREL: Oh, you don't have to worry any more, Skunk. Farmer Dullard has decided to leave a nice lot of brush along the creek where you like to live. He's even put out a garbage pail for your benefit . . . behind the barn.

SKUNK: He has! Well, what do you know!

SQUIRREL: And will you get fat cleaning up on those rats and mice! You too, Owl.

OWL: I can do with some rats and mice, I will admit.

MOLE: And me? How about me?

SQUIRREL: Farmer Dullard isn't such a dullard any more. In fact, he's thinking of changing his name to Dillard. He understands now who kept the cutworms and grubs under control. He's not going to worry about a few humps in his lawn.

MOLE: Ummm, it will be good to get my teeth in a cutworm again.

SQUIRREL: A cutworm. You can get your teeth in a million, more or less.

OWL: Well, fellow strikers, it looks as if we can all go back to our jobs. Farmer Dullard . . . Dillard . . . realizes he needs us as much as we need him.

WOODCHUCK: I second the m . . . m . . . motion.

SKUNK: I third it.

OWL: And may we never have to strike again, as long as we live. All in favor say "Aye."

ALL (*Except* BAT): Aye.

BAT (*Dreamily*): Me too.

THE END

Let's Plant a Tree

ALL: It's time to plant a tree, a tree.
What shall it be? What shall it be?

1ST: Let's plant a pine—we can't go wrong:
a pine is green the whole year long.
2ND: Let's plant a maple—more than one!
to shade us from the summer sun.
3RD: Let's plant a cherry—you know why:
there's nothing like a cherry pie!
4TH: Let's plant an elm, the tree of grace,
where robins find a nesting place.
5TH: Let's plant an apple—not too small,
with flowers in spring and fruit in fall.
6TH: Let's plant a fir—so it can be
a lighted outdoor Christmas tree.
7TH: Let's plant a birch, an oak, a beech,
there's something extra-nice in each.

ALL: It's time to plant a tree, a tree.
What shall it be? What shall it be?
It doesn't seem to matter much—
they all have special charms and such
in winter, summer, spring or fall.
Let's plant a . . .
           look, let's plant them *ALL*.

Planting a Pine

NOW I'm twice as tall as you,
little tree. You're tiny.
I am four feet, you are two,
with needles green and shiny.

I am twice as big, but oh,
soon I shall be smaller.
In a little while I know
YOU will be the taller.

Little tree, I'll never stand
more than two feet higher,
but you'll stretch above the land
like a tall green spire!

MOTHER'S DAY

Mother's Day Off and On

Characters

JUDY, *about 11*
ERIC, *about 10*
PATSY, *about 6*
FATHER
MOTHER

TIME: *Eight o'clock on the morning of Mother's Day.*
SETTING: *Two rooms of a house, the dining room and kitchen.*
AT RISE: JUDY *and* ERIC *are setting the breakfast table.* PATSY
is trying to help FATHER *in the kitchen.*

JUDY:
We've never been so nice and quiet.
ERIC:
We can do it, when we try it.
JUDY:
I bet Mom will think it's fun
To find, for once, that breakfast's done.
ERIC:
If only Dad won't burn the toast . . .
I saw him do it twice, almost.
Judy, I'm afraid he'll botch it.
JUDY:

328

I told Patsy she should watch it.

(*In the kitchen* FATHER *is puttering around.* PATSY *sniffs.*)

PATSY:

Daddy, look, the toast is burning.

FATHER:

Every time my back starts turning! (*Shakes the toaster*)
What's the matter, anyway . . .

PATSY:

Ssh . . . don't shout on Mother's Day
Or we never will surprise her.

FATHER (*Putting down the toaster*):

She is sleepier than wiser. (*He puffs out his chest.*)
I think I'm a magic-maker;
I got up . . . and didn't wake her.

(*In the dining room,* JUDY *and* ERIC *look over the Mother's
Day gifts on the table.*)

JUDY (*Feeling a package*):

Pat's present feels all bumpy.

ERIC:

Wonder what can be so lumpy.
Patsy won't let on, you know.

JUDY:

She said one thing about it, though:
She said it was the *best* she had.

ERIC:

She likes secrets . . . just like Dad. (*Picks up a package*)
His must be a box of candy.

JUDY:

Eric, wouldn't that be dandy!

ERIC:

Dad has something up his sleeve
In *addition*, I believe . . .
Something written in this letter. (*Picks up a letter*)

JUDY (*Impatiently*):
  If Mom won't wake up soon, I'll get her!
  Do you think my poem's all right?
ERIC:
  Sure. And my invention?
JUDY: Quite.
  Breakfast must be almost ready.
  (*There is a terrific crash in the kitchen.* FATHER, *picking up the teakettle to fill the dripolator, burns his hand. He drops the kettle with a crash.*)
PATSY:
  Daddy, hold the kettle steady.
FATHER:
  It's too late. It fell already.
  (JUDY *and* ERIC *run to see what happened. They all scurry around mopping up water and getting in each other's way. Just then* MOTHER's *voice is heard.*)
MOTHER (*Offstage*):
  Goodness, what a frightful clatter.
  Is there anything the matter?
JUDY:
  Mother's coming. Hurry! Hurry!
FATHER (*Wiping furiously*):
  We'll be through in time, don't worry.
PATSY:
  But we have to sing our song!
FATHER:
  Go ahead . . . I'll tag along.
  (JUDY, ERIC *and* PATSY *hurry to the dining room, awaiting* MOTHER's *appearance. When she comes in they begin to sing lustily to the tune of "Happy Birthday to You." Midway in the singing,* FATHER *appears, his apron rumpled and wet. He joins in.*)

CHILDREN:
>Happy greetings to you,
>Happy greetings to you,
>Happy Mother's Day, Mother.
>Happy greetings to you.

MOTHER (*Merrily*):
>What a lovely reception, my darlings, my dears.
>I haven't had so much attention in years.
>And look at the table—all set to perfection.

PATSY:
>And look at the presents.

ERIC: Yes, make an inspection!

FATHER:
>You *must* read the letter that's fresh from my pen.

PATSY (*Sniffing*):
>Oh, Daddy, the toast must be burning again.
>(FATHER *hurries to the kitchen to rescue the toast.* MOTHER
>*beams at the children and at the table.*)

MOTHER:
>I think I should take this occasion to mention
>That Mother's Day is an *exciting* invention.

ERIC:
>Invention! Just wait till you open up mine.

FATHER (*Returning breathlessly*):
>I rescued the breakfast, so everything's fine.
>Come, open your presents, and meanwhile we'll dine.
>(FATHER *and* JUDY *bring in things from the kitchen, and all
>sit at the table while* MOTHER *begins on her presents.*)

MOTHER:
>Now which shall I open up first? Let me see . . . (*Picks
>up gift*)
>This says, "From your Patsy." Hmmm . . . what can it
>be? (*Opens it*)
>Your ragdoll! Oh, Patsy . . .

ERIC (*Surprised*):
  Well, buckle my shoe!
JUDY (*Amused*):
  A ragdoll. Now, Mom, you'll have something to do!
PATSY:
  The best doll I have . . . and the best is for *you*.
MOTHER:
  Oh, thank you. But, darling, I give you fair warning
  I *may* need your help with this child, night and morning.
  (*That suits* PATSY. MOTHER *picks up another package, a
  large one.*)
  This package is heavy. (*Reads card*) "From Eric, with love."
  It's tied very tightly below and above.
  (*She finally gets it open and takes out four triangular pieces
  of wood. She wonders what the blocks are for.*)
  Oh, Eric . . . they're lovely!
ERIC: I cut them myself.
FATHER (*Bewildered*):
  My boy, are they bookends . . . to set on a shelf?
MOTHER:
  I hardly expect that was Eric's intention.
ERIC:
  Why, Dad, don't you see? It's a special invention:
  These blocks fit in corners. They're perfect for keeping
  The dust out . . . they're super to help Mom in sweeping.
  (ERIC *gets up and demonstrates.*)
MOTHER:
  How really amazing. How thoughtful. How clever.
FATHER:
  Corners for cutting off corners? I never!
  (MOTHER *picks up a small flat parcel.*)
MOTHER:
  Another nice present. I wonder what this is.
  It says, "To my Mother, with love and with kisses,

From Judy." (*Opens it*) You'd think it was *Christmas* today.
A beautiful hankie. (*Holds it up*) Look, isn't it gay?
And here are some verses . . . let's see what they say.

ERIC:
She made up that poem and it took her just ages.
It isn't so long, but she wasted whole pages!

FATHER:
I wasn't aware that this house held a poet.

MOTHER:
Just listen to this and, hereafter, you'll *know* it. (*Reads*)
For Mother on Mother's Day:
Half of your parents consists of a mother.
(Your father is also a half—he's the other.)
But though she is half, she is really three-quarters,
Because she stays home with her son and her daughters.

A mother, compared to a father, is smarter (FATHER *gives
a start.*)
About getting dinner . . . that's only a starter.
She also knows more about sewing and mending
And cleaning and ironing—the list is unending. (FATHER
gulps.)
She knows how to bake many things that are yummy
(Though carrots are better, she says, for your tummy.)
And oh, there are *so* many angles about her
We all would be lost in a minute without her!
(MOTHER *laughs*)
I'm glad for those *angles*, or I'd be too fat—
If I were all curving, you couldn't say that!
But, seriously, Judy, your verses are splendid.
You don't know how much I enjoy being commended.
And now, one more package . . .

FATHER: My gifts, though, are *two*.
I thought of a dozen red roses for you,

And then I decided a *choice* would be better,
As you will observe when you open my letter.
PATSY (*Suddenly*):
Oh, Daddy—the kettle. I bet you forgot
To put on more water.
FATHER (*Jumping up*):
The kettle—great Scot!
(FATHER *rushes to the kitchen to put water in the kettle.*
MOTHER, *amused, picks up the package and opens it. She
calls out*)
MOTHER:
What wonderful candy. Oh, thank you, my dear.
(FATHER, *pleased, hurries back, and sits down.* MOTHER *opens
the letter*)
And now for the letter. What choice have we here?
(*She begins to read aloud.*) "Dearest Wife and Mother. On
this beautiful occasion of Mother's Day, my first thought
was to buy you red roses as an expression of my deep love
and appreciation. But, on second thought, it occurred to
me I might give you a gift you would like even better. If
you prefer the roses, though, just say the word, my dear.
I have reserved some at the florist's until nine o'clock.
Here is my idea. Instead of roses, wouldn't you like to
have a complete rest and change on this Mother's Day?
Wouldn't you like to be *honorary* mother for the day, and
let me take over all your duties and responsibilities? Per-
haps there is a story you are eager to read or something . . ."
(MOTHER *looks up from the letter.*)
How *could* you have guessed it? Oh, that will be gay.
I'll read . . . and you handle my duties today.
ERIC (*To* FATHER):
It works out all right that today is a Sunday,
For, Dad, there's a *washing* to do every Monday.

MOTHER (*Finishing the letter*):

"And don't you worry one little bit. I am sure I will be
perfectly able to handle the duties of a modern mother."
(MOTHER *looks up with interest.*)
Modern mothers have it easy?
That's what you imply?

FATHER:

Oh, their lives are pretty breezy,
Matched with times gone by:
Take a good old-fashioned mother—
She was so immersed
In one labor or another . . .
Spinning, weaving, endless baking,
Quilting, making cheese,
Churning, soap and candle-making . . .
No more jobs like these.

MOTHER:

Yes, it's true that ceaseless toiling
Has a modern cure,
But . . .

JUDY: I hear the kettle boiling!

FATHER:

Kettle? (*Recollects himself*) To be sure.
(FATHER *rushes to the kitchen, fills dripolator, brings it in and
begins to pour a cup of coffee for* MOTHER. *Of course, the
water hasn't gone through yet, so some spills on the tablecloth.*)
You admit there's nothing to it—
Keeping house these days.
Just relax and watch me do it! (*Pats himself on the chest*)
Being efficient pays.

MOTHER:

Yes, of course, my dear. Take over!
I'm sure I shan't be missed.
All day long I'll be in clover . . . (*Looks mischievous*)

Better make a list
Of the things that must be finished
All in time for church.

FATHER (*Taking out pencil and paper*): Well? My zeal is undiminished.

MOTHER:
Don't leave me in the lurch!
First, the beds. And then the dishes.

FATHER (*Beginning to take notes, then turning to* PATSY *and* JUDY):
Daughters, make your plans
To carry out your mother's wishes!

JUDY (*Quickly*):
Mom always does the *pans*,
And cleans around the sink and table . . .

MOTHER:
Better put that down!
(FATHER *makes the note, and* JUDY *and* PATSY *go out, with amused backward glances.*)
Make a pudding. Are you able?
Don't give such a frown.
Start the pot-roast early—very,
Braise it long enough . . .

FATHER (*Puzzled*):
Braise? (*To* ERIC) Go get the dictionary. (ERIC *exits.*)

MOTHER:
Or else it will be tough.
Shell the peas, and make the salad,
Sweep the kitchen floor . . .
Dear, you look a little pallid.

FATHER (*Weakly*):
Is there any more?
(ERIC *comes back with the dictionary which he hands to* FATHER. *He also hands* FATHER *a sock.*)

ERIC:

Dad, you've got to do some mending.

My Sunday sock—just look.

FATHER (*Looking*):

The hole goes on without an ending!

But, son, I've got to *cook*.

(PATSY *comes running in with a dress. She goes to* FATHER.)

PATSY:

My Sunday dress must have a pressing. (*She points*)

Wrinkles here . . . and here.

FATHER (*With a sigh*):

I'm finding this a bit distressing.

MOTHER (*Much amused*):

Nothing to it, dear!

(JUDY *runs in with a light-colored jacket, and hurries to* FATHER.)

JUDY:

Daddy, find the spot remover.   (*Shows a spot*)

Help me get this out.

FATHER (*Desperately*):

Heavens, how can I maneuver

My poor way about?

MOTHER:

Modern mothers never worry—

Nothing to be done!

FATHER (*Looking at his watch*):

Almost nine! I'll have to hurry.

Gosh, I'll have to *run*.

(FATHER *dashes out, taking off his apron and banging into a chair as he goes.*)

MOTHER:

What a dreadful rush and clatter.

ERIC (*Going to window*):

You should see him sprint.

MOTHER (*Innocently*):
  I wonder what can be the matter.
  Can you give a hint?
JUDY:
  Perhaps he's gone to get the paper.
ERIC:
  Or maybe cigarettes.
MOTHER:
  It strikes me as a funny caper.   (*Then cheerfully*)
  But he'll be back, my pets.
ERIC (*Making a face*):
  I don't expect to like his dinner.
PATSY:
  He'll burn the meat, I fear.
JUDY:
  I guess by night we'll all be thinner.
MOTHER:
  Let's not shed a tear.
  I have a sort of inner feeling
  Things will turn out fine.
PATSY:
  Daddy's funny.
MOTHER: Most appealing!
JUDY:
  Daddy should resign—
  I mean, his trying to act for Mother.
ERIC:
  Yes, I think so, too;
  Each job is harder than the other,
  And what a lot to do—
  Cooking, darning, sweeping, pressing,
  Cleaning up the sink . . .
JUDY:
  Daddy said it was distressing.

MOTHER:

So easy, don't you think?

JUDY (*Thoughtfully*):

No. But, Mom, you're always cheerful.

PATSY:

You don't burn the toast,
Or drop the kettle. It was fearful.

ERIC:

Mom, you never boast,
But you handle things just dandy.

JUDY:

Yes, you always do.

MOTHER:

Thank you. Have a piece of candy?
(*She passes the candy box, then looks toward outer door.*)
Hmmm. I wish I knew . . . (*She turns to* ERIC.)
That sock . . . I'll darn it in a jiffy. (*Turns to* JUDY)
Nothing to that spot. (*Turns to* PATSY)
I'll make your dress look nice and spiffy
When the iron gets hot . . .
(*Just at that moment* FATHER *bursts into the room, panting,
with a bouquet of red roses in his hand. Proudly he rushes to*
MOTHER.)

FATHER:

Dear, a Mother's Day surprise!
Don't you think my choice is wise—
Much, much wiser than the other?
Roses . . . for the world's best mother!

THE END

That's the Way Mothers Are

GIRLS: What did she want for Mother's Day?,
     we asked when we were tiny.
       A pile of sand where it's fun to play,
       and a bucket new and shiny!

ALL: That's the way mothers are.

BOYS: What did she want for Mother's Day?,
     we asked when we were older.
       A camping kit and a water bag
       and a knapsack for her shoulder!

ALL: That's the way mothers are.

GIRLS: What did she want? Not anything
     as frail as flowers or candy!
       But a good strong rope (for a good strong swing),
       or a bobsled would be handy!

ALL: That's the way mothers are.

GIRLS: Now that we've found her out, at last,
     (after these years, who wouldn't?)
     we're making up for her "sandpile" past . . .
     though she always says we shouldn't!

ALL: That's the way mothers are.

Who?

1ST CHILD: Who's always there to help you out,
to soothe your doubt,
your tears, your pout,
to set your troubles right-about?
ALL: Mother!

2ND CHILD: Who's always quick to understand,
and lend a hand
to what you've planned,
who (most times!) thinks you're pretty grand?
ALL: Mother!

3RD CHILD: Who never wants to let you down,
who tries to drown
each fret and frown,
who's always doing things "up brown"?
ALL: Mother!

4TH CHILD: Who always has a smile to send,
a laugh to lend,
and love to spend?
Who's all in all, your chiefest friend?
ALL: Mother!

For Mother's Day

It isn't just on Mother's Day
that Mother likes a special smile.
Although we honor her in May,
it isn't just on Mother's Day
she likes the special things we say—
she likes them all the while!

Memorial Day

I

GROUP: It will be a day of flowers,
 honoring these graves of ours:
1ST GIRL: Lilacs heavy with the scent
 of countless Springs that came and went,
1ST BOY: Red geraniums in a pot
 on a green and hallowed spot,
2ND GIRL: Purple iris, deep-dyed blue . . .
 colors of the brave and true,
2ND BOY: Hawthorn, cherry, apple sprig—
 blossoms small and blossoms big,
GROUP: Flowers in bunches, wreaths, and bowers,
 honoring these graves of ours.

II

GROUP: It will be a day of flowers
 brightening the thoughtful hours:
GIRLS: All day long the flowers will glow
 near the crosses, row on row,
BOYS: All day long they will be bright.
 Then, upon the verge of night,
 lighting up the gathering gloom,
 there will be another bloom . . .

343

GIRLS: There will show, high up and far,
the blossom of the Soldiers' Star!

GROUP: The Soldiers' Star—the first to pay
its homage to the fading day,
rounding out a day of flowers
honoring these graves of ours.

NOTE: A good dramatic effect may be achieved by having the boys and girls in the first stanza carry the flowers mentioned in their lines as they enter.

Red, White, and Blue

RED for courage to do the right,
WHITE for faith with its guiding light,
BLUE for strength in carrying-through—
Hail to the red and white and blue!

The Soldiers Speak

"Place your flowers, but do not weep,"
the silent soldiers seem to say.
"We are peaceful where we sleep
on this bright Memorial Day.

"Think of us, but do not sigh,"
they seem to whisper on the breeze.
"We are peaceful where we lie
on this day of memories.

"Just to know that freedom thrives
and our banners proudly wave,
makes us know the best survives
of the gift of life we gave."

GRADUATION

Look to a New Day

Characters

MARK, *senior class president*
MISS GARTLAND, *faculty advisor*
SENIOR STUDENTS
BARTON, *a student*
SENATOR BLAKE
ANNE HUTCHINSON
ELIZABETH, *a Colonial woman*
COLONIAL WOMEN, *6 or 8*
BENJAMIN FRANKLIN, *at 16*
JOHN COLLINS
MR. BASCOM
MR. WOOLCOTT
COLONIAL FATHER
COLONIAL MOTHER
BOY
GIRL
VOICE OF THOMAS JEFFERSON
LUCY HOOPER
TWO SISTERS
JOHN GREENLEAF WHITTIER

SCENE 1

TIME: *The present.*

SETTING: *A classroom in a high school.*

AT RISE: MISS GARTLAND *and* MARK *stand talking at desk as* SENIOR STUDENTS, BARTON *among them, assemble for meeting. Some are already seated; others come in laughing and talking.*

MARK: The meeting will come to order. (*Waits for* STUDENTS *to take seats and settle down. Raps for order several times*) The sooner we get down to business, the sooner we can adjourn. (STUDENTS *become quiet.*) Since this is a special meeting for one special purpose, we'll dispense with the usual formalities. I'm sorry I had to call a meeting on such short notice.

MISS GARTLAND: It's all my fault, Mark. And I know it conflicts with Glee Club and Debating.

1ST BOY: And biology lab. I'll have to redo some experiments.

MARK: Well, I'm glad to see the class is pretty well represented anyway. We'll have to do the best we can. Miss Gartland, would you take over from here?

MISS GARTLAND: Thank you, Mark. (MARK *goes and sits with the others.*) As faculty advisor for the senior class, I thought you ought to know about the telegram I received this morning. I am counting on you to help me compose an answer. (STUDENTS *murmur curiously, ad lib, as* MISS GARTLAND *holds up a long night letter.*)

2ND BOY: Is all that just *one* telegram, Miss Gartland?

MISS GARTLAND (*Laughing*): I'll admit it's the longest one I ever received. It's from Senator Blake.

STUDENTS (*Surprised, murmuring*): Senator Blake!

MISS GARTLAND: You may not realize it, but I was instrumental in getting Senator Blake for our commencement speaker this year. The Senator and I went to school together, graduated from high school together. We haven't seen each other for years, but we've kept in touch more or less. When I heard that the School Board was having trouble deciding on a speaker, I suggested Senator Blake. He was born in our state, and you all know what an enlightened Senator he has been.

MARK: He ought to have something worthwhile to say on graduation night.

MISS GARTLAND: That's just it. He *wants* to have something worthwhile to say (*Takes telegram*), but listen to this. (*Reads*) THE TIME APPROACHES WHEN I MUST GET SOME THOUGHTS DOWN ON PAPER FOR THE GRADUATION ADDRESS I AM TO DELIVER AT YOUR SCHOOL. DO YOU REMEMBER THE SPEAKER WE HAD WHEN WE GRADUATED? NEITHER DO I. I DON'T REMEMBER HIS NAME OR WHAT HE LOOKED LIKE OR WHAT HE SAID. I CERTAINLY DON'T WANT TO BE THAT KIND OF SPEAKER NEXT FRIDAY NIGHT. BUT I FACE A DILEMMA. FOR THE PAST TEN OR TWELVE YEARS I HAVE BEEN OUT OF TOUCH WITH TEEN-AGERS EXCEPT IN A SUPERFICIAL WAY. AND SO I APPEAL TO YOU WHO HAVE BEEN VERY MUCH IN TOUCH WITH THEM. WHAT ARE YOUNG PEOPLE THINKING ABOUT THESE DAYS? WHAT ARE THEIR PROBLEMS? THEIR EXPECTATIONS? HOW DO THEY LOOK AT THE FUTURE? PLEASE HELP ME OUT. CALL COLLECT AS SOON AS POSSIBLE. MANY THANKS. IT WILL BE GOOD TO RENEW CONTACT WITH YOU AFTER ALL THESE YEARS. *Signed,* HANSON BLAKE. (*Puts telegram down*) It seems to me that graduates don't often get a chance like this . . . to hear a personalized address, as it were. And so Mark and I talked it over and decided a special class meeting was in order. I'm counting on you to help me answer that telegram. What *do* you have on your minds as you face the future?

1ST BOY: Problems!

1ST GIRL: Problems!

GROUP: Problems!

MISS GARTLAND (*Laughing*): Haven't we all? But I don't think a general answer like that would be of much help. *What* problems? Mark, why don't you start by telling us what problems you would like Senator Blake to give you some light on.

MARK: I'm lucky. I'm going on to college, and so the world isn't ending for me next Friday night when I get my diploma. But if I survive the next four years, there'll be plenty of problems to face.

MISS GARTLAND: What, for instance?

MARK: Getting a job, earning a living, doing something I like that someone will *pay* me for. That's not going to be simple, because so many of the interesting jobs have already been done or are being done. Why, by the time I'm through college even going to the moon may be commonplace! What's there left?

3RD BOY: That's what I say. Everything important has already been invented—television, sports cars, electricity.

2ND GIRL: Electricity didn't have to be invented, Jim. It was *there* all the time. Someone just had to think of harnessing it and putting it to use.

3RD BOY: Well, it's done.

MISS GARTLAND (*Making notes*): Worry about jobs. I suppose it's natural enough for you to be concerned about that.

4TH BOY: Jobs and money. Don't forget the money. With me that's more important than the job. I've got a whole list of things I want to buy . . . when I get the money.

MISS GARTLAND: I'll make a note of it.

2ND GIRL: And don't forget the world situation, Miss Gartland. I think we're all worried about that.

3RD GIRL: I'm not doing a lot of worrying. (*Tosses her head*) I'm just going to take things the way they come. I'm planning to have all the fun I can while the going's good. It may sound sort of cynical, but . . . (*Shrugs*) no one knows what the future will bring.

1ST BOY: That's what worries me. We're not in control.

4TH BOY: All I'm going to concentrate on is getting a sports car!

5TH GIRL: I'm planning to get married, and I want a home and family.

6TH GIRL: I'm planning to teach.

MISS GARTLAND: Good for you, Linda. It has plenty of problems, but lots of rewards, too.

2ND GIRL: What worries me is that I don't know *what* I want to do. There's something wrong with almost everything when I think about it. If I go to college, I'll have four years less of earning money on a job. If I don't go to college, I probably won't earn as much. Or is it better to go to business school? Or should I go on with my art? If Senator Blake can shed any light on my problems at graduation, he's a genius.

MISS GARTLAND: I think I'll put you down in one word, Dorothy. Uncertainty. (*To* BARTON, *who sits at back of room.*) Barton, what have you to say about it? We haven't heard a peep out of you.

4TH BOY: Bart doesn't have to talk. We all know he's going to Harvard, like all the Penningtons. (BARTON *stands.*)

BARTON: But I don't *want* to go to Harvard. And I hate to tell my father, because he's had me on the list for so long. I'd rather go to M.I.T. or Cal. Tech.

3RD BOY: Well, you can make a lot of money being an engineer these days.

BARTON: But it isn't money I'm after—just enough to get along on, that's all. And I'm not after fame, either. But I can't very well tell my family what I *do* want to do because they'll think I need my head examined.

MISS GARTLAND: Aren't you going to tell *us,* Barton?

BARTON: You'll probably think I'm crazy, too, but I've always wanted to help people in underdeveloped countries with their problems—irrigation, farming, education . . . any jobs that need to be done. But how does a person get started in that sort of thing? (*Sits*)

MISS GARTLAND: I'm sure Senator Blake won't think you need your head examined, Barton. I'll see that you get a chance to talk to him. (*Looks at notes*) I think this ought to give the Senator a pretty good idea of what you seniors are thinking about. I'll call him.

MARK (*Standing*): Meeting adjourned.

MISS GARTLAND: And thank you all for coming. I trust that thirty years from now you will still remember the speaker at your graduation exercises and what he had to say.

CURTAIN

* * * * *

SCENE 2

TIME: *Graduation night.*

SETTING: *A speaker's stand and some chairs are at one side of the stage. At center are a table and some chairs.*

AT RISE: SENATOR BLAKE *is speaking.* MARK *sits beside him. A few* STUDENTS *may be seated onstage, if desired.*

BLAKE: Now that I have touched upon some of your personal problems, my young friends, let me emphasize again that narrowing our vision to personal problems is not the best approach at a time like this. Jobs and pay checks are secondary to the larger problems of the kind of world we are to live in. You, every one of you, must contribute to the give-and-take of our democratic way of life if America is to survive as a leader among nations. Archibald MacLeish has said that America was promises. He was right. America was promises of freedom, a new life, a new start, a new day. But to put it another way, America was challenges . . . and it still is challenges . . . to make those promises come true.

Our American way of life with its priceless rights and liberties did not come to us by chance. It came through the "blood, sweat, and tears" of countless Americans who had ideals for their country and the stamina to try to realize them. What we need today, and that is where you come in, is the same sort of vision our forefathers showed.

Take the struggle for religious freedom. We have to go back to colonial America to see how it was secured. The first settlers came to our shores as rebels against the established church of England. They sought freedom to worship in their own way, and they found it. But no sooner had they established their own form of worship than they expected everyone else to conform to it. What had become a promise fulfilled for some became a challenge to others.

Anne Hutchinson, whose name you all recall, was one of the courageous ones who took a stand. Let us go back to the fall of 1637. A group of women are gathered in the Boston home of Mistress Hutchinson to listen to her ideas. (ANNE HUTCHINSON, ELIZABETH *and* COLONIAL WOMEN *enter and go to table. Stage lights dim. A spotlight shines on group at table.* ANNE *stands in center of group.*)

ANNE: As I have told you before in these meetings, dear friends, I believe in a covenant of grace—based upon direct intuition of God's love and grace . . . *not* upon obedience to established rules of church and state. Salvation comes through faith alone! Church and state should be kept separate and apart. What right has government to force any form of religion upon us? Everyone should be free to worship as his conscience dictates.

1ST WOMAN: That is what Roger Williams believed, too, and we all know what happened to him.

2ND WOMAN: Banished from Salem in the depths of winter! He all but lost his life fleeing into the wilderness. If he hadn't known some friendly Indians . . .

ANNE: Ah, but he didn't lose his life. And think what he has done with it! His colony at Providence is a haven of freedom where anyone is free to worship as he pleases. How different from Boston! Is it not a sad thought, my friends, that religious dissenters are no more free here than they were in old Boston in England? To think that those who fled from intolerance should impose their own brand of intolerance on others!

3RD WOMAN: Aren't you fearful about speaking so openly, Mistress Hutchinson? The very walls have ears these days.

ANNE: How can we meet the challenge if we are afraid to speak openly?

4TH WOMAN: Please take care, for your own sake, and the sake of your family and friends!

ANNE (*Nodding*): I know . . . the elders are calling me too independent in my thinking. Perhaps, my friends, it will be best to give up our meetings for a few weeks. I am willing to face any trial in defense of my convictions . . . but that is no reason why you should suffer with me. Until this talk of "independent thinking" blows over, we can examine our religious beliefs in private and in silence.

1ST WOMAN: I can't imagine your keeping silent, dear Anne, if an occasion arises to speak up for tolerance and freedom.

ANNE: Come what may, I will take my stand in Boston, as Roger Williams took his in Salem. My husband and my children support me in this. Whatever happens I will find the strength to meet the test, since I do not trust in my strength alone. Goodbye now, my friends . . . until we meet again. (WOMEN *exit*. ELIZABETH *remains*.)

ELIZABETH: I must speak to you alone, Anne. I'm afraid you don't realize how serious the situation is.

ANNE: Why, Elizabeth, who is talking against me besides the lords-brethren?

ELIZABETH: They themselves are powerful enough, goodness knows. More than ever they are taking a stand: there shall be *no* dissenting opinions in New England, no authority besides the authority already here. I fear you are to be charged with heresy, Anne. (*Shudders*)

ANNE: Rev. John Cotton is on my side. He wields great influence.

ELIZABETH (*Hesitating*): I . . . I am sorry to be the one to tell you. Rev. Cotton is weakening, withdrawing his support. My husband tells me that John Cotton is veering to the side of your persecutors.

ANNE: How can it be? Four years ago John Cotton and I were on the same ship coming to New England. We talked freely together then and we have talked freely many times since. He has agreed with my ideas of inner illumination from the first.

ELIZABETH: First is not last, Anne. Believe me when I tell you he is no longer on your side.

ANNE (*Slowly, shaking her head*): If John Cotton takes this step, he will become a bitter, disillusioned man living with a shrinking horizon. How often it happens . . . when one gets a certain amount of power and prestige, he cannot bear to endanger it. More and more he will seek safety in conformity.

ELIZABETH: Former Governor Winthrop and the Rev. John Wilson and most of the other leaders oppose you, as you well know. Governor Vane was on your side, but he has seen fit to go to England. That leaves only your brother-in-law among those of authority . . . the Rev. John Wheelwright.

ANNE: He will not desert me.

ELIZABETH: But how can he help you? Oh, Anne, my husband

predicts that your brother-in-law will be banished by the General Court in its next session.

ANNE (*Quietly*): Then I shall be without defenders when my turn comes to stand trial.

ELIZABETH: Couldn't you change your mind and conform . . . outwardly, at least?

ANNE: No. I believe that everyone should have the freedom to worship as he pleases. I cannot say or act otherwise.

ELIZABETH: Then, my dear, dear Anne, I know not what will become of you! Banishment can mean death by starvation . . . or even worse, massacre at the hands of Indians. (*Spotlight goes out.* ANNE *and* ELIZABETH *exit. Stage lights come up again on* SENATOR BLAKE *at speaker's stand. This lighting procedure is repeated for following spotlight scenes.*)

BLAKE: As you know, Anne Hutchinson was tried and sentenced to banishment. The Rev. John Wilson cast her out of the church as if she were a leper. In the spring of 1638 she and her family struggled through the wilderness and made their way to Rhode Island, where they founded a colony for dissenters.

Anne Hutchinson was not the first to fight for religious freedom in America, nor was she the last. But her courageous voice helped make America a land where church and state became wholly separate. We need more Anne Hutchinsons and their vision today.

Another milestone of yesterday was the fight for freedom of speech and press. From the time the first printing press was licensed by the crown at Cambridge, Massachusetts, until the trial of John Peter Zenger almost a hundred years later, the crown censored the printed word. No such thing as free speech and free printing existed in those days. Boston's first newspaper was suppressed after only one issue.

As the years went by, adventurous souls established other newspapers, but all had to be licensed by the royal governor. And all had to watch their step.

Take James Franklin's experience, for instance, in publishing the fourth newspaper established in the colonies. His troubles began in the summer of 1722, the year after his weekly *New England Courant* was licensed in Boston. He printed an anonymous letter criticizing the government's failure to protect the coast against pirates. For this, he and his apprentice were hailed before the Council. The apprentice was none other than Benjamin Franklin, sixteen years old.

In the print shop the morning after the hearing, Benjamin was busily at work when John Collins, a bookish young friend of his, came to see him. (BENJAMIN FRANKLIN *enters, writing with a quill pen. He sits at table and continues writing as* JOHN COLLINS *enters.*)

JOHN (*Out of breath*): Morning, Ben. (*Looks around furtively*) Where is James?

BENJAMIN (*Getting up*): It's perfectly safe, John. The master of the print shop is not here.

JOHN (*Relieved*): I had some books to deliver in this end of town. Ran all the way so I could stop to see you, Ben. What happened yesterday before the Council? Where's James? Are they going to do anything to you?

BENJAMIN: Briefly, my brother James will be enjoying a month in jail.

JOHN: Jail! For printing a letter that stated a simple fact! The government *isn't* protecting the coast against pirates, and everyone knows it.

BENJAMIN: But the King and his government are beyond criticism, remember. Of course, it's ridiculous. I don't always agree with James, but here's one time I applaud him. I'd have printed that letter, too . . . *somebody* has to take a stand for freedom of speech.

JOHN: I trust you didn't say that to the Council. What happened to you at the hearing, Ben?

BENJAMIN: The Council examined me . . . without getting any information . . . admonished me . . . not very severely . . .

dismissed me . . . assuming that a mere apprentice could do
no harm. If they only knew!

JOHN: Knew what? What do you have up your sleeve? (BEN-
JAMIN, *smiling broadly, begins to cavort about room.*)

BENJAMIN (*Singing to tune of "Pop! Goes the Weasel"*):
>A penny for a pot of ink,
>A penny for a taper,
>The Council gets its feelings hurt
>And pop! goes the paper.
>All around the printing press
>The waiting letters caper,
>Till Benjy puts them all in place
>And out comes the paper!

JOHN: You mean . . . you mean you're going to print the paper
yourself while James is in jail? (*Voices are heard from offstage.*) Someone's coming.

BENJAMIN: Wait, John. That must be Bascom and Woolcott.
Friends of my brother's. They usually come in about this
time with bits for the paper—"Serious, sarcastic, ludicrous
or otherways amusing." They won't stay long. Wait around
and maybe you'll hear some news. (BASCOM *and* WOOLCOTT
enter. They nod at BEN, *ignore* JOHN.) Good morning,
gentlemen.

BASCOM (*Looking around*): Then it's true. James isn't here?

WOOLCOTT: We heard he'd been taken in, censured, and im-
prisoned for a month, but couldn't believe it.

BENJAMIN: It's true. He wouldn't tell who wrote the offending
letter, of course. I hope you brought your usual items for the
paper.

BASCOM: What paper? With your brother in jail, how can the
paper be published?

BENJAMIN: I intend to publish it, to the best of my ability.

WOOLCOTT: But you're only a lad, Ben.

BENJAMIN: Maybe I am only sixteen but surely you will admit that experience is more important than age. I've been working here in the print shop for four years, composing type, reading proof, working the press. The *New England Courant* will be published this week as usual, and I'll appreciate it if you gentlemen will favor me by continuing to write for it.

BASCOM: Well! Indeed we will, lad.

BENJAMIN: I hope to get in a few rubs against the government myself if the occasion arises. And that reminds me, gentlemen, I found another of those letters from Mrs. Silence Dogood under the door when I came to work this morning.

BASCOM: Ah, Silence Dogood! She has been too silent lately for my liking. I could take more of her.

WOOLCOTT: Yes, even though it is a torment not to know who she really is. Hasn't your brother found out yet?

BENJAMIN: Not that I know of. (*Goes to table, picks up paper.*) Here, gentlemen, would you be so kind as to look this over and tell me what you think. (*Hands them letter. Turns to JOHN*) In case you don't know, John, Mrs. Dogood is one of our most popular contributors.

BASCOM (*Sharply*): Oh-oh, listen to this. (*Reads bit aloud*) "There can be no such thing as public liberty without freedom of speech; which is the right of every man as far as by it he does not hurt or control the right of another . . ." Excellent! Excellent, Mrs. Dogood! But how's the government going to like it, eh? No such thing as liberty without freedom of speech! And here's James Franklin in jail for printing a simple little truth about the government. Woolcott, why can't we discover this mastermind among our friends who writes the Dogood letters?

WOOLCOTT (*Shrugging*): Perhaps the writer is not among our friends, Bascom. I can think of no other explanation. (*Looks at letter again*) There's more . . . listen . . . "Whoever would overthrow the liberty of a nation must begin by subduing the freedom of speech . . ." Gentlemen, where is our liberty under the present royal government of England? It is time someone spoke out, and if that someone is our much-admired Silence Dogood, so much the better!

BENJAMIN: Then you think I'm justified in printing the letter in the next issue of the *Courant?*

WOOLCOTT: Print it, Ben. And if trouble comes of it, we'll stand behind you.

BENJAMIN: Thank you, sirs. I value your advice . . . and also what you write.

BASCOM: Come, Woolcott, come, we must ferret out some lively reading for this brazen young editor of the *New England Courant.* (*To* BEN) We'll be back. (*They exit.*)

BENJAMIN (*Laughing*): I planned to print the Dogood letter anyway, whether they agreed or not. But I feel encouraged to have them agree. Someone has to bring our grievances out into the open. What's a newspaper for if not to express itself and the thoughts of its readers?

JOHN: Ben, who is this Silence Dogood? Doesn't anyone really know?

BENJAMIN: So far just the person who writes the letters knows. But his best friend will know shortly.

JOHN: How do you know *that?*

BENJAMIN: Because . . . swear you'll never tell, John, by word or look. (JOHN *raises his right hand*) I know because *I* am Mrs. Silence Dogood! (BENJAMIN *and* JOHN *exit.*)

BLAKE: Benjamin Franklin's daring words about freedom of the press, printed under the pseudonym of Mrs. Silence Dogood, escaped the eye of the censor. The *New England Courant* existed for five more lively years.

In 1734 came that famous case for freedom of the press, the Zenger case. When Zenger was found "not guilty" on charges of seditious libel against the royal governor, the cause of freedom leaped ahead. But the battle was not really won until the end of the century, when freedom of speech and of the press were written into our Bill of Rights, along with other freedoms that had to be fought for.

And what freedoms were they? The freedoms the colonists up and down the Atlantic seaboard were deprived of by the tyranny of England. The people of the mother country had already won these rights from the King, but Parliament refused to grant them to the colonists. Every one of the rights that we take for granted today the colonists had to fight for. "No taxation without representation" echoed throughout the colonies, as you well remember.

Look in on a typical household in Boston a few months after the Boston Tea Party. A family sits gloomily around the table—father, mother, and two teen-age children. (COLONIAL FATHER, MOTHER, BOY and GIRL *enter and go to table*.)

FATHER: The port of Boston closed by act of Parliament! I can't believe it. Haven't we a right to live? Our whole existence depends on ships coming and going.

BOY: We all get punished for the action of a few in dumping that tea into the harbor. And why shouldn't the tea be dumped, anyway? What right has Britain to tax our tea without our consent?

GIRL: Parliament had to back down on the stamp tax. They had to back down on the taxes on paint, lead, and glass, too . . . because we refused to pay them, even with the British regiments here. To assert their authority they kept the tax on tea, and then we dumped it into the harbor. It's really funny when you think of it.

BOY: We'll starve to death before we consent to their tyranny . . . if that's what they want.

MOTHER: I'm afraid we *will* go hungry, very hungry indeed. When the stores run out of food, what then? Where will more come from, with the port closed?

FATHER: Bottled up, that's what we are. Trade cut off. Business ruined. They're making an example of us to the rest of the colonies. They've singled us out.

BOY: It's up to us to fight back. And we *will* fight back. (*Leans over confidentially*) I was down at the tavern again this afternoon, and there's plenty of talk of rebellion. We're going to form a band of minutemen to uphold our rights. Don't tell me I'm too young to join! We have to take our stand now before more troops are quartered on us . . . we have to meet this challenge. (*The family exits.*)

BLAKE: You know how the Revolutionary War began—with British troops from Boston fighting with minutemen at Lexington and Concord. And you all know how it ended, how we gained our independence from England and set up our own government under our own Constitution. But the Constitution contained no guarantee that the new government would not in its turn become tyrannical. There were no provisions that protected the rights of the people against the government. Listen to what Thomas Jefferson had to say about it:

JEFFERSON'S VOICE (*On loudspeaker*): "I disapproved from the first moment the want of a bill of rights to guard liberty against the legislative as well as executive branches of the government, that is to say, to secure freedom in religion, freedom of the press, freedom from unlawful imprisonment, freedom from a permanent military, and a trial by jury in all cases determinable by the laws of the land."

BLAKE: Many other Revolutionary patriots felt like Jefferson and insisted that a Bill of Rights be written into the Constitution. And so, in 1791, we got our first ten amendments, guaranteeing our right to life, liberty and the pursuit of happiness.

But only the rights of free white men were protected; the slaves had no rights. Those rights still had to be fought for by men of vision. One such man was the New England poet John Greenleaf Whittier. We go to New York late in the summer of

1837 to look in on a friend of Whittier's who has the young poet very much on her mind. Lucy Hooper is talking to her two sisters. (LUCY *and her* SISTERS *enter and sit at table.* LUCY *carries some pamphlets.*)

1ST SISTER: Is your friend Mr. Whittier calling again tonight, Lucy?

LUCY: Oh, I hope so.

1ST SISTER: I'm not sure these late hours . . .

2ND SISTER (*Interrupting*): To say nothing of the excitement . . .

1ST SISTER: Are good for you. You're not overly strong, you know.

LUCY: But I never feel tired when I talk to John Greenleaf Whittier. I feel inspired. I've written so many poems since he came to New York. I hope his work with the American Anti-Slavery Society goes on forever and ever.

2ND SISTER: What a warm friendship you two have developed in such a short time!

LUCY: In addition to our interest in poetry, we think alike on so many things. (*Holds up pamphlet*) I've read all John's poems, and now I have begun on his prose. This is his first piece on the slavery question, written four years ago, when he was twenty-six.

1ST SISTER (*Bending over to see title, reading slowly*): "Justice and Expedience . . . or Slavery Considered with a View to Its Rightful and Effectual Remedy, Abolition." (*Thumbs pages*) Goodness, Lucy, it looks formidable.

LUCY: Not at all. I've marked certain places. (*Takes pamphlet*) Listen. (*Finds place, reads eloquently*) "I desire peace—the peace of universal love—the peace of a common interest—a common feeling—a common humanity. But so long as slavery is tolerated, no such peace can exist. Liberty and slavery cannot dwell in harmony together . . . Peace! there *can* be no peace between justice and oppression—truth and falsehood—freedom and slavery."

1ST SISTER: I never thought of the problem in just that way.

LUCY (*Turning pages*): And this: "When the Declaration of Independence and the practice of our people shall agree, when Truth shall be exalted among us; . . . when all the baneful pride and prejudice of caste and color shall fall forever, then, and not till then, shall it go well for America."

2ND SISTER: He almost makes me want to join the abolitionists! How did he get this engrossing interest in slavery, Lucy?

LUCY: Through William Lloyd Garrison, who published John's first poetry. That was the start of their friendship. Mr. Garrison printed other poems, and his stirring editorials persuaded John to become an abolitionist.

2ND SISTER: But there is a great deal of hostility against abolitionists, isn't there, even in the North?

LUCY (*Nodding*): John Greenleaf Whittier has been all but ostracized socially because of his anti-slavery beliefs and activities. And two years ago he and a lecturer from England were attacked by a mob in Concord. It hasn't been easy. (*Sound of knock is heard.* LUCY *looks up expectantly;* SISTERS *notice her eagerness.*)

1ST SISTER (*Rising*): Perhaps that is Mr. Whittier now. (WHITTIER *enters, bows to* SISTERS *politely, hurries to* LUCY.) Come, sister. (*The two exit.*)

WHITTIER: Have you seen the new moon over the rooftops, Miss Lucy, with the bright star near by? Very low in the sky now . . . I wonder if we can see it from your window. (*They stand together, looking.*) There! It will be down in a few minutes.

LUCY: How beautiful. I used to think stars were children of the moon.

WHITTIER: Perhaps they are. (*They turn back to their chairs.* LUCY *picks up the pamphlet.*)

LUCY: I've been telling my sisters all about your pamphlet.

WHITTIER: Oh, but you don't know all about it! How it cost me a new suit and a much-needed pair of shoes! You see, I printed five hundred copies to distribute, and that took a large part of my year's earnings. So I had to go without the new suit and shoes.

LUCY: Have you regretted it?

WHITTIER: Not for a moment. Not even after a wealthy merchant came along and paid for the publication of five thousand copies. (*Smiles*) But how right my Quaker father was. Neither poetry nor pamphlets buy a great deal of bread!

LUCY: One does not live by bread alone, remember.

WHITTIER: You are right. I have dedicated myself to a cause, and that sustains me when bread fails. Oh, by the way, Miss Lucy, I have a bit of news.

LUCY: Another poem published?

WHITTIER: No, an editorial this time, in the *Pennsylvania Freeman*, and a letter accompanying the acceptance. My work with the Anti-Slavery Society in New York will not last much longer. There will soon be an opening on the *Pennsylvania Freeman* which I think I shall accept.

LUCY (*Distressed*): You will be leaving New York?

WHITTIER (*Noticing her disappointment*): Yes, for Philadelphia. Oh, but not for a few months. We shall still have time for some good talks. Come, read me your latest poem. (LUCY *and* WHITTIER *exit*.)

BLAKE: The next spring John Greenleaf Whittier became editor of the *Pennsylvania Freeman*, writing some daring editorials for it. Then in a few months Pennsylvania Hall, in which his office was located, was burned to the ground by a hostile mob. Whittier set up another office in Philadelphia, and his work went on. Several years later letters from Lucy Hooper's sisters brought him the sad news of her death. The sisters told of the depth of Lucy's affection for him, and he wrote back contritely. (WHITTIER *enters, writing. He speaks slowly as he writes*.)

WHITTIER: "I admired and loved her; yet felt myself compelled to crush every warmer feeling. . . . Poverty, illness and our separate faiths—the pledge that I had made of all the hopes

and dreams of my younger years to the cause of freedom—
compelled me to steel myself against everything which tended
to attract me . . . the blessing of a woman's love and a
home." (*He exits*.)

BLAKE: For thirty years Whittier worked for the abolition of
slavery. His voice was not the only one by any means, but it
was a strong one. For thirty years he fought on behalf of those
unfortunate people who had been captured, chained, brought
to our shores and sold into slavery against their will and
against the principles of humanity. Then, in the midst of the
Civil War, Abraham Lincoln signed the Emancipation Proclamation and freed the slaves with one mighty stroke of the pen.

It takes Whittier's kind of dedicated purpose to make
visions come true.

By now, you are perhaps wondering what these forays into
the past have to do with you and the new life you are facing.
Why worry, you ask, about rights that are already ours,
handed down in the Constitution and its amendments? Who
can take away these freedoms which we hold in our hands?

The answer, my friends, is not so much *who* can take them
away as *what*. It is true we have our rights on paper . . . but
we must keep defending them again and again. The responsibility is on your shoulders and mine. We have to be as courageous and determined to *keep* our rights as our forefathers
were in winning them.

And may I say that we have another responsibility in this
era of One World . . . the responsibility of sharing our rights
with others. We no longer live in the kind of world the colonists knew . . . when it took three months for the May-
flower to sail across the Atlantic, and ten days of hard riding
for Jefferson to cover the three hundred miles from Monti-
cello to the Constitutional Convention in Philadelphia.
Today, in a matter of hours, jet planes can cross continents

and oceans. Today trouble in India or Africa or Asia is potential trouble for us in America.

But how can we share our freedoms, you ask?

One of your own graduates has a good, down-to-earth answer. I am pleased and encouraged to hear that, above all else, he wants to work in underdeveloped countries, helping to build schools, irrigate land to grow crops, and teach good health habits. Many such jobs are available through the Peace Corps. We aren't all in a position to help in that way, but there are things we all can do. We can start right here at home by giving everyone an equal chance—regardless of race, color, or creed. We can respect others' rights. We can set high standards in our work instead of just trying to get by. Above all, we can face every challenge to our ideas with the same courage Americans had when our country was finding its way to freedom. (SENATOR *gathers up his notes, as* MARK, STUDENTS *and audience applaud enthusiastically.* MARK *rises and shakes* SENATOR'S *hand. Then* MARK *turns to audience, motioning for silence.*)

MARK: On behalf of the graduates, I wish to thank Senator Blake for a talk we shall long remember. He has made us see that our worries about jobs and pay checks are small indeed, compared to the exciting challenge of upholding and improving our American way of life. In all humility I say that we will do our best to carry on in the spirit that made America great. (*Curtain*)

THE END

The Mountain Trail

1st Boy: The mountain trail is a steep trail
and rocky-rough and bare.

All: But most of the trails are steep trails
that get you anywhere.

1st Girl: The mountain trail is a hard trail
with pitfalls left and right.

All: But most of the trails are hard trails
that reach a beckoning height.

2nd Boy: So over the rocks we scramble!
2nd Girl: With never a mind to stop!
All: And few of us care it's a steep trail
for thought of the mountain top!

School Again!

BOY: Part of me's sad,
and part of me's glad,
and part of me's in-between:
the weather is clear
as crystal this year
and maple trees still are green,
but . . .

ALL: It's pencil and pen
and counting by ten
and reading and writing at—school again!

GIRL: Part of me's gay
and part of me's gray
and part of me's sort of blue:
the summer was free
as wind in a tree,
but summer is mostly through,
so . . .

ALL: It's paper and pen
and spelling, and then
arithmetic problems at—school again!

BOY *and* GIRL: Part of me blinks,
and part of me winks
as mischievous as an elf:
for where'd be the fun
now school has begun
to stay at home *by myself!*
So . . .
GIRLS: It's Nancy!
BOYS: And Glenn!
GIRLS: And Kathy!
BOYS: And Ken!

ALL: Hello there, hello there,—it's school again!

Autumn Leaves

1ST CHILD: Leaves are falling,
     falling from the hedge,
2ND CHILD: falling from the ivy
     on the window ledge,
3RD CHILD: falling from the poplar,
4TH CHILD: falling from the pear,
ALL: falling, falling, falling
     through the hazy air.

5TH CHILD: Leaves are flashes
     of yellow and brown,
6TH CHILD: orange and crimson
     fluttering down,
7TH CHILD: big leaves,
8TH CHILD: broad leaves,
9TH CHILD: middlesized,
10TH CHILD: small—
ALL: Showers of confetti
     in honor of fall!

A Gypsy Month

ALL: September is a gypsy month
        with gypsy things to do:
GIRLS: It dresses trees in red and gold
        with jewels of sun shot through.
BOYS: It makes the sleepy summer hills
        look brassy-bright and new.
GIRLS: It splashes color down each path
        and polishes each view.
BOYS: It decks the burnished countryside
        with scarfs of every hue.
GIRLS: It dangles leaves like butterflies
        against a sky of blue.
ALL: September is a gypsy month,
        a glowy, showy gypsy month,
        a dancing, prancing gypsy month . . .
        and we are gypsies too!

Leaf Boats

ALL: The pond was full of little boats
floating up and down,
with stems for masts, and colored sails—
golden, red, and brown.

BOYS: Some went fast.
Some went slow.
Some had holes
and couldn't go.

GIRLS: Some went east.
Some went west.
Some just sat'|
and took a rest.

ALL: The pond was full of little boats
(more than just a few),
but where they sailed and where they went
no one ever knew!

Polar-Bear Pines

ALL: Oh, every pine is a polar-bear zoo
when the fluffity, puffity storm is through,
for every branch holds a bear or two
when the fluffity storm is through.

GIRLS: Maybe-bears,
play-be-bears,
big and small and baby bears!
BOYS: Slumpy bears,
humpy bears,
never cross-and-grumpy bears!
ALL: Oh, every branch holds a bear or two
when the puffity storm is through.

GIRLS: They cling to the branches or lie down flat
out in the pine-tree zoo.
BOYS: Or balance themselves like an acrobat
(a *very* hard thing to do).
ALL: And they all are wonderfully white and fat,
such fluffity bears to marvel at,
when the puffity storm is through.

ALL: Oh, every pine is a polar-bear zoo
when the rollicky, frolicky storm is through,

for every branch holds a bear or two
when the frolicky storm is through.

GIRLS: Droopy bears,
stoopy bears,
single ones and groupy bears!
BOYS: Flimsy bears,
limbsy bears,
full-of-fun-and-whimsy bears!
ALL: Oh, every branch holds a bear or two
when the rollicky storm is through.

GIRLS: They cling to the boughs where they fell last night
out in the pine-tree zoo.
BOYS: They sprawl on the branches or hold on tight
(a *very* hard thing to do).
ALL: And they all are wonderfully soft and white
and make such a rollicky, frolicky sight
when the frolicky storm is through, is through,
when the rollicky storm is through.

Wee Little Feb.

1ST GIRL: "Dear little
queer little
mere little Feb.—
just twenty-eight days!" said Jan.
"*Why*, now,
do I, now,
have three days more?
It sounds like a senseless plan."

1ST BOY: "Sweet little
neat little
fleet little Feb.—
just twenty-eight days!" March said.
"*See*, now,
take me, now,
I've three days more.
Why so?" And he shook his head.

2ND GIRL: "Trim little
slim little
prim little Feb.!"
said April and June and May.
"*Who*, now,

can view, now,
her short little life,
and not wipe a tear away?"

2ND BOY: "Fair little
spare little
rare little Feb.!"
said August, July, and Sept.
"*Where*, now,
is there, now,
a grain of sense
in the manner the months are kept?"

3RD GIRL: "Bright little
slight little
quite-little Feb.!"
December told Nov. and Oct.
"*Queer*, now,
that we're, now,
so big and strong,
and she is so little. I'm shocked!"

3RD BOY: Shy little
spry little
wry little Feb.
smiled up with her face alight:

ALL (*Soft chorus*): "Near ones,
and dear ones,
don't fret for me.
I don't mind my size a mite!"

"Strength isn't,
length isn't
everything!

I'm noted in other ways:
Who, now,
of you, now,
is quite so full
of wonderful holidays?

"Lincoln,
I'm thinkin',
belongs to me.
And Washington's mine! Ahem,
who, now,
has two, now,
such famous dates?
I'm something because of *them*.

"Also
recall, so
you'll fret no more—
St. Valentine lives with me!
Come, now,
who's glum, now?
Not wee little Feb.!
I'm gay as a month can be."

To a Groundhog on February 2

ALL: Wake up, sleepyhead!
    Put your dreams away.
    Everyone is waiting
    for what you have to say:
GIRL: Will your shadow make a blot
    on the snow today or not?
BOY: Will the sun start turning hot?
    Will the month be cold, or what?
    Hurry, sir, and tell us on this Groundhog Day.

ALL: Wake up, sleepyhead!
    What's a little snow?
    If your shadow follows you,
    back inside you'll go.
BOY: Will the coming six weeks be
    wintry, cold, and shivery?
GIRL: Balmy, warm, and summery?
ALL: Groundhog, what's your prophecy?
    Better put your *glasses* on, so you'll really know!

Rain on the Roof

(Starts very slowly, gets faster and faster)

1st Child : With a peck
                a raindrop comes,
                like a bird to peck at crumbs.
2nd Child : Then another.
3rd Child : Then some more,
                sharper, louder than before.
4th Child : Faster, faster,
                rain-birds flit
                to the roof to peck on it.
5th Child : Dozens,
6th Child :   hundreds,
                neck to neck:
7th Child : Peck, peck,
8th Child : Peck, peck,
All :   Peck-peck-peck.

Early Crocus

BOY: A chubby little crocus,
GIRL: A nubby little crocus,
BOY: A fubby little crocus
    peeked up to see the sun.
GIRL: Before the cold was over,
BOY: Beside a sleepy clover,
ALL: It looked the garden over—
    before the snow was done.

GIRL: A little snowbird spied it,
BOY: And for a moment eyed it,
GIRL: Then settled down beside it
    and said to it:
ALL: "Oh, dear,
    I hope you brought your mittens
    and furs, like willow-kittens . . .
    or you'll get chilled to bittens
    so early in the year."

Who Is It?

GIRLS: We know someone—
        try to guess!
1ST CHILD: She wears a gold hat.
2ND CHILD: She wears a green dress.
3RD CHILD: She wears glass slippers
        the color of rain.
4TH CHILD: And around her neck
        is a dandelion chain.
5TH CHILD: She scatters flowers
        over the hills,
        some of them plain
        and some with frills.
6TH CHILD: She listens when robins
        and blackbirds sing.
7TH CHILD: And she laughs at winter,
        because she's . . .
BOYS: SPRING!

May Day

BOY: You heard the screen door open?
GIRL: You heard the hinges squeak?
BOY: You heard the doorknob rattle—
      before you got a peek?

GIRL: You heard the porch boards creaking
      beneath some hurrying feet?
BOY: You saw a little shadow
      go flitting down the street?

GIRL: And then you found a basket
      with flowers inside, you say?
ALL: To think you had forgotten
      it was the first of **May!**

PRODUCTION NOTES

The Weaver's Son

Characters: 3 male; 2 female.
Playing Time: 20 minutes.
Costumes: The women wear long full skirts, aprons, dark bodices and long-sleeved blouses. Domenico and the two boys wear hose and long-sleeved doublets.
Properties: Basket of tangled yarn.
Setting: A combination work-room-living room. If possible, a loom or spinning wheel should be in one corner of the room. A plain work table is at center, and near it are several stools. Other furnishings—chairs, piles of wool, etc.—may also be included.
Lighting: No special effects.

Day of Destiny

Characters: 10 male.
Playing Time: 20 minutes.
Costumes: All the characters wear hose and long-sleeved doublets. The sailors wear faded blue, the page, green, and Columbus, dark blue. Columbus may wear a cape and hat.
Properties: Book, cup, bird, lantern.
Setting: All that is needed is a backdrop showing a ship's rail, some masts, and some ocean. If desired, ropes, kegs, masts, etc., may be placed around the stage.
Lighting: No special effects.

Ghosts on Guard

Characters: 4 male; 3 female.
Playing Time: 15 minutes.
Costumes: Mrs. Briggs wears a housedress. Mr. Briggs is dressed in a white shirt and sheets. Harry wears a shirt and short trousers until Mr. Briggs dresses

384

him as a ghost. The rest of the children wear masquerade costumes and masks.

Properties: Scene 1: Pins, rope. Scene 2: Paper bags, laundry soap, tick-tack, noise-maker, rope.

Setting: Scene 1: The living room of the Briggs' home. The room may be furnished with a few chairs and a table. Scene 2: In front of the Briggs' home. A few "bushes" or "trees" are all that is necessary. Note: If desired, this play may be produced without any scenery at all.

Lighting: Scene 1: Bright lights. Scene 2: Dimmed lights or a dark stage with a spotlight.

effects offstage: an abrupt clang, a discordant crash, and the clear sound of a bell.

Setting: The living room of the Dawson home. Chairs, tables and lamps are placed around the room to make it look attractive and comfortable. In one corner of the room, downstage, a gauze curtain is hung; the flashbacks take place behind this curtain.

Lighting: If possible, thè lighting behind the gauze curtain should be a little dimmer than the lighting on the rest of the stage.

Note: This play could be used as a radio play with very little change.

THE VOICE OF LIBERTY

Characters: 6 male; 4 female.
Playing Time: 30 minutes.
Costumes: The Dawson family and Gram wear everyday modern dress. Isaac, William and Stephen wear costumes suggesting the colonial period.
Properties: Instruments that will make the proper sound

ONCE UPON A TIME

Characters: 11 male; 5 female; Reader may be either male or female; as many male and female characters as desired may take the parts of the Old Woman's children, although 4 male and 4 female actors are all that is necessary.
Playing Time: 20 minutes.

Costumes: The Reader wears everyday dress. The Old Woman wears a long full skirt, white blouse, and tight bodice. Her children can wear everyday clothes or peasant costumes. The Baker's Man is dressed in white and has a tall white chef's hat. Whizzer wears a long full black cape and a tall black hat. A book on a string is tied around his neck. Although costumes for the book characters are desirable, they are not necessary, since each character is identified in the text. If costumes are worn, they can be copied from illustrations in the various books.

Properties: Book for Reader, platter with pie for Baker's Man, wand for Whizzer, white gloves and fan for White Rabbit, small cake for Alice, umbrella and carpet bag for Mary Poppins, bow and arrow for Robin Hood.

Setting: All that is needed is an easy chair for the Reader, a stool, a table, and a few chairs. A telephone is on the table. There are exits at left and right. (The Children can sit on the floor.)

Lighting: No special effects.

TREASURE HUNT

Characters: 13 male; 11 female; more if desired.

Playing Time: 20 minutes.

Costumes: Miss Brooks and the children are dressed in modern clothing. The characters from books are dressed in appropriate costumes. For suggestions, consult the books mentioned in the play.

Properties: Thimble, stuffed cat, slippers, compass, rolls, bow and arrow, "tail," flowers, box of candies.

Setting: Scene 1: A sidewalk in front of the school, or a corridor. This scene may be played in front of the curtain. Scene 2: A classroom. Miss Brooks' desk is downstage right. Chairs or desks for the children are placed in rows facing Miss Brooks.

Lighting: No special effects.

Unexpected Guests

Characters: 6 male; 6 female.

Playing Time: 10 minutes.

Costumes: All the characters wear typical Pilgrim costumes.

Properties: Cooking equipment, food, buckets, nuts, wood, peas.

Setting: A kitchen-living room in a Pilgrim home. At the end of the room is a large fireplace. The simple furniture has been moved against the walls to make room for work tables holding cooking equipment and food. On the upstage wall is a window, and near the window a long sheet of paper which Mistress Winslow consults.

Lighting: No special effects.

Angel in the Looking-Glass

Characters: 3 male; 5 female.

Playing Time: 20 minutes.

Costumes: Modern dress. Lucy wears a white flowing robe typical of the angel's costume in a Christmas pageant.

Properties: Pins, tape measure, halo.

Setting: Before the curtain there is a large full-length mirror placed on one side of the stage. The stage itself is divided into three "apartments." In the Youngs' apartment are two chairs and a table. In Aunt Martha's apartment are an overstuffed chair and two hassocks. In Zorlova's apartment are a chair and a modernistic dressing table. On the dressing table is a telephone. Note: This play may be produced without any scenery at all; the apartments may be indicated by signs.

Lighting: No special effects.

Time Out for Christmas

Characters: 3 male; 1 female; 24 male or female.

Playing Time: 20 minutes.

Costumes: Rag Doll wears a long dress with white apron and black shoes. Teddy Bear is dressed in a costume to suggest what he is. Tick and Tock are dressed in the same costumes—small pointed hats, shirts with matching shorts. The Days wear very simple costumes and each one wears a large cardboard letter with its numeral printed on it.

Properties: Handkerchiefs for Rag Doll and Teddy Bear, half-finished present.

Setting: On one side of the stage there is a large clock whose hands point to almost 12 o'clock. The face of the clock may be painted on a large sheet of wrapping paper and pinned to a screen. It should be large enough so Tick and Tock can come from behind it. On the other side of the stage there is a large calendar. This may also be painted on wrapping paper (a winter scene at the top and December printed in large letters beneath) and pinned to a screen. A few small chairs complete the setting.

Lighting: No special effects.

A CHRISTMAS TREE
FOR KITTY

Characters: 2 male; 4 female; male and female extras.

Playing Time: 10 minutes.

Costumes: Everyday dress. Willa, Martha, Mike and the Carolers wear outdoor clothing.

Properties: Small Christmas tree with ornaments, catnip ball, tissue paper, ribbons, wrapping, bow of red and green ribbon, plate of cookies, tag.

Setting: The living room may have a couch, chairs, lamps, etc. The only essential furnishing is a table at center which holds the little tree.

Lighting: No special effects.

THE SPIRIT OF CHRISTMAS

Characters: 2 male; 4 female; Reader and Spirit may be either male or female.

Playing Time: 10 minutes.

Costumes: The Spirit of Christmas is dressed in a red and green jester's costume. He wears a long, pointed cap with a little bell on his head, and bells are attached to the tips of his shoes with silver ribbon. The rest of the characters wear appropriate modern dress.

Properties: Trays of cookies, coffeepot, milk bottles.

Setting: No setting is necessary, although the stage may be decorated with Christmas greens.

Lighting: No special effects.

THE CHRISTMAS CAKE

Characters: 2 male; 1 female; Narrator may be either male or female.

Playing Time: 10 minutes.

Costumes: Everyday dress. Mrs. McGilly could wear a long full skirt; she puts on an apron when she enters, and when she goes out she takes off the apron and puts on a cloak.

Properties: Mixing bowl, spoon, paper with "recipe" on it, whittling knife, paper, kindling, pan for cake batter, half-finished carving for Boy, cherries.

Setting: The McGilly kitchen. A table and two chairs are at center. Cooking equipment is on the table and on one of the chairs are Mrs. McGilly's apron and cloak.

At right is a stove, and near the stove a box of kindling. Upstage center is a window.

Lighting: No special effects.

ABE'S WINKIN' EYE

Characters: 4 male; 4 female.

Playing Time: 25 minutes.

Costumes: All the characters wear plain working clothes of the period. Mrs. Lincoln and the girls wear long skirts. The boys and Mr. Lincoln can wear overalls and work shirts.

Properties: Jacket, knives, vegetables, corn bread, honey, eggs, iron skillet, bowl, spoon, water pail, cans containing "shortening" and "sugar," stone.

Setting: The interior of the Lincoln cabin. There is one door and one window. The cabin is simply furnished, but clean and neat. Cooking is done at a rude fireplace, upstage center. Pots and pans hang near the fireplace. A four-poster bed stands in one corner, a home-made bed cleated to the wall in another corner. There are several chairs and benches, a table, and a cupboard in the room. A rag rug is on the floor. A ladder at one end of the room leads to the loft.

Lighting: No special effects.

NEW HEARTS FOR OLD

Characters: 3 male; 3 female.

Playing Time: 20 minutes.

Costumes: Modern dress.

Properties: Valentines, newspaper, cardboard box containing old-fashioned valentine, heart-shaped box, perfume bottle and satchet bag, red paper, scissors, plate of tarts, large red heart-shaped candy box, small package containing perfume bottle.

Setting: A comfortably furnished living room. At one end of the room (the living room part) is a small table with valentines on it. Near the table are some chairs. At center are two large armchairs. At the other end of the room is a large dining table with six chairs around it. One door leads to the kitchen, another to an outer hall.

Lighting: No special effects.

HEARTS, TARTS AND VALENTINES

Characters: 6 male; 3 female; male and female extras.

Playing Time: 20 minutes.

Costumes: The Reader wears everyday clothing. All the rest of the characters are dressed in appropriate fairy tale costumes with hearts on them.

Properties: Book of fairy tales, megaphone, platter covered with napkin, piece of lace, envelopes, valentines, plate of tarts.

Setting: The kingdom of the King and Queen of Hearts. No furnishings are necessary except a throne upstage center for the King.

Lighting: No special effects.

WASHINGTON MARCHES ON

Characters: 26 male; 7 female; male and female extras. (This is a maximum cast; many of the parts may be doubled up.)

Playing Time: 25 minutes.

Costumes: If costumes are used, all the characters should wear costumes appropriate for the time and place of their particular scenes.

Properties: Paper, ink, quill pen, packet of mail, map, magnifying glass, tripod, sewing, newspapers, knitting, letters, Bible, books, flags.

Setting: On stage are two chairs and a table holding paper, ink and quill pen. If a blackboard is used, it should be placed at a downstage corner of the stage.

Lighting: No special effects.

WHAT NOW, PLANET EARTH?

Characters: 13 male; 10 female; 5 male or female for Moderator, Scientist, Librarian, Historian, and Reporter.

Playing Time: 30 minutes.

Costumes: Modern, everyday clothes for members of audience, Moderator, panelists. Late nineteenth-century clothing for Marsh and Scribner. Appropriate nineteenth-century farmers' clothing for Sadie, Father, Mother. Worn farm clothing for Fred, Ruth, and Billy. Everyday clothing for Rachel Carson and Mrs. Carson.

Properties: Crumpled tin can; papers; newspaper clippings; books; manuscripts; shovel; letters in envelopes.

Setting: Stage is furnished for panel discussion. At left is a table with five chairs behind it, and name plates before each place reading, from left to right: MODERATOR, SCIENTIST, LIBRARIAN, HISTORIAN, REPORTER. At right are three chairs and a desk.

Lighting: Spotlight, as indicated in text. Other lights dim when spotlight comes up on desk area.

Sound: Live or recorded music to "This Land Is Your Land" or "America the Beautiful," as indicated in text.

TROUBLE IN THE AIR

Characters: 13 male; 12 female; 1 male or female for

M.C.; 4 or more male or female for Chorus; 1 male offstage voice for Radio Voice; as many male and female extras as desired for Children and Townspeople. Except for Chorus, M.C., Young Woman, and Businessman, parts may be doubled.

Playing Time: 45 minutes.

Costumes: Everyday, modern dress. If desired, characters may wear costumes suggesting their roles. Young Woman carries briefcase.

Properties: Script for M.C.; briefcase containing papers, gas mask, notebook, and pencil; mailbag containing letters; book.

Setting: A sparsely-furnished stage. A lectern for M.C. and chairs for Chorus are at center. At left is a park bench, and at right are small table and several chairs. Exits are at right and left.

Lighting: No special effects.

Sound: Radio Voice speaks through microphone or loudspeaker from offstage.

ON STRIKE

Characters: 8, either male or female.

Playing Time: 15 minutes.

Costumes: The characters may be dressed completely to look like the animals, or may have only marks of identification like a red breastplate for the Robin. Or they may simply have signs pinned on them with the names of the animals. Owl wears glasses.

Properties: Book and watch for Owl, handkerchief for Robin, notes for Squirrel.

Setting: A clearing in the woods. Several trees, stumps and bushes should be placed around stage.

Lighting: No special effects.

MOTHER'S DAY OFF AND ON

Characters: 2 male; 3 female.

Playing Time: 20 minutes.

Costumes: Modern dress.

Properties: Dishes, silverware, toaster, kettle, dripolator, doll, triangular pieces of wood, hankie, candy (the four gifts are wrapped with paper), letter, pencil, papers, dictionary, sock, dress, jacket, bouquet of red roses.

Setting: Two rooms of a home, the dining room and the kitchen. In the dining room there is a table with five chairs. There is also a table in the kitchen. The rest of the equipment may be imaginary, and the division between the two rooms may be indicated by placing the furniture in them near the right and left walls of the stage.

Lighting: No special effects.

LOOK TO A NEW DAY

Characters: 11 male; 13 female; and female extras.

Playing Time: 30 minutes.

Costumes: Everyday modern dress for all of the characters in the present-day scenes. The characters from history wear clothing appropriate for the period in which they lived.

Properties: Scene 1: Gavel for Mark; telegram for Miss Gartland. Scene 2: Speech for Blake; quill pen, papers for Benjamin Franklin; pamphlets for Lucy Hooper; pen and paper for Whittier.

Setting: Scene 1: A classroom. A desk is downstage, and rows of chairs for students face the desk. Scene 2: A speaker's stand and some chairs are at one side of the stage. At center are a table and some chairs.

Lighting: If possible, a spotlight should be used in the historical scenes.